THE COMPLETE IDIOT'S GUIDE® TO

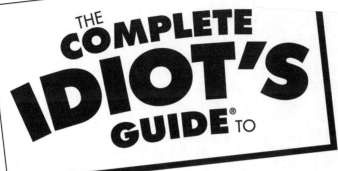

Business Law

by Cara C. Putman, J.D.

ALPHA

A member of Penguin Group (USA) Inc.

To Eric, Abigail, Jonathan, and Rebecca, who endured my long nights of writing, and smiled the whole time.

ALPHA BOOKS

Published by the Penguin Group

Penguin Group (USA) Inc., 375 Hudson Street, New York, New York 10014, USA

Penguin Group (Canada), 90 Eglinton Avenue East, Suite 700, Toronto, Ontario M4P 2Y3, Canada (a division of Pearson Penguin Canada Inc.)

Penguin Books Ltd., 80 Strand, London WC2R 0RL, England

Penguin Ireland, 25 St. Stephen's Green, Dublin 2, Ireland (a division of Penguin Books Ltd.)

Penguin Group (Australia), 250 Camberwell Road, Camberwell, Victoria 3124, Australia (a division of Pearson Australia Group Pty. Ltd.)

Penguin Books India Pvt. Ltd., 11 Community Centre, Panchsheel Park, New Delhi—110 017, India

Penguin Group (NZ), 67 Apollo Drive, Rosedale, North Shore, Auckland 1311, New Zealand (a division of Pearson New Zealand Ltd.)

Penguin Books (South Africa) (Pty.) Ltd., 24 Sturdee Avenue, Rosebank, Johannesburg 2196, South Africa

Penguin Books Ltd., Registered Offices: 80 Strand, London WC2R 0RL, England

Copyright © 2009 by Cara C. Putman

International Standard Book Number: 978-1-59257-852-8
Library of Congress Catalog Card Number: 2008939795

11 10 09   8 7 6 5 4 3 2 1

Interpretation of the printing code: The rightmost number of the first series of numbers is the year of the book's printing; the rightmost number of the second series of numbers is the number of the book's printing. For example, a printing code of 09-1 shows that the first printing occurred in 2009.

Printed in the United States of America

Note: This publication contains the opinions and ideas of its author. It is intended to provide helpful and informative material on the subject matter covered. It is sold with the understanding that the author and publisher are not engaged in rendering professional services in the book. If the reader requires personal assistance or advice, a competent professional should be consulted.

The author and publisher specifically disclaim any responsibility for any liability, loss, or risk, personal or otherwise, which is incurred as a consequence, directly or indirectly, of the use and application of any of the contents of this book.

Most Alpha books are available at special quantity discounts for bulk purchases for sales promotions, premiums, fundraising, or educational use. Special books, or book excerpts, can also be created to fit specific needs.

For details, write: Special Markets, Alpha Books, 375 Hudson Street, New York, NY 10014.

Publisher: *Marie Butler-Knight*
Editorial Director: *Mike Sanders*
Senior Managing Editor: *Billy Fields*
Senior Acquisitions Editor: *Paul Dinas*
Development Editor: *Lynn Northrup*
Senior Production Editor: *Megan Douglass*
Copy Editor: *Michael Dietsch*

Cover Designer: *Bill Thomas*
Cartoonist: *Steve Barr*
Book Designer: *Trina Wurst*
Indexer: *Johnna Van Hoose Dinse*
Layout: *Ayanna Lacey*
Proofreader: *Laura Caddell*

Contents at a Glance

Appendixes

Contents

Introduction

Business law is in many ways not a distinct area of law, but a compilation of many disciplines. First, you have to understand the framework of our unique form of government. Then you'll need to understand the role that regulation plays in today's business environment. Don't forget about understanding the different ways a business can be set up with the laundry list of advantages and disadvantages. Then there are contracts, property, employment law … the list could go on and on.

While each business law class is different in who teaches it and what that professor will emphasize, the general principles don't change. And that's what *The Complete Idiot's Guide to Business Law* is designed to help you with. As we spend the next 300 or so pages exploring the law, the driving philosophy behind this book is to give you the tools you need to understand the vocabulary and basic principles. I've used examples to help illustrate the principles, but I have not relied on case law. Each textbook picks different cases. Those cases are a helpful way to understand how courts apply the law, but there are thousands of them. Instead I've focused on core principles—what you have to know to understand this area of law.

We'll have some fun along the way, too. I wouldn't teach this class if I didn't enjoy it!

How This Book Is Organized

This book is organized into seven parts. Each part is organized into chapters that expand on the core themes. You can read the parts in order or pick the part that relates to your current reading for your business law text. You may also find that looking at this book chapter-by-chapter works best. The table of contents can be very helpful in pinpointing which chapter and part address the area of business law you need.

Part 1, "The Legal, Ethical, and Judicial Environments," looks at how the federal and state legal systems interrelate. We will also look at the sources of law as well as individual rights. Then we'll explore how disputes are resolved through the court system and which court should hear a case. We'll also take a quick look at ethics and how they frame legal issues.

Part 2, "The Regulatory Environment," discusses how regulations play a strong role in today's business environment. Governments use regulation to control businesses' actions and to enforce laws. We'll specifically look at how regulations impact price and monopolies and other anticompetitive behavior. Then we'll examine administrative agencies and the role they play in enforcing, overseeing, and prosecuting regulations. Finally, we'll take some snapshots of the federal agencies.

Part 3, "Formation of a Business," explores the different ways a company can be formed. We'll compare and contrast corporations and partnerships in their many iterations as well as the limited liability corporation hybrid. As we look at each, I'll highlight the advantages and disadvantages of both so that you'll be able to determine which form works best in each situation.

Part 4, "Contracts and Sales," explores the complex world of contracts. We'll look at the key elements to a contract, with an eye on how offer and acceptance works. Then we'll examine the requirements for a contract, such as writing, consideration, capacity, and how to handle typical problems with contract formation. Next we'll examine the rules that apply when a contract is breached and the remedies available to the parties. Next, we'll consider how sales contracts under the Uniform Commercial Code are different from other contracts. Finally, we'll look at what happens with title and risk of loss as goods are transferred.

Part 5, "Employment and Agency Law," is one of my favorite sections because it contains a lot of information that you can use right now. We'll start with a look at agency law and then compare that to employment law. We'll close the part with an examination of equal employment opportunity law.

Part 6, "Property Law Basics," covers the unique rules that apply to property law. We'll start by looking at real property and the rules that apply to the different forms of real property. We'll also discuss how real property is owned and transferred. Then it's on to personal property with a final chapter on intellectual property.

Part 7, "Financial Law," starts by reviewing securities law. Then it's off to explore negotiable instruments (don't worry—just think checks and mortgages and you're on the right track). Then we'll survey business crimes and torts.

That's it! By the time you've read Chapter 25, you will have a good grasp of the basic principles of business law. Congratulations!

Extras

To help you even further, you'll find small boxes with special items of interest in each chapter. You'll immediately see a clue to the subject matter of each box by the little cartoon at the top. Here's what you'll find:

Consultation

Here you'll find helpful hints that illuminate a subject.

def•i•ni•tion

Check these boxes for definitions of legal terms and other words that may be unfamiliar to you.

Citations

These boxes share helpful information that expands on the topic at hand.

Stay Out of Jail

Check these tips regarding steps to avoid, when to be careful, and when to seek help.

Acknowledgments

Thanks to Paul Dinas, my acquisitions editor at Alpha Books, for the opportunity. It has been a true pleasure to work with you. Marilyn Allen, thanks for believing I was the right person to write this book. Ron Benrey, thanks for introducing me to Marilyn.

To the attorneys and staff at Bennett Boehning & Clary: it has been a pleasure to work and learn with you. I can't think of anywhere else I'd rather practice the law. To the students in my Business Law classes at Krannert: I *love* teaching this class and helping you learn the law. To my professors and fellow students at George Mason University School of Law: there was no better place to get started. To Senior Judge Loren Smith for choosing me to clerk for him—that was an amazing year of watching the courts work from the inside.

Finally to my family: Eric, for supporting me in all my endeavors and believing I could do this; and to Abigail, Jonathan, and Rebecca, for being such troopers and good sports as I wrote three books at once.

Trademarks

All terms mentioned in this book that are known to be or are suspected of being trademarks or service marks have been appropriately capitalized. Alpha Books and Penguin Group (USA) Inc. cannot attest to the accuracy of this information. Use of a term in this book should not be regarded as affecting the validity of any trademark or service mark.

Part

The Legal, Ethical, and Judicial Environments

To understand business law, you need to understand the legal, ethical, and judicial backgrounds. This part will examine each area.

We'll start with the Constitution and a look at the state and federal systems. Then we'll look at the court systems and which court should be used in the event of a dispute. Then we'll examine ethical frameworks. By the time you've read this section, you'll have a roadmap for the chapters and topics to come.

Chapter 1

States Versus the Federal System

In This Chapter

- ◆ An early vision of our government

- ◆ What is Federalism?

- ◆ The role of states in Federalism

- ◆ Legal vs. individual rights

- ◆ Powers retained by the federal government

- ◆ Limits placed on the federal government

The foundation of the law in the United States is the balance of power between the federal and state governments as expressed in the Constitution. This chapter will consider what the Founders tried to accomplish when they created the federalist system with its checks and balances. We'll also look at how the federal and state systems balance each other. Finally, we'll examine the balance between legal and individual rights.

Our Founding Fathers Had a Vision ...

Since people started living together, they have searched for the best system of government. The Founding Fathers were no different: men like George Washington, the first president; Thomas Jefferson, the third president and author of the Declaration of Independence; and James Madison, the fourth president and Father of the Constitution. In the 1780s when the Founding Fathers were establishing the government of the United States, they knew several things they did not want. They did not want a king. They did not want an aristocratic system. And they did not want a marketplace closed to ideas and religion.

Instead, the Founders believed society should be an open market where ideas were exchanged and people could work to make their lives better. Our Constitution strives to provide that by allowing people maximum freedom to do what they want so long as it doesn't infringe on the rights of others.

Citations
For a great and easy to read look at the Constitution, be sure to pick up *The Complete Idiot's Guide to the U.S. Constitution* by Tim Harper (see Appendix B).

The men who became the Founding Fathers were well-educated men, well-versed in the history of governments. They knew the writing of Greek philosophers like Aristotle and Solon. They'd studied Cicero and other Roman thinkers. They knew the history of the Magna Carta and how for the first time the law was king and had to be followed by everybody. But they looked for something more that hadn't yet grown out of the English Common Law.

These men had lived through the days of taxation without representation that led to the American Revolution. They had risked everything on the idea that "men are created equal and endowed by their Creator with certain inalienable rights," as Thomas Jefferson phrased it in the Declaration of Independence.

They had also experienced the league of friendship that the Articles of Confederation created in 1781. They saw how a loose confederation would not work as the former colonies tried to solidify their independence from Britain. Some call the Articles a transition constitution, one that was better suited to war than peace. And that's what the Founders decided. By 1787 because of conflicts among the federated states over trade and commerce, they knew something had to change.

When the men gathered in Philadelphia in 1787, some notable revolutionary leaders such as Patrick Henry were absent, unconvinced that the Articles needed to change.

The key question remained whether the states needed a strong central government or the loose confederation that already existed. James Madison became the unofficial architect of the Constitution while Gouverneur Morris did most of the actual drafting.

They quickly decided that, while they needed a more centralized government, they did not want the risk of one branch accumulating so much power that a monarchy developed. Thus developed the idea of separation of power and checks and balances. While we take this system for granted, it was a revolutionary concept at the time. Not only would the federal government be balanced among its branches, there would also be a balance among the states and the state and federal government. The Bill of Rights, the first ten amendments to the Constitution that were added almost immediately, provided protection for individual rights in the face of government.

Between December 1787 (Delaware with a unanimous vote) and 1790 (Rhode Island in a close vote), all 13 states approved the Constitution.

Balance of Power Between State and Federal Governments

"We the People of the United States, in Order to form a more perfect Union, establish Justice, insure domestic Tranquility, provide for the common defence, promote the general Welfare, and secure the Blessings of Liberty to ourselves and our Posterity, do ordain and establish this Constitution for the United States of America." From the moment those words were penned, the United States has been on an ideological journey to balance the rights of people against the State.

While the text of the Constitution focuses on the federal government, the Tenth Amendment addresses states' rights. Under the Tenth Amendment, "[t]he powers not delegated to the United States by the Constitution, nor prohibited by it to the States, are reserved for the States respectively, or to the people." This amendment, which could appear as an afterthought, represents the belief of the Founders that any unenumerated powers were reserved to the individual states. The federal government has only the powers listed in the Constitution. All other powers flow to the states. Then the individual states can do what they choose. And that is why states have widely varying laws. New York may decide that it's important to have laws that limit the right of citizens in one area, while Wyoming doesn't bother to legislate that area.

The Tenth Amendment protects the self-identity and self-rule of the individual states. This concept of states' rights was very important for the first 150 years. However, beginning in the early 1940s, the power of the Tenth Amendment was whittled away by Supreme Court cases, in particular those that gave the federal government broad powers under the Commerce Clause. In addition, the Civil Rights movement of the 1960s further nullified the power left in the Tenth Amendment.

The current view is a battle between two viewpoints. One position states that by being part of the federal government, states have given some of their power to the federal government. Under that, states' rights are a political issue that are best governed by electing representatives to Congress who will act as the state wishes when passing laws. The second is illustrated by a couple of recent Supreme Court cases that place limits on Congress to force states to act through federal regulations. The Court has held that the federal government cannot place its burdens on the states.

Sources of Law

Law is created in many ways:

♦ *Statutory law* is created when legislative bodies make law. This occurs at the federal level through Congress, the state level through the state houses, and even locally when city councils pass ordinances.

♦ *Regulatory law* is created through administrative regulations. Often, a statutory law will give an agency authority to create new regulations to enforce the law.

♦ *Private law* is created by the parties to contracts. It refers to the rules and regulations parties agree to in their contracts. The terms of the contract state the limitations the parties place on their actions within that contract.

def•i•ni•tion

Stare decisis, let the decision stand, is the principle that prior case law should serve as a precedent and control future decisions of courts. A **precedent** is a court decision that becomes the law for a particular problem in the future.

♦ *Case law* is created when judges publish their decisions or legal opinions; it refers to the law expressed in the published opinions of courts. This source of law has been around for hundreds of years. Under the principle of *stare decisis*, courts must honor prior case law, also called *precedents*. While prior cases should serve as a guide, courts have some flexibility to overturn a prior decision if they find it was incorrect.

♦ *Common law* is the body of law that has grown over hundreds of years in England and the United States. Common law consists of foundational principles that were then recognized by the courts and incorporated into their opinions.

◆ *Substantive law* establishes principles and creates, defines, and regulates rights and liabilities. *Procedural law* sets the rules that must be followed to enforce rights and liabilities. For example, substantive law states that you can't murder someone. Procedural law sets the steps that must be followed to prosecute some-one accused of murder.

Our System of Federalism

Federalism can be defined as a political theory where the government has a central unit that is made up of subunits. In other words, the United States is a federal system, because we have a federal government that is made up of 50 states. The citizens are responsible to both the federal and state governments, and the states have a voice in the federal government through the elected representatives. This was more true prior to the passage of the Seventeenth Amendment. Prior to the Seventeenth Amendment, U.S. Senators were elected by the state houses. After that amendment, the U.S. Senators are elected by popular vote. Thus, they no longer report to the states but to the voters.

Under our federal system, some powers are reserved specifically to the states such as education, while others are reserved to the federal government, like foreign policy. Granted powers are those enumerated to the federal government in the Constitution. For the federal government those include the right to provide patent and copyright protection, establish the post office, and have an army and navy. Finally, there are con-current powers that the state and federal governments share. These include protecting the health, safety, and general welfare of the public. For example, kidnapping can be a federal or a state crime. Both entities can tax citizens.

The Balance Between the Three Branches of the Federal Government

The first three Articles of the Constitution establish a separation of powers between the three branches of the U.S. government. This is an attempt to keep one branch from overpowering the other branches.

◆ Article I addresses the legislative branch. The legislative branch consists of the Congress, which is made up of the House of Representatives and the Senate. Originally, the House was to be elected by popular vote, and the Senate by the state houses. Now, both are elected by popular vote. Congress passes legislation that is in line with the enumerated powers listed in Section 8. Those include tax-ation, borrowing money, and regulating commerce. Section 9 provides limits on what Congress can do, while Section 10 prohibits the states from taking certain actions like imposing duties on goods or entering treaties or alliances with other countries.

- ◆ Article II addresses the executive branch. This article delineates the powers and responsibilities of the president. The president can make treaties with other nations if two thirds of the Senate concur. He is Commander in Chief of the military and shall fill vacancies that occur during Senate recesses. He also appoints judges and ambassadors. Most of his actions must receive the concurrence of the Senate to be valid.

- ◆ Article III addresses the judicial branch. Federal judges are appointed by the president and approved by the Senate. The Constitution established the Supreme Court, but left the design of the lower courts to Congress.

Federal judges hear cases involving the Constitution, the federal laws, and treaties. They also have jurisdiction to hear conflicts between parties that are residents of different states. However, a state may not be sued in federal court.

The role of the judiciary is to tell the executive and legislative branches which of their laws and regulations are unconstitutional. By doing so the court declares the law to be illegal and nullifies it. This power to nullify laws provides a check to Congress and the president from overreaching their constitutional limits.

Federal Supremacy

When there is a conflict between federal and state laws, the federal law reigns supreme. For example, the First Amendment provides that there is freedom of speech and the freedom of the press. A state can't pass a law that prohibits journalists in that state from reporting on the activities of the governor. That would be an unconstitutional restriction on the freedom of the press.

States can't regulate below the federal level. Let's say the Securities and Exchange Commission (SEC) issues regulations enforcing the Sarbanes-Oxley Act (see Chapter 3) that require a certain report to be filed each quarter. A state decides that filing is too burdensome for companies registered within its borders and passes a law that states companies formed within its borders are exempt. That law is unconstitutional because a state cannot override or supersede a federal law.

State Authority and Power

The states by nature of being part of the United States have delegated certain powers to the federal government. Those include the power to declare war, determine the currency, and have a post office. States maintain the power to adopt laws that fall under the police power: laws designed to protect the general welfare, health, safety, and morals of their citizens.

As I've mentioned, federal law prevails over state laws when there is a conflict between the two. But how can you tell if there's a conflict? Look at the language used. Does the state law cover a new area? Or does it address the same area as the federal law? If it's the same area, the state law cannot contradict or conflict with the federal law. Instead, state law can fill the gaps left by federal law. State law can also address areas untouched by federal law. For example, since *Roe v. Wade*, the federal law has been that abortion is legal in many instances, but not all. However, states can address and fill the gaps unaddressed by the federal right to privacy. For example, the Supreme Court has held that state law can address parental notification.

In addition, if it's clear from the language of the law that Congress intends that the states not legislate or regulate, then the federal government has preempted state action. Confusion occurs when Congress is silent. Does that silence mean states can regulate or that Congress intended that neither the federal nor state governments could regulate? That often depends on the facts of the situation and the language used by Congress.

Legal Versus Individual Rights

The U.S. Constitution, state constitutions, laws, and regulations provide for a balance of legal and individual rights. Legal rights stem from the Constitution and allow us to require people to act or not act. We also have duties to act in accordance with those rights and the laws. Individual rights are guaranteed by the Constitution. Many of those rights are articulated in the Bill of Rights and include freedom of speech, the freedom from unwarranted search and seizure, and the right to assistance of counsel in criminal cases.

What About Federal Powers?

The federal government has many powers that are delineated in the Constitution. These powers are granted because they are necessary to administer the national government.

Regulating Commerce

The need to standardize commerce was a key motivator for calling the 1787 Constitutional Convention. To this day, regulating commerce remains a key power of the federal government. This power flows from Article I, Section 8, Clause 3—also known as the Commerce Clause—which states the power "[t]o regulate commerce with foreign nations, and among the several states, and with the Indian tribes." For the first 150 years, the Supreme Court held that his clause created the federal government's power to control or regulate the flow of commerce as it crosses state lines, but *only* as it crossed state lines.

Between 1937 and 1946 this power expanded dramatically. By 1946, it had expanded to allow Congress to regulate businesses. For example, federal agencies have argued that the Commerce Clause applies to companies if they use credit card machines. That tenuous connection with interstate commerce is sufficient. Courts have also held that the Commerce Clause applies to marijuana grown for personal medicinal use.

Today the Commerce Clause allows Congress to legislate activities that are economic in nature. If there is merely an economic impact, that is not sufficient and the Supreme Court may declare the law unconstitutional.

Stay Out of Jail

The Supreme Court has used the Commerce Clause to prevent states from interfering with interstate commerce through regulations and laws. For example, states have attempted to use taxation and tariffs to inhibit interstate commerce. Courts will also examine regulations that have the effect of providing a competitive edge to local businesses over out-of-state businesses. —

Financial Powers

The federal government has three financial powers: taxing, spending, and banking. The Constitution provides that the federal government can levy and collect taxes as long as the revenue is used for a public purpose. The government can also spend money collected through taxes or borrowed to pay the debts of the government and provide for the defense and general welfare. Finally, the government can create and regulate banking. It has chosen to do that through the Federal Reserve System.

Limitations on the Government

The Constitution also provides protections to individuals and businesses. These protections are key to the liberties that are the hallmarks of the U.S. system.

Due Process

Due process is the idea that the laws should be applied fairly to all. Due process rights are found in the Fifth and Fourteenth amendments. The Fifth Amendment applies due process to federal laws. When the Fourteenth Amendment passed, it expanded the application of due process to the states.

There are two types of due process: procedural and substantive. *Procedural due process* applies in the criminal setting from investigation and arrest through the trial and appeal. The key question courts ask is whether an individual has been deprived of life, liberty, or property and what procedural process should be given to that individual. Those questions include: Are the laws applied fairly? Is the law too vague? Does the law lean toward guilt? If the answer is yes to any of these questions, the law is unconstitutional under procedural due process. Bottom line, the government must follow the law and procedural rules when taking an individual's or business's freedom or property.

def•i•ni•tion

Due process is the principle of fairness under the law, the idea that legal procedures must be applied equally to avoid prejudicial or unequal treatment under the law.

Consultation

Procedural due process recognizes the rule of law applies to all equally. The government must play by the rules when applying the laws. When we ask the how question, if the answer is not acceptable, courts may find the law unconstitutional. I like this way of phrasing it: we can't be harmed by the loss of freedom or property at the hands of the government unless the judicial rules are followed and our rights aren't violated.

Substantive due process focuses on the content of the law. It asks *why* about laws and examines whether the law infringes on fundamental constitutional liberties. So a law may pass with appropriate procedural due process, but still violate substantive due process because the substance or topic of the law is unconstitutional. Substantive due process has been used to strike down laws regarding abortion, confining non-dangerous mentally ill persons, and affirmative action.

Equal Protection of the Law

Equal protection of the law protects the ideal that the government must treat its citizens equally. In general, equal protection applies to the actions of governments. Private individuals and entities can discriminate. The government cannot treat one person or group with preference over another. Instead, laws must be applied equally. If there is no justification for a difference in how groups are treated, then the law, regulation, or treatment violates the Constitution.

The underlying law or regulation may be constitutional. But it may be applied in a way that discriminates against one group and thus violates the principle of equal protection. For example, in *Yick Wo v. Hopkins*, the Supreme Court found that while a regulation regarding laundries was constitutional, it was applied in a way that discriminated against a class of owners.

The Least You Need to Know

- The Founding Fathers adopted a democratic republic with power balanced between the states and three branches of the federal government.

- Federalism is the political form where the government has a central unit that is made up of subunits.

- The federal government has separation of powers to distribute authority between the executive, legislative, and judicial branches.

- The states can legislate and regulate in areas where they are not preempted or prohibited by federal laws and regulations.

- Due process and equal protection are principles which limit the actions of the government and require the laws to be applied equally.

Dispute Resolution and Court Systems

In This Chapter

- ◆ Understanding the legal lingo
- ◆ Federal court jurisdiction
- ◆ State court jurisdiction
- ◆ How state and federal courts differ
- ◆ What happens in court

Contracts are designed to avoid disputes by making the intentions and responsibilities of the parties clear. In a similar way laws provide requirements and expectations for how individuals and businesses will act. However, disputes will arise even under a carefully crafted contract. People will break the law. In those situations, dispute resolution or the court system is used to resolve the dispute or prosecute the crime. This chapter surveys federal and state jurisdiction before turning to how to determine which law applies.

Terminology You Should Know

As you'll learn with many areas of the law, there are key terms you need to understand before we explore the principles (see Appendix A for many more definitions):

- *Courts* are the government tribunals or bodies that hear and decide disputes and other matters brought before them. Each court has jurisdiction to hear certain kinds of cases. Courts have authority to hear either federal or state disputes.

- *Jurisdiction* is the power, right, or authority of the court to hear and determine or apply the law. These may be criminal or civil cases. Dollar amounts may be used to determine whether a case can be heard in federal court or the state court that is appropriate for the controversy. For example, in federal court, the amount in controversy has to be $75,000 or more; small claims court is $5,000 or less.

- *Subject matter jurisdiction* refers to a court's ability to hear a case based on the nature of the dispute. It is the ability to hear a certain kind of case.

- *Personal jurisdiction* gives the court authority to bring the parties before it and hear the complaint against them. A key question is whether a court can be forced to bring someone from one state in to another state in order to hear the complaint against that party.

- *Original jurisdiction* is the authority to hear a case when it's brought before the court.

- *Special jurisdiction* reflects the specialized nature of some courts. Juvenile courts only hear cases involving minors. Family courts only hear disputes involving domestic relations issues. Small claims courts only hear cases involving dollar amounts that vary by state but are usually much smaller than $10,000.

Consultation

Small claims courts are an example of subject matter that is also special jurisdiction. These state courts have jurisdiction over parties as long as the dispute does not reach a dollar threshold. Personal jurisdiction revolves around the question of whether the court can bring a party into its courtroom. For example, the small claims court has jurisdiction over the parties even if they are from different states. But a federal court wouldn't unless the parties were from different states *and* the controversy involved more than $75,000.

- *General jurisdiction* means a court can hear most disputes brought before them. Sometimes the plaintiff (the person bringing the suit) will be able to choose between multiple courts when determining where to file the action.

- *Appellate jurisdiction* is the power select courts have to hear appeals from other courts or administrative agencies. Appellate courts are examining the cases to determine whether *reversible error* occurred. Reversible error is one so serious the appellate court will set aside the decision of the lower court. The court will either affirm and uphold the lower court's decision or reverse it.

So how does jurisdiction work? Let's take the Court of Federal Claims, a court of special jurisdiction because the United States is always the defendant. In the tax cases it hears, the Court of Federal Claims has concurrent jurisdiction with the Tax Court and U.S. District Courts. The plaintiff can choose in which court to raise its claim. The Court of Appeals for the Federal Circuit hears any appeals from decisions of the Court of Federal Claims.

Federal Court Jurisdiction and Systems

The Constitution states that federal courts can only hear cases and controversies; that means the courts can't create disputes to resolve. A court cannot hear hypothetical legal questions. Federal question jurisdiction allows federal courts to decide cases that involve the United States Constitution or laws, the United States government, or controversies between states or the United States and other governments. In other words, federal courts can hear cases that involve federal laws or the federal Constitution.

Federal courts may also hear cases that involve diversity of citizenship of the parties. This primarily occurs when the parties are from two different states or from the United States and another country. However in diversity cases, the dispute must involve a potential damage amount of $75,000 or more.

Federal Court System

The federal courts have three levels. District courts hear the original dispute. If a party is unsatisfied with the district court decision, it can file an appeal. The appeal is usually heard by one of the thirteen courts of appeal that are located around the United States. The final recourse is to appeal decisions of the Court of Appeals to the Supreme Court.

Consultation

Federal courts have exclusive jurisdiction over bankruptcies. Because Congress has determined that bankruptcies are best addressed in a standardized manner, federal courts determine all bankruptcies. Individuals and businesses use the bankruptcy process when they must liquidate their assets or reorganize their finances due to insolvency.

◆ **District courts:** The district courts are the trial courts of the federal court system. They have original jurisdiction to hear both civil and criminal cases. The courts must have original jurisdiction to hear the civil cases. To recap, those judicial requirements are that a federal question be involved or that diversity of citizenship combined with alleged damages of $75,000 or more be at stake.

Several federal district courts have limited jurisdiction. In addition to the Court of Federal Claims, the Tax Court, Court of Veterans Appeals, Court of International Trade, Indian tribal courts, and bankruptcy courts have specialized jurisdiction to hear only certain categories of cases.

◆ **U.S. Courts of Appeals:** Once the court has reached a decision in the district court, the matter is not necessarily ended. Either party may appeal that decision to a court of appeals. By appealing, the party asks the appellate judges to review the trial court or jury's decision for reversible errors.

There are 12 geographically based courts of appeal in the federal system. There is also the specialized Court of Appeals for the Federal Circuit, which hears appeals from the Court of Federal Claims, district courts, the United States Court of International Trade, and the U.S. Court of Appeals for Veterans Claims. It has jurisdiction to hear appeals that involve the subject matter of government contracts, patents, trademarks, federal personnel, veteran's benefits, international trade, and certain monetary claims against the United States.

def•i•ni•tion

In an *en banc* hearing, a full panel of the judges from the Court of Appeals hears the case.

In the typical appeal, a panel of three judges from that court of appeals will hear oral arguments or decide the appeal solely from the written briefs. In some cases, an *en banc* panel of the court will decide the case. This usually occurs when the court feels that a significant issue is at stake or when one or both parties request an *en banc* hearing and the court agrees.

◆ **Supreme Court:** The United States Supreme Court is the final arbiter of what the Constitution means and accordingly of which laws, regulations, and government actions are constitutional. The Supreme Court also hears appeals from state supreme courts where a constitutional issue is at issue or where a state court has overturned a federal regulation. In the majority of cases that it hears, the Supreme Court is the final appeal. However, in rare cases it has original jurisdiction. Those cases affect ambassadors, other public ministers and consuls, and those in which a state is a party.

Nine justices serve on the Supreme Court, although the Constitution allows that number to change as needed.

State Court Jurisdiction and Systems

The structure of state courts varies by state. I'll discuss the basic pattern, but each state will have variations on this. For example, Indiana calls its final appellate court the Supreme Court. New York calls one of its courts of original jurisdiction supreme court, and its final appellate court is called the Court of Appeals. Some states have town and city level courts. Others start at the county level. Some have highly specialized courts for areas like family law and drug courts. Others leave all subject matters to the general courts.

As a general rule, state courts have jurisdiction over almost all divorce and child custody matters, probate and inheritance disputes, real estate, and juvenile matters. They also hear all criminal cases arising under state law, contract disputes, and personal injury cases.

The structure of the court systems will follow this general pattern:

◆ **Trial courts:** All states will have a general level of trial courts. These courts will hear criminal and civil matters, and depending on the state will have varying restrictions. These courts have original jurisdiction, and are called many things including superior court, circuit court, or district courts.

◆ **Specialty courts:** These can take many approaches. Some common specialty courts include family law courts, juvenile courts, and probate courts. Juvenile courts will hear cases involving juveniles accused of committing a crime as well as children in need of services.

◆ **Small claims courts:** Many states also have small claims courts. These courts often have a dollar limit and only hear disputes up to that threshold. These courts provide a forum for disputes to be settled without the added expense of an attorney. Small claims courts often have their own procedural rules which are more relaxed than those the other courts use. An example of a common dispute these courts handle is lease violations.

◆ **Appellate courts:** Most states have appellate courts that serve a similar function to the federal appellate courts.

◆ **Supreme courts:** The state supreme court is the final court of review. And as with the federal Supreme Court, the state courts do not have to hear each appealed case. However, if a case involves federal subject matter, the state supreme court opinion can be appealed to the U.S. Supreme Court.

Comparing State and Federal Courts

Now let's look at how the state and federal court systems compare and differ.

The federal court system is structured under Article Three of the Constitution, which created the Supreme Court and allows Congress to create all lower federal courts. The parties to a federal lawsuit can appeal to Court of Appeals with jurisdiction. Then a party can ask the Supreme Court to review the decision, but the Supreme Court isn't required to do that.

The state courts are established under the state constitutions and laws. Many state courts have specialty jurisdiction that is limited to areas like probate and family law. Parties can appeal to the intermediate court of appeals and then may ask the highest state court to hear the case. Limited state cases are eligible for review by the Supreme Court.

Federal judges are nominated by the president and confirmed by the Senate. Federal judges are appointed for life and can only be removed from office by impeachment for misbehavior. State court judges are selected in varied ways including election, appointment by the governor for a term, appointment for life, or some combination of those methods.

As I discussed earlier, federal courts hear cases dealing with the constitutionality of laws, cases about U.S. laws or treaties, disputes between two or more states, bankruptcy, and cases involving ambassadors and public ministers. State courts hear most criminal and contract cases, probate, personal injury, and family law cases. State courts are the final courts to hear state law and constitution cases.

Court Procedures

This section will review the basics steps and vocabulary of court cases and procedures. When we're done, you'll understand what happens during the cases.

The Parties

The plaintiff is the party who files the civil lawsuit. In the criminal setting the prosecutor files the charges. The defendant is the person sued in the civil or criminal setting. The judge oversees the trial. If there is a jury, the judge decides the law and the jury decides the facts. Without a jury, the judge decides both.

Steps in a Lawsuit

The first thing a plaintiff does, after finding an attorney and picking the court, is file a complaint. The complaint outlines the parties, facts, law that applies, and relief wanted. The complaint and summons are then served on the defendant according to the applicable trial rules.

The defendant can respond to the complaint in several ways. If the defendant fails to respond, the court enters a default judgment against the defendant and awards the damages or relief the plaintiff sought. The defendant can file an answer, which addresses each of the plaintiff's allegations and raises defenses to the plaintiff's claims. Or the defendant can file pre-answer motions that allege that the plaintiff's complaint or some portion of it should be thrown out. In a summary judgment motion, the defendant argues the plaintiff has raised no genuine issue of material fact and therefore the judge can make a decision for the defendant based on the law. The defendant could also file a Motion to Dismiss that asks the court to dismiss the complaint because even if everything the plaintiff alleged was true, the plaintiff could not recover.

Motions to Dismiss and Summary Judgment Motions can be filed by either party. The plaintiff can file them on the defendant's counterclaims, and the defendant files them on the plaintiff's claims. In either case, filing such a motion can simplify complex cases and reduce the expense of litigation by resolving some matters without a trial.

If the defendant files an answer, it can assert counterclaims against the plaintiff. In many cases both parties feel they have been wronged, so there are claims on both sides.

Consultation

An early question in lawsuits is which law to apply. For procedural issues, the state law of the court will be used. If parties are from different states, substantive law could come from either state. The default rule is the law of the state where the contract was formed prevails. However, the parties can choose which law to apply within the terms of the contract. In personal injury cases, the court will use the law of the state where the accident occurred.

Once the complaint is filed and the defendant has an opportunity to respond, discovery begins. Discovery is the process used by the parties to uncover the evidence related to the claims or crimes. Modern trials have very few opportunities for surprise—despite what you see in movies and on TV. This is largely because of discovery. Discovery is broad because the rules allow the parties to obtain evidence that is relevant to the claims.

Discovery serves two primary purposes: to obtain documents from opposing parties and to obtain testimony that can be used in trial. Documentary evidence is obtained primarily through requests for production. Testimony can be obtained through interrogatories, requests for admissions, and depositions.

Depositions are the form of evidence that you're likely familiar with. Depositions are taken to learn a witness's testimony before the trial or to preserve testimony that otherwise won't be admitted because of the unavailability of the witness. Because depositions are sworn testimony, they can be used to impeach a witness who tries to change their testimony at trial. Affidavit and deposition testimony can also be used to support summary judgment motions.

Expert witnesses are used in cases that involve an area of expertise. If the claim involves an injury or illness, a medical doctor may serve as an expert to explain the injury or illness to the judge and jury. An expert witness can be used if scientific, technical, or other specialized knowledge will help the trier of fact understand the evidence or determine a matter of fact.

Trials

Trials are governed by the rules of trial procedure and criminal procedure. Regardless of whether a trial is civil or criminal, several elements are the same.

The first thing that happens in many trials is that a jury is selected. The size of the jury will vary under state law, but the jury must be composed of representative members of the community where the jury is selected. The jury pool will be examined by the judge and then by the attorneys to determine whether there is any reason a potential juror should not serve. Each party is allotted a certain number of preemptory challenges, which allow it to disqualify a juror without giving a reason. Challenges for cause allow a party to strike a juror for bias, admitting a relationship with a party, personal knowledge of the facts of the case, or any other reason that would indicate the juror can't be impartial. Once the parties' preemptory challenges and challenges for cause have been exhausted or the required number of jurors is reached, the jury will be sworn in and seated.

Attorneys for the parties will then make opening statements to the judge or jury. This is each party's opportunity to introduce the judge and jury to the case. Then all parties will have the opportunity to present their evidence through witness testimony and documents or other exhibits. Evidence must be relevant to the questions of the case as well as admissible. Otherwise, the court must not allow it to be entered as evidence. A witness will undergo a direct examination by the party who called him or her. Then the witness will be cross-examined by opposing counsel, before being redirect-examined. This process can go back and forth between counsel until all questions for the witness are exhausted. However, the party calling the witness must have the opportunity to ask the last question of that witness.

If at the close of the plaintiff's or prosecutor's evidence, the defendant believes that insufficient evidence was entered to prove the case, it can move the court for a directed verdict. The directed verdict basically alleges that the plaintiff failed to meet its burden of proof and the case must be dismissed. Even if the evidence offered were 100 percent true, the plaintiff could not recover. If the court denies the motion, the trial proceeds to the defendant's defense.

After the close of the evidence, the parties make closing arguments. A motion can also be filed for a mistrial. A mistrial can be requested when it is necessary to have a new trial to avoid a great injustice. In the new trial, a new jury must hear the case.

If a jury hears the facts, then the jury will receive instructions and verdict forms from the court prior to retiring to reach a verdict. The parties submit proposed instructions and verdict forms to the court ahead of time. After the jury returns with its verdict, a party may file

> ### Citations
>
> A party might file a motion for a mistrial if testimony or argument had been presented that prevents a party from getting a fair trial. That may include evidence that the defendant has insurance, inviting the jury to step into the plaintiff's position by using the Golden Rule, or arguing an issue that has not been presented through evidence or testimony.

a motion for a judgment notwithstanding the verdict. It may also request a new trial again.

After the trial the parties must decide whether they will appeal the court's or jury's decision. If not, the judgment must be executed. If the judgment includes monetary damages, a secondary action may be filed to have the losing parties wages garnered until the judgment is paid.

Alternatives to Litigation

Alternative dispute resolution (ADR) is a growing alternative to full-blown litigation. As courts become overloaded with more cases, the judges may urge the parties to utilize ADR methods including arbitration and mediation.

Arbitration is an alternative that allows the parties to present their evidence to a trained expert. That expert evaluates the disputed area and issues a binding opinion. Parties may agree to arbitration as a term of their contract. In other cases, arbitration may be required by statute. Arbitration is often cheaper than a full trial. It allows the parties to have a trained third party hear and decide the case without all the full expenditure of time and expense a trial requires.

Mediation is similar to arbitration, but the results are not binding on the parties. It's much easier for one side to walk away from mediation at any time. In mediation the mediator is neutral and acts as a messenger between the parties. The mediator can also educate the parties on the likely success or failure of their claims and defenses.

Other alternatives exist, but arbitration and mediation are most often used.

The Least You Need to Know

- Jurisdiction is the power, right, or authority of the court to hear and determine or apply the law. These may be criminal or civil cases.

- Courts must have subject matter and personal jurisdiction to hear a case.

- State and federal court systems are similarly structured with lower courts of original jurisdiction whose decisions may be appealed to appellate courts and finally to supreme courts.

- Trial procedures are similar in both federal and state courts: a complaint is followed by motions that can dismiss or narrow the claims, followed by a trial if settlement has not been reached.

Chapter 3

Business Ethics

In This Chapter

- ◆ A framework for decision-making
- ◆ The value of business ethics
- ◆ Working through ethical dilemmas
- ◆ The impact of the Sarbanes-Oxley Act

The economy has slowed to the point that the conglomerate Jackson works for has asked him to choose which of its four plants to shut down. Jackson needs a framework to decide how to make that decision. Which one should he use?

A manager has instructed Ellen to falsify entries in the corporate books. She doesn't feel comfortable doing it, but isn't sure she can risk her job by saying no. What should she do?

These situations arise in the business environment and force individuals to make difficult decisions. Ethics is the system of moral precepts that can help employers and employees decide which course of action to take. This chapter will illustrate a few of the ethical frameworks people can use when faced with decisions in a business setting.

Defining Business Ethics

Ethics is the system of moral principles that govern our actions. Put another way, ethics is the search for right and wrong. Ethics provides a framework for making decisions in all contexts, but recent events have highlighted the importance of this area in the business world. As a result of ethical breaches in large companies that led to their collapse and billions of dollars in losses, the government has turned its attention to enforcing ethical standards in the workplace.

def•i•ni•tion

> **Ethics** is a branch of philosophy designed to provide people with a framework for making decisions. **Business ethics** focuses on the goal of balancing profits with the values of society and individuals.

Ethical dilemmas are constantly evolving as technology develops. The Ethical Resource Center defines the ethical dilemmas of the twenty-first century as privacy issues, financial mismanagement, intellectual property theft, cyber crime, and international corruption. In a world that is vastly different than the Leave-it-to-Beaver world of the 1950s, what should *business ethics* look like?

Ethics from the Law

One ethical framework draws moral standards from codified law. Under this approach, the test of whether an action is justified is whether it is legal. This approach is frequently used in the business context. It's a relatively flexible approach because the law can be altered as the perceived need for ethical standards changes. For example, under codified law, businesses extend warranties to purchasers and failing to meet those warranty standards is unethical behavior.

When the law is the standard, ethics will evolve as judges apply it to new areas. As a result, what was ethical before may become unethical behavior. For example, prior to the Emancipation Proclamation it was perfectly legal to own slaves. Accordingly, from a positive law approach, it was also ethical. But since the Emancipation Proclamation and laws passed after the Civil War, slavery is illegal. The law changed and moved the ethical boundaries with it.

Under this approach, Jackson asks himself if it's legal to close a plant. If the company isn't doing anything illegal, it has the right to close any plant that it chooses. However, Jackson still feels unsettled and unsure what to do. Ellen has concerns that the bookkeeping magic she's supposed to work isn't legal, but her boss has given her an explanation that seems right. After all, she'll only have to do it once.

Universal Standards for Ethics

Universal standards for ethics arise from several fronts. Fundamentally, this approach holds that ethics are set and cannot be changed by the shifting winds of the law. Instead, there is a *natural law* that sets the standards we should live by. This framework allows civil disobedience because sometimes the laws do not comply with a higher ethical standard.

Individuals such as theologian and philosopher Thomas Aquinas (1225?–1274) believed that natural law derived from the nature of the world and the nature of humans. That is, there are clear moral constraints—actions that are always right or always wrong regardless of what the culture or law state.

def•i•ni•tion

Natural law refers to standards of conduct derived from traditional moral principles or God's law and will.

Continuing the slavery example, it was morally and ethically right for the individuals in the north who had stops on the Underground Railroad to help the slaves escape to Canada. Even though there was a law on the books that made those actions illegal, a higher moral standard compelled them to act contrary to the law.

Ellen knows that it's wrong to lie, and that's what doctoring the books feels like. She drafts a resignation letter but hopes she doesn't need to turn it in since she's the primary breadwinner for her family and caregiver to her husband, who is terminally ill. Jackson evaluates his instructions to choose a plant to close and can find nothing about the situation that violates natural law. It's simply a decision that has to be made for the good of the company. Feeling somewhat better, he conducts his analysis and makes a recommendation.

Situational Business Ethics

Situational business ethics, or moral relativism, calls for individuals to look at the underlying situation and make decisions based on those facts. While there may be large absolutes, those can only be understood and applied in the context of the current situation. For example, natural law states that stealing is wrong. Situational ethics might agree in general that stealing is wrong, but someone who is starving might find stealing justified. Do the motivations and circumstances excuse and justify the actions? If the answer is yes, the action is ethical.

Citations
Businesses may choose to rely on situational ethics in an international context because what is illegal (think bribery) in the United States is ethical and expected in other corners of the world.

Jackson evaluates the facts about each plant, and ultimately decides to keep three of them because he has friends employed at each. Situationally, that seems like the best approach. Sure, some people will lose jobs, but at least it won't be people he knows. And he can justify the decision with a cost analysis. Ellen decides that she can doctor the books this once, because she needs her job. With her husband's terminal illness, they can't afford to lose her insurance.

Business Stakeholder Theory

The business stakeholder theory looks at ethics from the viewpoint of the different constituencies a company has. *Stakeholders* are groups that share a common interest. The problem is that the needs and goals of the varying groups often conflict. Under this approach, business must find the right balance between the stakeholders where they interact so together they can create value.

Let's say a company is considering taking a potential cancer treatment into drug trials. One set of stakeholders are the company's shareholders: their goal is to maximize profits and dividends. The FDA, as the regulatory agency overseeing the trials, has an interest in how the trials are conducted. People with the cancer the drug is designed to treat are also stakeholders. They want a cure, but may be adversely impacted by unknown side effects. And employees want to see the company grow while maintaining their jobs. These various interests can collide. The business stakeholder model balances the diverse needs as it searches for the ethical course of action.

def•i•ni•tion

Stakeholders are those who have an interest in the activities of a corporation. This group may include shareholders, employees, vendors, customers, or governments.

Under this analysis, the decision-maker should follow these steps to reach a decision:

1. Define the problem.

2. Identify who could be injured by the proposed plan.

3. Define the problem from the perspective of the stakeholders.

4. Decide whether the decision-maker would be willing to tell his family, supervisor, CEO, and the board of directors about the planned action.

5. Determine whether the decision-maker would be willing to testify before a community meeting, a congressional hearing, or a public forum to describe the plan.

After considering these elements, the decision-maker should reach a decision about whether to take the contemplated action.

As these steps indicate, it's important under this analysis to first articulate the impact of the decision on the various stakeholders. But then, the decision-maker has to decide whether he or she can defend the decision in public. Or, as I like to put it, are you willing to defend the action if the decision is exposed on the front page of the local paper or *The New York Times*? (More on this a little later in the chapter.)

This framework can be used to decide whether to act in a legal manner—will I help myself to money from the corporate account? But it also helps companies decide whether to do more than the law requires. Employers have no legal obligation to offer their employees options like telecommuting or dental and vision insurance (usually). However, employers may decide to offer it as a way to maintain a qualified workforce. In the stakeholder analysis, the employees need or ask for greater flexibility or insurance benefits, and the company decides the benefit it receives in exchange is valuable.

This stakeholder analysis can also be used to address issues like the social responsibility of a company. Will the company actively engage in environmental issues like Ben & Jerry's or will it take an approach that believes the money should go to shareholders so that they can support the causes that are important to them? Neither is right or wrong, but companies can land on different sides of the issue.

Jackson uses a stakeholder analysis to evaluate which plant to close. Each community needs the plant as a source of jobs. However, one of the plants will need substantial upgrades to comply with new EPA regulations. There have been whispers in the company that it is releasing toxins into water sources. Jackson recommends that plant be closed. Ellen looks at the situation from all sides. She decides that she's going to go with her gut and refuse to adjust the profit-and-loss statements. Her manager finds someone else who is willing to move the numbers.

The Importance of Business Ethics

All this discussion of the frameworks for making ethical decisions is great, but why does it matter? In addition to the need for standards that company scandals like Enron and WorldCom highlight, there are sound business reasons to behave in an ethical way.

The capitalist system succeeds in no small measure because companies build trust, make sound financial decisions, and build solid reputations. Ethical lapses threaten each of these.

Impact on Trust

Trust is essential in a capitalist system. Trust means that others can rely on the character, strength, and integrity of a business. Without trust, investors would be reluctant to invest capital in companies. Employees would be hesitant to work day in and day out for those companies. Customers enter contracts with companies because they believe they can trust the companies to honor the obligations.

Yet, in a survey conducted by Gallup for the Better Business Bureau that was released in October 2007, 18 percent of adult respondents said their trust in businesses they regularly deal with had decreased. In the same survey, they rated honesty and fairness as essential elements for a company to win their trust.

Many of the recent scandals have led to this decrease in the trust the public has in large companies. Not only are Enron and Arthur Andersen affected. Those companies' breach of trust affects the trust the public is willing to extend to other companies.

Impact on Financial Performance

Ethics also has an impact on the financial performance of companies. Studies suggest a direct correlation between the way companies ethically treat stakeholders and the financial performance of that company. These studies find that if investors want a solid return from their investments, investors should invest in companies that are consistently candid in their financial standards. While this tidbit seems self-evident, the number of companies caught in accounting and other ethical scandals highlights the importance of investors being able to trust the books of companies.

Stay Out of Jail

When company scandals like WorldCom, Enron, and Adelphia broke, nobody expected anyone to actually go to jail. But executives and management from each company spent time in jail for the company's financial fraud. Enron CEO Jeff Skilling got 24 years, former WorldCom CEO Bernie Ebbers got 25 years, and former Adelphia CEO John Rigas was sentenced to 15 years. Notice that Bernie Ebbers and John Rigas were not the CEOs at the time the scandals broke.

Impact on a Company's Reputation

Each scandal becomes a black eye on that company's reputation. With an ethical breach, the company loses the public's trust, which affects the company's reputation. That in turn affects the willingness of the public to purchase from that company for years to come.

Many companies have a clear understanding of the value of their reputations. As a result, some hire search engine optimizers (SEOs) to manage their reputations on the Internet. SEOs find ways to create positive content about the client and push the bad information down the search engine rankings. Is it ethical to actively manage a reputation? Or is it image management like a publicity campaign?

Business Regulation

Business regulation often grows out of an area where an industry ceases to police itself—often due to an ethical breach. Congress steps in to legislate and agencies to regulate when Congressional studies uncover abuses. For example, the Federal Trade Commission (FTC) began policing consumer debt after Congress passed the Fair Debt Collection Practices Act when Congress found evidence of abusive, deceptive, and unfair debt collection practices. The Securities and Exchange Commission (SEC) promulgated regulations for financial disclosures regarding derivatives after several companies and local governments lost huge sums of money due to their investments. When businesses act ethically, the companies can often avoid the cost and arbitrary nature of regulation.

Resolving Ethical Dilemmas

So how should ethical dilemmas be rectified? In theory, it's nice to know about ethics, but the challenge is in applying it to real-life issues. There are several frameworks or sets of questions that can be used to take ethics from the theoretical to the practical. In the following sections we'll take a closer look at three of these approaches, any of which can help managers decide which course of action is the most ethical in a particular situation.

Blanchard and Peale Three-Part Test

Dr. Ken Blanchard, management expert and author of *The One Minute Manager*, and Dr. Norman Vincent Peale, the author of *The Power of Positive Thinking* and pioneer of

Christian psychology, collaborated on this ethical approach that revolves around three ethics checks. In it, they recommend asking three questions when confronted with an ethical dilemma:

1. Is the proposed action legal?

2. Is the action balanced?

3. How does the action make me feel?

When examined within this framework, the correct action to take should become clear. If the action isn't legal, the analysis can stop there since it's rarely ethical to act in an illegal manner. If the action passes that test, is it balanced to the needs of the various groups that will be impacted? This question requires a look at the stakeholders and the impact of any decision on those groups. Finally, how does the decision make you feel? If in your gut the decision still doesn't feel right, that's your last indication that the decision isn't right. This personalization of the decision allows the manager to determine how he or she physically responds to the ethical decision.

Front-Page-of-the-Newspaper Test

In many ways this is the clearest and simplest of the proposed frameworks. This is also called the New-York-Times Rule. The basic idea is to ask with each ethical decision, is the result of this decision something I want to read about on the front page of *The New York Times, Wall Street Journal, USA Today*, etc. in the morning? Is it a decision I would be comfortable telling my grandmother? If the answer to either question is no, then the decision is probably unethical. It forces the decision-maker to visualize the possible public disclosure of his action and determine whether he is willing to accept those costs.

Laura Nash Model

Laura Nash, an author and educator who has focused her career on business ethics, developed a 12-step model to help managers reach ethical decisions. The questions focus on the various angles of the problem:

1. Have you defined the problem accurately?

2. How would you define the problem if you stood on the other side of the fence?

3. How did this situation occur in the first place?

4. To whom and to what do you give your loyalty as a person and member of the corporation?

5. What is your intention in making the decision?

6. How does this intention compare with the probable results?

7. Whom could your decision or action injure?

8. Can you discuss the problem with the affected parties first?

9. Are you confident that your position will be valid over a long period of time?

10. Could you disclose without qualm your decision or action to your boss, the board of directors, your family, or society as a whole?

11. What is the symbolic potential of your action if understood?

12. Under what conditions would you allow exceptions to your stand?

The purpose of this model is to examine a decision from the perspective of all stakeholders. It also highlights how the manager would feel if the decision is thrust into the media spotlight. After answering these questions, a manager should be able to determine whether a decision is ethical for them.

Sarbanes-Oxley Act of 2002

Congress passed the Sarbanes-Oxley Act of 2002 (SOX) as a direct response to the dramatic collapse of several large companies and loss of shareholder value due to accounting irregularities. Sarbanes-Oxley provides a comprehensive regulatory framework for regulating external accounting firms as well as internal audit functions. The failure to abide by Sarbanes-Oxley can result in jail time and civil fines.

The legislation is sweeping and cannot be covered in detail in this book. However, there are certain principles and compliance areas from SOX that every business law student should know. Keep in mind that the overarching goal of SOX is to regulate corporate governance and financial practices with strict compliance criteria. While there are eleven titles in SOX, there are six key compliance sections, which I'll discuss in detail in the following sections.

Certification of Periodic Financial Reports

Section 302 requires that periodic financial reports include the following certifications:

- ◆ That the signing officers reviewed the report

- ◆ That the report is not misleading and does not contain any material untrue statements or material omissions

- ◆ That the financial statements fairly present the financial condition of the company

- ◆ That the signing officer is responsible for internal controls and has reviewed those within 90 days

- ◆ That the report contains a list of any deficiencies in the internal controls and information on any fraud to the auditors and audit committee

- ◆ That the report details any significant changes in internal controls or related factors that could have a negative impact on internal controls

The purpose of this section is to provide a person who is ultimately responsible for any financial misstatements or fraud.

Accuracy of Financial Statements

Section 401 requires companies to ensure that their financial statements are accurate and presented in a way that does not contain incorrect statements. It also requires disclosure of off-balance sheet transactions, arrangements, obligations, and other relationships the issuer has with unconsolidated entities or other persons, which may have a material or future impact on the company's financial condition.

Enhanced Conflict Provisions

Section 402 provides for enhanced conflict of interest provisions. Specifically, personal loans to directors or executives are no longer allowed, except in very rare circumstances.

Internal Controls

Under Section 404, management is required to file with each annual report an internal control report. That report should state the responsibility of management for establishing and maintaining adequate internal controls and procedures for financial reporting along with an assessment of the effectiveness of those internal controls. This section also requires the external auditor to sign off on the company's assessment of its internal controls.

Real-Time Issuer Disclosures

Section 409 requires companies to make real-time disclosures to the public of any material changes in the financial condition or operation of the company. Thus, if a material change occurs between annual reports, the company must issue a special report so the public is informed of those changes in real time rather than waiting until the next report.

Criminal Sanctions

Under Section 802 anyone who knowingly alters, destroys, mutilates, conceals, covers up, falsifies, or makes a false entry in an attempt to interfere with an investigation could go to jail for up to 20 years. And any accountant who conducts an audit must keep the audit or review work papers for a period of five years.

Stay Out of Jail

Section 802 was a direct response to the shredding that Arthur Andersen employees did when the Enron investigation started. Shredding was never a good idea after an investigation started, but now it could lead to stiff penalties plus time in jail.

The Least You Need to Know

- At its core, business ethics are the principles and values that govern decisions and actions within a company.

- A company that acts ethically will have higher trust, a better reputation, and higher shareholder value.

- Ethical dilemmas can be solved by asking basic questions such as whether the action is legal, whether it considers the stakeholders, and whether it can be explained on the front-page of a newspaper.

- The Sarbanes-Oxley Act of 2002 provides tighter regulation of the financial statements and reports of companies as well as external auditors.

Part

2

The Regulatory Environment

It's hard to operate in today's world without colliding into government regulations. While the United States attempts to have a free-market marketplace, the reality is that governments, both federal and state, actively regulate the marketplace. Here you'll learn the key principles and players in government regulation of business.

We'll start with a look at the basics of regulation and antitrust regulations. Then we'll examine the role of administrative agencies and international trade. While there are hundreds of federal agencies, we'll end this part with a look at the history and roles of 11 agencies that many businesses interact with.

Chapter **4**

Government Regulation of Business

In This Chapter

- ◆ Regulation in a free enterprise system

- ◆ Why regulate prices?

- ◆ Government regulation of monopolies and other forms of unfair competition

- ◆ Remedies for anticompetitive behavior

In this chapter we're going to explore the way government, particularly the federal government, regulates business. The government regulates business for many reasons, most of which are focused on providing the most competitive environment possible for business. The intent is to create a business environment that benefits the consumer by providing better goods at a lower cost.

Regulation Versus Free Enterprise

The Supreme Court has held that the federal government may regulate business for any reason as long as it advances the government's economic needs. States may regulate business as long as the regulations don't interfere with interstate commerce or the federal government's activities. States set the limits on what local governments can regulate. So what local governments can do fluctuates from state to state.

In a true *free enterprise* system, the government would not be involved in business. Instead, it would stand back and allow the market to dictate what actions businesses take. If consumers didn't like how a business operated, they would take their business to other companies. As a result, the "bad" companies would change their behavior to keep their customers.

def•i•ni•tion

A **free enterprise** system is one where business is regulated by supply and demand rather than government interference through regulations and subsidies.

In a market economy businesses try to respond to the needs of customers. In real life, the market doesn't always respond quickly enough to problems. Thus, the federal and state governments step in with regulations that direct the actions of the companies.

Governments cycle through times of regulation and deregulation. When companies abuse their freedom, the government steps in with regulation. When the economy shifts because of new technology, the regulations may be lifted.

For example, in the early 1980s the federal government broke up Ma Bell because it acted in a monopolistic manner that harmed consumers. Ma Bell consisted of 24 companies that provided local phone service, AT&T for long distance, a research and development lab, and a manufacturing company. On January 1, 1984, Ma Bell was broken into seven regional Bells with AT&T keeping the long-distance service. Twenty years later, the face of telecommunications is dramatically different. There is competition for local calls; there are hundreds of providers of long-distance service; and consumers can purchase their phone service through cable providers and other Internet sources. The government is more open to consolidation among telecommunications firms because the market has changed.

Why Government Regulates Business

The primary goal of government regulation is to protect the public from harm. One way the government protects the public is to regulate false advertising and labeling of products. The Federal Trade Commission (FTC) bears the majority of this burden by preventing fraud, deception, and unfair business practices. The FTC enforces federal laws that protect consumers and provides information that helps consumers avoid fraud and deception.

It also sets health and purity standards for cosmetics, pharmaceuticals, and foods. Let's look at the U.S. Food and Drug Administration (FDA). The FDA plays the lead role in regulating this area. The FDA regulates under the mandate to improve patient and consumer safety while increasing access to new medical and food products. The FDA also regulates to improve the quality and safety of manufactured products and the supply chain.

Attempts to deregulate are not always successful. In the late 1970s the federal government began deregulating thrifts, organizations like savings and loans that are formed to hold deposits for individuals. This deregulation, in combination with economic factors like falling inflation and collapsing housing prices, in the mid-1980s led to the collapse of the savings and loan industry. The Financial Institutions Reform, Recovery and Enforcement Act of 1989 (FIRREA) was enacted to save the savings and loan industry by increasing federal oversight.

The tension between regulation and deregulation ebbs and flows. When several large companies like Enron, WorldCom, and Adelphia imploded in the early 2000s due to accounting irregularities, Congress responded by passing the Sarbanes-Oxley Act (see Chapter 3). Once Congress acts, the agencies create regulations the companies must follow and the oversight to make sure the companies follow those regulations. So expect this cycle to continue.

Citations

To learn more about the role of the federal government in regulating businesses, check out the following websites:

◆ Food and Drug Administration: www.fda.gov

◆ Federal Trade Commission: www.ftc.gov

◆ Consumer Litigation branch of the Civil Division of the Department of Justice: www. usdoj.gov/civil/ocl/index.htm

---

Federal Antitrust Enforcers

Antitrust laws are enforced in three basic ways. The federal laws are enforced by civil enforcement actions by the Federal Trade Commission (FTC), criminal and civil enforcement actions by the Antitrust Division of the Department of Justice (DOJ), and lawsuits brought by private parties asserting damages from the anticompetitive behavior. The FTC and DOJ have overlapping jurisdiction, but have developed separate areas of expertise. The agencies also will consult with each other prior to starting an investigation to avoid duplication.

In addition to these two agencies, state attorneys general play a role by bringing suits under federal law on behalf of businesses and consumers from their states. This is in addition to any actions they may bring under state law. Nineteen states joined the Department of Justice in its 1998 suit against Microsoft. Private individuals may also bring suit under the federal laws.

There is also a growing area where international organizations are also involved in antitrust on a multinational level. This can be seen with the ongoing litigation saga Microsoft has endured where it has fought legal battles in the United States and internationally. According to the FTC, there are more than 100 foreign competition agencies. That's a lot of antitrust law and regulation for businesses to monitor.

Regulation of Prices

The regulation of prices happens at the state and federal levels. It can occur when consumers purchase products, but also by limiting interest rates, or instituting rent controls. Because the state laws vary by state but echo federal principles, here we'll focus on the federal principles.

Price-Fixing Under the Sherman Antitrust Act

Congress passed the Sherman Act in 1890 as a response to the large trusts that had developed in steel, sugar, and other areas of the economy. The Federal Trade Commission (FTC) Act and Clayton Act were passed in 1914 to prevent unlawful mergers and anticompetitive business behavior. The Supreme Court has found that violations of the Sherman Act are automatically violations of the FTC Act. The core purpose of these laws is to protect consumers by encouraging businesses to operate efficiently and keep costs down and quality up.

A key principle in this area is that competitors cannot engage in price-fixing. Price-fixing—any agreement to charge an agreed-upon price or set maximum or minimum prices—is a form of collusion that is prohibited by Section 1 of the Sherman Antitrust Act. Horizontal price-fixing occurs when competitors get together on pricing. Let's say several competitors are at the same business networking luncheon.

While there, they discuss the prices they charge on a make and model of laptops they all sell. As they talk, they decide they could all make more money if they set the price at the same level. This is horizontal price-fixing and is illegal.

Citations
The Sherman Act is one of two primary federal laws used to prevent antitrust activities. Section 1 states: "every contract, combination in the form of trust or otherwise, or conspiracy, in restraint of trade or commerce among the several Sates, or with foreign nations, is declared to be illegal. Every person who shall make any contract or engage in any combination or conspiracy hereby declared to be illegal ..." Price-fixing is covered by this section.

Because price is a sensitive part of competition, if competitors engage in price-fixing, it can also be monopolistic behavior. That's because if competitors collude to set prices, they are often trying to prevent new competition.

Price-Fixing Under the Clayton Act and Robinson-Patman Act

The Clayton Act and Robinson-Patman Act also prohibit price discrimination. Section 2 of the Clayton Act prohibits anyone engaged in commerce to "discriminate in price between different purchasers of commodities of like grade and quality ... where the effect of such discrimination may be substantially to lessen competition or tend to create a monopoly in any line of commerce, or to injure, destroy, or prevent competition with any person who either grants or knowingly receives the benefit of such discrimination ..."

The key language is "substantially to lessen competition or tend to create a monopoly." So how does price discrimination accomplish that?

One of my favorite cases that illustrates price discrimination is the Utah Pie Company case. In this case, three outside competitors entered the Utah pie market. Their entries resulted in a price war—not anticompetitive in and of itself. What made this action unconstitutional is that several of these companies charged a higher price for the same pie in other states. Because of that fact, the court determined that the only reason the companies would charge lower prices was to push the Utah Pie Company out of the Utah pie market. That is predatory pricing because the companies intended to harm the Utah Pie Company.

Under the Robinson-Patman Act price discrimination occurs when sellers charge competing buyers different prices for the same commodity or provide different allowances for the competitors. Allowances include items like compensation for advertising or services like repairs. Price discrimination in this context isn't always illegal, because it may cost more to get a product to one customer over another. For example, the shipping costs may be higher for one. Robinson-Patman applies to commodities and purchases, not services and leases. To be a violation the goods must be of like grade and quality, there must be a likely harm to competition, and the sales must usually be interstate.

Price-fixing also isn't illegal under Robinson-Patman if the lower price results from the seller attempting to meet a competitor's price or service offered to that customer. What the pie companies did in the Utah Pie Company case was predatory pricing because they priced below cost with the intent of harming competition by forcing out a competitor. That is never legal. The price difference may also be justified by different costs in the sale, delivery, or manufacture of the goods.

Permitted Price Discrimination

In addition to the two forms of allowable price discrimination under the Robinson-Patman Act, price discrimination is allowed in select circumstances. Those include when the difference in grade, quality, or quantity justifies the price difference. It is also justified when a different method of production is used or the quantity is different. Maybe the goods have deteriorated in a way that justifies the price difference. A close-out sale on a particular line of goods to move the remaining stock can also justify the price difference.

Regulation of Monopolies and Other Forms of Unfair Competition

The Sherman Act and Clayton Act do more than address price-fixing. These laws also are designed to prevent monopolies and other forms of unfair competition.

Tying and Bundling Products

In addition to the price discrimination discussed above, Section 1 of the Sherman Act prevents tying of product and monopolization of markets. Products are tied when the seller conditions the sale or lease of a product the buyer wants on purchase or lease of a second item it doesn't want. For tying to violate the Sherman Act, the seller must have appreciable economic power in the tying market.

A close cousin to tying is the bundling of products. Bundling occurs when related products are sold as one unit. In a sense newspapers are bundled to consumers. If I purchase a newspaper I pay a fixed rate for the entire paper. I can't pick and choose the sections I will actually read and pay only for those. The terms bundling and tying are often used interchangeably by the courts.

The distinction is that tying always includes coercion on the part of the seller, and bundling doesn't. Tying also will often include a slow-selling or unknown product. Bundling can occur because consumers actually want the products bundled. If I purchase a printer, I expect it to come with ink or toner. Those products are bundled together for my convenience. However, if the printer company ensures that nobody can compete with it on the sale of replacement toner, the product may now be tied.

Economists tend to believe that tying and bundling can be good for the economy.

In the Microsoft case that was originally filed in 1998, one charge against Microsoft was that it tied its products. Microsoft required computer manufacturers that wanted to use its software to purchase Internet Explorer. Because Microsoft had a near-monopoly in operating systems, it was in a monopolistic position, and the United States and other plaintiffs successfully argued that Microsoft used the tying to keep competitors out of the market.

Per Se Violations

A small number of anticompetitive behaviors are per se violations of the antitrust laws. *Per se* means that it's a violation just because the act happened. All the plaintiff must do is show the violations occurred and move to a determination of damages. The Supreme Court has held the following are always per se violations:

♦ Competitors agree to divide markets

♦ Group boycotts

♦ Price-fixing in both vertical and horizontal arrangements

♦ Tying, though this trend is changing to a rule of reason review

If a company engages in any of these activities or agreements, they have violated antitrust laws, specifically the Sherman Act. Because they are per se violations and always illegal, these items do not require a trial on the law. However, courts are shifting to require market analysis in tying cases, which is fact intensive, using a rule of reason analysis.

Stay Out of Jail

Don't assume that every monopoly is illegal. Sometimes a monopoly is the truly most efficient arrangement in a free market. Other companies either don't have the interest in a market or are unable to make the product as efficiently or inexpensively as the monopoly holder. Or the monopoly holder is doing nothing to actively prevent competitors. In those situations, the monopoly is legal.

Antitrust Examination of Mergers and Acquisitions

The Sherman Act does not speak to businesses becoming too big unless they take monopolistic action. However, the Clayton Act prohibits companies from merging with or acquiring another if "the effect of such acquisition may be substantially to lessen competition, or to tend to create a monopoly." The Federal Trade Commission and Antitrust Division of the Department of Justice are charged with reviewing proposed mergers. Periodically you'll see headlines about mergers that have either been approved or denied by one or both of these agencies. In multinational mergers, the companies will also need to receive approval from foreign governments.

This requirement to give premerger notification to the FTC and DOJ is designed to limit the loss incurred if companies are told to divest postmerger. It also reflects the reality that most mergers benefit the consumer because they increase competition and allow the firms to operate more efficiently. But the government is watching for those mergers that could lead to higher prices, fewer goods and services, or less innovation. The agencies are most concerned about horizontal mergers, those between direct competitors. They review more than 1,000 merger applications a year, and approve more than 95 percent with many of the balance approved once changes are made.

Legal Competitor Dealings

Not all dealings between competitors are illegal. In fact, those interactions can be procompetitive when they allow firms to move into new areas of business both with products or by expanding geographic markets. In addition, competitors often interact in trade associations, joint ventures, and professional groups.

For example, a large pharmaceutical company like Eli Lilly will often form a joint venture with a much smaller pharmaceutical that has a drug it needs help marketing. The smaller company had the expertise and luck to identify a new compound, but it needs assistance with sales and marketing that a large company like Eli Lilly can offer. Because the drug might not be available without the larger company's involvement, it's not anticompetitive for two firms in the same industry to join together for the purpose of manufacturing, marketing, and selling that drug.

The problem occurs when these interactions between competitors lead to the companies not acting independently or the competitors are now able to wield market power together that they did not have independently. The key analysis regulators make is whether the agreement brings procompetitive benefits or anticompetitive harms.

The same rule of reason or per se analysis is used to evaluate these agreements between competitors. If the agreement is so likely to cause anticompetitive harm that they violate antitrust laws *per se*. The harm is so obvious that a fact-finding trial isn't required. If the harm isn't as obvious than the rule of reason will be used, requiring fact finding into the overall competitive effect. Remember, rule of reason analysis is flexible and varies depending on the nature of the agreement and market.

Remedies for Anticompetitive Behavior

There are two different types of remedies for anticompetitive behavior. Sometimes civil remedies of money damages or injunctions will be issued. In other cases, criminal remedies are available.

Civil Remedies

Plaintiffs can seek an injunction against the defendant for violating the antitrust laws. If the plaintiff is an individual or business, then they can seek treble damages. If the suit is a class-action brought by a state attorney general, then the attorney general can seek damages to reimburse the buyers who have been harmed by the price discrimination or fixing. Structural remedies and injunctions are often the remedies for mergers and acquisitions.

Criminal Remedies

The DOJ can seek criminal remedies under the Sherman Act. Those remedies include a maximum fine of $10 million against a corporation per incident. The maximum fine against an individual is $350,000, but that person can also be sentenced to up to three years in jail or both for the anticompetitive behavior. The DOJ obtained a criminal fine of $250 and $500 million against BASF Ag and F. Hoffmann-La Roche in 1999. In 2003 in 41 criminal cases, it obtained $107 million in fines and an average sentence of 21 months.

Old Laws Applied to Today's Marketplace

One challenge enforcers have today is that the laws they enforce were created to deal with the economy of the late 1800s and early 1900s. That economy was more stagnant than today's fast-paced, technology-based one. So the question is whether the laws even work. The Microsoft case is a great example of this. The case was fast-tracked from the moment it was filed in May 1998. Yet, by the time the D.C. Court of Appeals issued its decision at the end of June 2001, technology changed. Did the facts that led to the case filing still exist? Was Microsoft a natural monopoly? These questions will likely be asked more in the future as old laws are applied to a rapidly changing economy.

The Least You Need to Know

- The federal government actively regulates businesses to ensure that consumers are protected and the market is as open as possible.

- Price-fixing is a per se violation of the Sherman Act and always illegal; however, the courts recognize that there are limited occasions when price discrimination between buyers is legal.

- Antitrust laws also prevent monopolistic behavior which prevents competition or substantially limits it.

- Civil and criminal remedies can be obtained against violators and those include treble damages and jail time.

Administrative Agencies

In This Chapter

- ◆ Understanding the unique role of administrative agencies
- ◆ Agencies wield legislative power
- ◆ Agencies wield executive power
- ◆ Agencies wield judicial power
- ◆ Appeal of the agency's action
- ◆ The complexities of international trade

The first permanent administrative agencies weren't created until after the late 1800s. Administrative agencies serve as an extension of the government to regulate businesses. These agencies operate as the government's presence to enforce the laws. This chapter will examine agencies and the roles they play in the business arena.

Administrative Agencies' Unique Role

Administrative agencies are granted authority to act on behalf of the legislative branches of governments. Officially, administrative agencies are official government bodies that have the power and authority to direct and implement portions of government legislation. Generally, an agency does this by creating regulations that apply the law to specific situations. Then the agency enforces that law.

While the first administrative agency was created in 1789 to administer Revolutionary War soldiers' pensions, the first permanent administrative agency was created by Congress in 1887. The Interstate Commerce Commission was authorized by Congress to regulate commerce among the states, especially related to transportation issues. Since this numerous agencies have been created to facilitate the enforcement of laws.

Citations

While this chapter focuses primarily on federal agencies, it's important to note that agencies also exist at the federal and state levels. The state and local agencies often mirror the purposes of the federal agencies. Regardless of the level they function on, all are charged with enforcing and implementing legislation. States will also have laws that are similar to the Administrative Procedure Act (APA) to govern and limit the actions of state agencies.

Federal Administrative Procedure Act

Federal agencies are governed by the Federal Administrative Procedure Act (APA). The APA provides the rules and procedures the federal agencies must follow as they propagate and enforce regulations. It is designed to bring uniformity to the administrative process across agencies.

While our system of government is usually broken into three distinct groups: executive, legislative, and judicial, the agencies usually fill all three functions. Because agencies have wide authority to act in these three areas, they are subject to strict regulation and review by the APA. The APA requires agencies to operate in an open manner by maintaining open records, open meetings, and public announcement of agency guidelines. All three are important to maintain accountability regarding the agency's actions.

Open Records

The Freedom of Information Act (FOIA) combines with the APA to require federal agencies to make their records available to the public on request. The FOIA ensures the public access to public records. If a citizen requests records in writing, the federal agency must provide those records unless the request falls within one of nine exemptions. The exemptions include things like national security, confidential business information, or when it would infringe on personal privacy. In general, the exemptions are designed to prevent individuals or companies from gaining access to information that could be used to injure the person or company that provided the information to the government. The presumption is that the exemption does not apply, and the burden is on the person asserting the exemption to show that it does in fact apply.

FOIA covers all agency records that were created or obtained by a federal agency and are at the time the request is filed, within the control and possession of the agency. A request should be filed with each agency's FOIA office. The law requires the agencies to maintain instructions on how to file FOIA requests in a public manner—most agencies contain the important information on their website.

Open Meetings

The APA also requires that agency meetings be open except in limited circumstances. Meetings that involve deliberations of the agency must be open to the public. The agency must publicize the meeting at least one week ahead of time. The notice must also be published in the *Federal Register*. While there are numerous exceptions to the requirement that the meetings be open to the public, the law has created a standard that brings uniformity to the agencies and their exposure to public scrutiny. This portion of the APA is found at 5 U.S.C. 552b and is called the Government in Sunshine Act. The act was passed in 1976 to bring the actions of the agencies into public view except in limited circumstances.

Public Announcements

The APA also requires that agencies make public the way they operate. This is accomplished by publishing the rules, principles, and procedures the agency follows. One aspect of this is that the agency must publish proposed rules and regulations. The public then has an opportunity to comment on the rules before the agency can adopt the final version. The agencies also have public hearings on some proposed rules.

Agency's Legislative Power

An agency utilizes *legislative power* when it creates regulations. Regulating is a necessary part of filling any gaps left by Congress in implementing laws. The APA provides strict guidelines for agencies to follow as they create regulations.

def•i•ni•tion

Legislative power is the power to make laws by creating and passing regulations with public input.

Before it can act, the agency must receive authority from Congress. This authority will come from the enabling legislation, that is the legislation the agency will enforce. The authority to regulate is broad. If Congress failed to address a necessary area the agency will oversee, the agency can create rules and regulations to cover the missed areas. This issue often arises when technology has advanced in ways Congress couldn't anticipate or chose not to address. In general, the courts will defer to the administrative agency's decisions on rule making in areas that are not clearly covered by the law.

The agency fills its legislative function as it creates regulations. The first step is that Congress must pass a law that gives jurisdiction to a particular agency to make rules and regulations. Sometimes an existing agency will be given authority for the new area. Other times, Congress will create a new agency for the purpose of enforcing a law. For example, the Americans with Disabilities Act broke new ground. New regulations had to be created to elaborate on and enforce the new law. Part of that new responsibility was given to the Equal Employment Opportunity Commission (EEOC). The EEOC already existed, but the ADA gave it authority to operate in a new area of law.

Stay Out of Jail

Agencies must conduct studies prior to rule making, in part to establish the necessity for the new regulation. The agency must follow the same steps when rescinding a rule that it did when creating the rule. If an agency conducted studies prior to creating the rule, it cannot withdraw a regulation or rule without conducting studies that show the rule is no longer needed.

Once authority has been established, the agency must conduct research and explore different methods to regulate the area. The agency must conduct a cost benefit analysis of the proposed regulations and solutions.

Proposed regulations must be published in the *Federal Register.* That provides public notice that the proposal is under consideration. A proposed regulation must also be published in the relevant trade publications. At the same time, the agency must publish a regulatory flexibility analysis, which examines the impact of the proposed rule on small entities.

Following the regulation's publication in the *Federal Register*, the public must have a minimum of 30 days for public comment. Any person or entity that is affected by the proposed comment can submit their comments in writing or by attending one of the public hearings.

After the agency has received the public comments it has several options. It can pass the rule, modify the rule, or withdraw the rule. If it modifies the rule, and if the change is significant, the agency must publish the amended version in the *Federal Register* and allow additional public comments.

The steps to passing a regulation are summarized in the following figure.

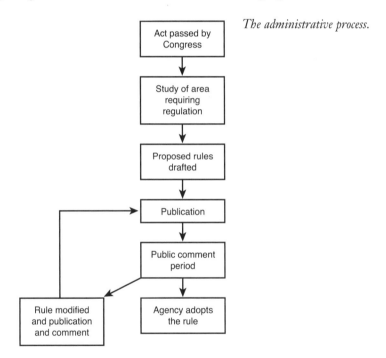

The administrative process.

An Agency's Executive Power

In exercising its *executive power*, an agency has the full power to investigate cases. It can call witnesses and require those witnesses to produce documents and other evidence. Regulations can be enforced as law just as any statute or court decision. Agencies can investigate and determine if a company or individual has violated any regulation. Agencies are limited by the rules of evidence when conducting searches.

def•i•ni•tion

Executive power is the power to execute the laws.

An Agency's Judicial Power

Agencies also act through *judicial power* to serve as judge and conduct hearings on violations. In this sense the agency serves as a court; this authority is limited to act as a court even though they are not courts.

As with a court, someone must file a complaint to start the judicial process. The complaint is served on the named company or individual. An investigation may be conducted by the agency, or the parties will exchange discovery. Then the agency will hold a hearing.

def•i•ni•tion

Judicial power is the power to act as a court and hear matters related to the agency's regulations.

The hearing will be before an administrative law judge (ALJ). While a party may have a right to a jury trial in true judicial proceedings, a jury is not available in agency proceedings. The ALJ hears the complaint, swears in witnesses, evaluates the evidence, and then makes an action recommendation to the head of the agency.

Consent decrees—informal settlements enforced by the agency—can be used by the parties to avoid litigation. Consent decrees can be effective when the alleged wrongdoer is told before a complaint is filed about the possible problems. Then the offender is more likely to work with the agency to rectify any wrongs or correct its behavior. The parties may also reach a settlement at anytime prior to the end of a hearing.

The ALJ will make a recommendation to the agency head. The agency will usually draft an opinion setting forth the facts and reasoning behind the ALJ's decision. This is an important step if a party appeals the agency's decision.

The agency can impose a penalty and issue orders that bind the regulated party. Some laws also give the agency authority to issue cease and desist orders. Those orders allow an agency to stop a party from continuing to act in a way that violates the law. An agency may make an initial determination without conducting a hearing, unlike litigation, which leads to either a trial or a settlement.

Appealing the Agency's Action

Often a regulated party will not agree with the results of the ALJ hearing. When that is the case, the regulated party will want to appeal the decision. Before an appeal can be made, that party must exhaust its remedies before the agency. This means it must wait to appeal until after the agency has issued a final decision. However, there are instances in which the Supreme Court has stated that a hearing must be held because an appeal is not a sufficient remedy.

There are occasions when an appeal can be raised prior to a final decision. Those include occasions when 1) available remedies would not provide relief; 2) irreparable injury will occur without immediate judicial relief; 3) an appeal within the agency would be worthless; or 4) the plaintiff has raised a substantial constitutional question.

Once the party has exhausted its remedies, courts can review the case on the following bases. Courts can review procedural issues. These arise when an agency fails to follow the procedures required by the APA and other laws. If substantive law or fact issues are involved, the court can review those. If the court disagrees with the agency's interpretation, it will overturn the agency's ruling. If the question is one of fact, the court will accept the agency's interpretation if there is substantial evidence to support it. The court will not overturn it simply because it would have interpreted the facts differently.

The courts will also review cases where the question is whether the case was beyond the jurisdiction of the agency. The court will sustain the agency's action if substantial evidence supports it. Finally, the courts will review agency actions that are arbitrary and capricious. This situation will arise if an agency changes its prior decisions or actions. If the agency does not explain its reversal, the action is arbitrary and will be reversed. The general rule is that an agency decision will not be reversed unless there is an error of law or an abuse of discretion. Courts will rarely find that an action was arbitrary or capricious.

International Trade

International trade has its own complexities and is ever evolving. Because of that evolving nature, I'll focus on a couple of fundamental principles that apply regardless of the countries involved.

When dealing in the international arena, it's important to remember that law grows out of culture, history, and social context, so the law of a country will be a unique reflection of that country's experience. Those differing views will lead to differing approaches to areas like antitrust, commerce, and crimes. For example, bribing government officials to oil the wheels of commerce is not illegal in many countries, although it is in the United States.

Which Law Applies?

When a transaction occurs domestically, the question is which state's law applies. Occasionally, there will be a question whether state or federal law applies. When the transaction is between parties in different countries, you have to determine which country's laws apply. Will it be the seller's country or the importer's country laws that apply? To determine that you should first look at the language of the contract. Often the parties will set the prevailing law in the contract through a *choice-of-law provision*.

def•i•ni•tion _____

A **choice-of-law provision** is a contract clause that sets which law will apply should a dispute develop.

If they did not, a treaty will often set the choice of law. Many countries have entered trade treaties for the purpose of governing the transactions between their citizens. One that may be covered in your class is the United Nations Convention on Contracts for the International Sale of Goods (CISG). This treaty deals with the contracts for the international sale of goods.

Arbitration

The parties to an international contract may prefer arbitration to litigation based on the added expense of international trials. Look in the contract for a clause that sets that all disputes must be resolved via arbitration or other dispute resolution process.

Important International Trade Organizations and Treaties

A number of international organizations provide structure to international transactions. Here are a few of the key players:

- ◆ **General Agreement on Tariffs and Trade 1994 (GATT):** 126 governments signed this agreement beginning in 1947 and continuing through the most recent version in 1994. Policed by the World Trade Organization (WTO), the purpose of this agreement is to promote trade without discrimination and protect members against *tariffs*.

def•i•ni•tion _____

Domestically, a **tariff** is a government-approved schedule of charges that can be made by a regulated business like a carrier; internationally, it's a tax imposed by a country on goods crossing its borders.

A key concept in GATT is that signatories to the agreement cannot give one country favored status over other signers. This is known as most-favored nation status, which requires that any privilege granted to a third country after two parties have contracted on the same subject matter is extended to the other party to the treaty. Under this treaty, all signing nations are equal, with none having a special advantage over another. The exceptions come when there is a regional group that can trade among themselves with special preferences. These regional groups include the North American Free Trade Agreement (NAFTA) and the European Union (EU).

♦ **United Nations Convention on Contracts for the International Sale of Goods (CISG):** The CISG, as it name suggests, provides uniform rules for the international sale of goods. The influence of Article 2 of the Uniform Commercial Code is clear in CISG. However, the CISG does not cover the sale of goods for personal, family, or household uses and the sale of watercraft, aircraft, natural gas, or electricity. Neither does it cover letters of credit, auctions, and securities. Contracting parties have the ability to opt out of the provisions of the CISG. However, if they do not affirmatively opt out, then the contract is governed by CISG.

♦ **European Union (EU):** The European Union is the outgrowth or development of the European Economic Community. The Union provides four main items to the member countries. First, the European Council sets broad policy guidelines for the member countries. Second, the European Commission initiates actions against violators. Third, the European Parliament fills an advisory legislative role with limited veto powers. Fourth, the European Court of Justice serves as the judicial arm of the EU.

♦ **North American Free Trade Agreement (NAFTA):** NAFTA is an agreement between Mexico, Canada, and the United States eliminating tariffs between the three countries over a 15-year period. NAFTA opens markets for a large section of goods as well as lowers barriers to U.S. investments in the member countries.

Governmental Regulation

Governmental regulation continues to exist in the international arena. That regulation mirrors many areas that national governments regulate, with the same purpose: to protect its citizens and businesses from outside competitors. Here are some of the ways that the government regulates in the international business arena:

♦ **Export regulations:** The United States controls the export of goods and technology. Unless a license is required by the regulations, domestic businesses no longer need a license to export goods. The Department of Commerce's

Exporter Assistance Staff is available to help businesses determine whether a license is needed. The Commerce Control List contains the items that export is controlled. The list also identifies why an item is controlled. Reasons include national security, crime control, short supply, and more. Civil and criminal charges can be brought against U.S. manufacturers who fail to obtain a required license.

◆ **Intellectual property:** The United States has regulations governing the importation of counterfeit intellectual property. Think CDs. Often CDs are pirated and manufactured in other countries, and then imported in to the United States. This infringes on the copyright of the artists on the CDs. Remedies available to the copyright holder include injunctions, seizure and destruction of the counterfeit goods, and damages and attorneys' fees.

Stay Out of Jail

Some goods are called gray market goods. These goods are made by a foreign business that has a license to manufacture them from the trademark holder. However, those goods are then imported to the United States to compete against the goods domestically. U.S. law prohibits the importation of those goods unless the U.S. trademark holder gives written consent.

◆ **Antitrust:** Restraints of trade can occur in the international market, just as they can domestically. See Chapter 4 for more on domestic antitrust regulation. Antitrust laws are designed to protect American consumers from anticompetitive behavior of domestic and foreign corporations. It also protects corporations from outside antitrust coalitions that are created to attempt to exclude others from an international marketplace.

◆ **Securities regulation:** U.S. securities regulations can be violated internationally as well as domestically. When this occurs, the laws can be enforced, but may intersect with international laws. U.S. courts have jurisdiction when the violations affect U.S. citizens living here if the act occurred domestically or abroad or to U.S. citizens living abroad if the action occurred in the United States. It does not apply to foreigners outside the United States unless the action occurred within the United States. The SEC is sometimes stymied in its enforcement efforts by foreign countries' secrecy laws.

◆ **Barriers to trade:** Countries will sometimes use tariffs as a barrier to trade. They will also institute other controls against the free movement of investments, goods, and services. As stated above tariffs are a tax imposed on goods entering a country. In the United States the Customs Service imposes the tariff after determining the value of the imported goods. An import quota is an example of a nontariff barrier to trade.

The Least You Need to Know

♦ Administrative agencies are granted authority to act on behalf of the legislative branches of governments and utilize legislative, judicial, and executive powers.

♦ Proposed regulations must be published in the *Federal Register* and followed with a public comment period.

♦ A regulated party must exhaust all of its remedies before it can appeal the agency's decision.

♦ International agencies also have treaties and regulations that must be followed.

Chapter 6

Federal Agencies

In This Chapter

♦ Agencies that oversee the financial market

♦ Agencies that oversee employment law

♦ Agencies that oversee environmental regulation

♦ Two more miscellaneous agencies

Regulations require an agency to enforce them. While states have their own agencies that enforce business regulations, this chapter will examine federal agencies. Federal agencies run the gamut from Amtrak to the Ballistic Missile Defense Organization to the Farm Credit Administration. There are literally hundreds of departments and agencies listed at www. usa.gov. We can't look at every agency, but we'll review the big players that enforce the regulations businesses most often face.

Financial Market Agencies

There are dozens of agencies that regulate financial markets. Many of them are highly specialized like the Commodities Future Trading Commission, Federal Reserve Board, and Federal Deposit Insurance Corporation. Unless you're in banking, you will have little occasion to interact with these agencies.

And because of their highly specialized nature, they are rarely covered in a global business law class. There are three federal agencies that are likely to be covered and more likely to be encountered. Those are the Department of Justice, Securities and Exchange Commission, and Federal Trade Commission.

Department of Justice

The Department of Justice (DOJ) and its 40 components exist to enforce the laws and defend the interests of the United States. It also works to ensure public safety against foreign and domestic threats, works with states to control crime, and works to ensure fair and impartial administration of justice for all Americans. These missions are much broader than financial markets alone, however, it has mandates to enforce antitrust laws and to try federal white-collar crimes.

Many familiar departments fall under the DOJ, including Attorney General; Bureau of Alcohol, Tobacco, Firearms and Explosives; Immigration and Naturalization Service; and the Federal Bureau of Investigation. While the functions are different, they all work toward enforcing the laws of the United States.

The Antitrust Division has spent more than 60 years protecting the competitive process by enforcing the antitrust laws. The Antitrust Division enforces the Sherman Act and Clayton Act, which I discussed in Chapter 4. The Department of Justice brings criminal and civil enforcement actions to prohibit monopolies and antitrust behavior by businesses.

Stay Out of Jail

The DOJ can seek criminal remedies under the Sherman Act. Those remedies include a maximum fine of $10 million against a corporation per incident. The maximum against individuals is a fine of $350,000, up to three years in jail, or both for anticompetitive behavior. The DOJ obtained a criminal fine of $250 and $500 million against BASF Ag and F. Hoffmann-La Roche, a pharmaceutical company, in 1999 for conspiracy to suppress and eliminate competition in the vitamin industry. Executives from these companies also paid fines and spent time in U.S. jails. In 2003 in 41 criminal cases, it obtained $107 million in fines and an average sentence of 21 months.

The Civil Division represents the United States in a host of areas. Key areas include recovering money owed to the United States or victims of fraud, loan default, bankruptcy, violation of consumer laws, or unsatisfied judgments. It also enforces consumer protection laws. If a company violates any of these areas, this division can bring suit against it.

The Criminal Division's main focus is on counterterrorism and more traditional crimes like drug and organized crime, but it also plays a role in white-collar federal crimes. It enforces federal laws regarding intellectual property, asset forfeiture and money laundering, and fraud. Fraud involves corporate, securities and investment fraud, financial institution and insurance fraud, and government program and procurement fraud.

Securities and Exchange Commission

The Securities and Exchange Commission (SEC) regulates the U.S. securities markets. Its mission is to "protect investors, maintain fair, orderly and efficient markets, and facilitate capital formation." The goal of the laws and regulations that the SEC oversees is to ensure that all investors have access to certain information about companies and investments prior to buying stock. Companies are required to make public disclosures of financial and other information. The SEC oversees this public disclosure and enforces violations.

The hope is that with this transfer of information, the capital markets will be more active, efficient, and transparent. The SEC oversees securities exchanges, securities brokers and dealers, investment advisors, and mutual funds. The SEC has power to bring enforcement actions against the individuals and companies that violate the laws or regulations. The typical investigation involves insider trading, accounting fraud, and providing false or misleading information.

The framework for the SEC to oversee the securities markets comes from the Securities Act of 1933, the Securities Exchange Act of 1934, the Investment Company Act of 1940, and the Sarbanes-Oxley Act. The Securities Act of 1933 requires that investors receive financial and other significant information before the security is offered for public sale, and prohibits deceit, misrepresentations, or fraud about the sale of securities. The Securities Exchange Act of 1934 created the SEC and gave it disciplinary powers and required publicly traded companies to make periodic reports. The Investment Company Act of 1940 regulates the organization of companies that are primarily in investing, reinvesting, and trading in securities whose own securities are offered to the public. Finally, Sarbanes-Oxley gives the SEC authority to oversee reforms to corporate responsibility, financial disclosures, and accounting fraud. (See Chapter 22 for more on these laws.)

As with many of these agencies, the SEC oversees rule-making to implement legislation Congress has passed. Because the statutes the SEC enforces are broad, the rule-making process allows the SEC to provide guidance on how the law is interpreted and will be applied. The rule-making process follows the steps outlined in Chapter 5: release of the concept, rule proposal with comment period, and then rule adoption.

The role of the SEC has expanded in the aftermath of accounting scandals at large firms like Enron, WorldCom, and Adelphia, thanks to Sarbanes-Oxley. The SEC's duties and authority is carried out by the Division of Corporate Finance, Division of Trading and Markets, Division of Investment Management, and Division of Enforcement. The Division of Enforcement can utilize civil action by filing a complaint with a U.S. District Court and seeking an injunction or monetary damages. It may also pursue administrative action such as sanctions in a proceeding in front of an administrative law judge.

Federal Trade Commission

The Federal Trade Commission (FTC) was created in the Federal Trade Commission Act of 1914 with the purpose of preventing unfair methods of competition. Since that time, the FTC has developed into an agency that does much more. It oversees consumer protection and competition in many sectors of the economy. The Wheeler-Lea Amendment gave the FTC broad authority to prevent "unfair and deceptive acts or practices."

The Bureau of Consumer Protection protects consumers against unfair, deceptive, or fraudulent business practices. The Division of Advertising Practices enforces federal truth-in-advertising laws with a focus on claims of foods, drugs, dietary supplements, and anything else claiming a health benefit; tobacco and alcohol advertising; protecting children online; and claims made in newspapers, through direct mail, or on the Internet.

The Division of Consumer and Business Education plans and implements campaigns aimed to educate consumers. It also partners with four other agencies on www.consumer.gov. This site is designed to be a one-stop shop for consumers regarding consumer issues with links to free annual credit reports and the national do not call registry.

The Division of Enforcement ensures enforcement of administrative and court orders in consumer protection cases. It conducts investigations and prosecutes civil actions involving fraudulent, unfair, or deceptive marketing and advertising practices. And the division enforces consumer protection laws, rules, and guidelines.

The Division of Financial Practices develops policy and enforces laws related to financial and lending practices that affect the consumer. The Division of Marketing Practices monitors fraudulent marketing. The Division of Privacy and Identity Protection oversees issues related to consumer privacy, credit reporting, identity theft, and information security.

The Bureau of Competition is the branch of the FTC empowered to prevent anti-competitive mergers and other antitrust practices discussed in Chapter 5. It reviews proposed mergers and other business activities for anticompetitive behavior. If it finds such behavior, the Bureau will recommend formal law enforcement action.

The Bureau of Economics supports the efforts of the FTC by evaluating the economic impact of the FTC's actions. It provides economic advice for the enforcement of antitrust and consumer protection enforcement. It studies the effects of legislative options and regulations. And it analyzes markets and industries.

> **Citations**
>
> The Bureau of Competition enforces Section 5 of the Federal Trade Commission Act, Sections 1 and 2 of the Sherman Act, Sections 7 and 7A of the Clayton Act, and other provisions which prohibit certain forms of price discrimination, tying, and interlocking directorates and officers.

Employment Law Agencies

Several agencies play an active role in overseeing employment laws and policies. The four we'll examine here are the Department of Labor, Equal Employment Opportunity Commission, National Labor Relations Board, and Occupational Health and Safety Administration. As with the prior section, there are many more we could examine, but these are the biggest players most likely to be covered in a text.

Department of Labor

The Department of Labor was created by a law signed in 1913. Its purpose was to "foster, promote and develop the welfare of working people, to improve their working conditions, and to enhance their opportunities for profitable employment." Since its earliest days the department has tried to balance the needs of labor, business, and the public at large.

The current mission of the department is to foster and promote the welfare of the job seekers, wage earners, and retirees of the United States by improving working conditions, protecting retirement and health care benefits, strengthen collective bargaining, and tracking employment trends. The laws it oversees include those guaranteeing a safe and healthy working environment, minimum and hourly wage and overtime pay, freedom from employment discrimination, and unemployment insurance.

The Department of Labor has numerous divisions, each focusing on a different segment of its directive and the laws it enforces. They include the Employee Benefits Security Administration, Mine Safety and Health Administration, and Bureau of Labor Statistics.

Equal Employment Opportunity Commission

The Equal Employment Opportunity Commission (EEOC) was created by Title VII of the Civil Rights Act of 1964 with the purpose of eliminating employment discrimination in the workplace. The EEOC coordinates all regulations, practices, and policies; interprets laws; and monitors employment discrimination programs.

The EEOC enforces Title VII of the Civil Rights Act, the Equal Pay Act of 1963, the Age Discrimination in Employment Act of 1967, Sections 501 and 505 of the Rehabilitation Act of 1973, Titles I and V of the Americans with Disabilities Act of 1990, and the Civil Rights Act of 1991. Several of these laws are examined in Chapter 18. In a nutshell, the EEOC enforces these laws because they all contain some type of employment discrimination. The EEOC will investigate claims of discrimination. If it finds discrimination, it may prosecute the case, reach a settlement, or allow the claimant to pursue litigation on his or her own.

Consultation

If you're looking for employment law resources, here are two websites that are loaded with excellent information, guidance, and resources:

◆ Equal Employment Opportunity Commission: www.eeoc.gov

◆ U.S. Department of Labor: www.dol.gov

National Labor Relations Board

The National Labor Relations Board (NLRB) is an independent agency that enforces and administers the National Labor Relations Act (NLRA). See Chapter 17 for an explanation of that law. The NLRA governs interactions between unions and employers and guarantees the right of employees to organize and bargain collectively. The NLRA also provides that employees can't be forced to organize into unions. The NLRB was created by Congress in 1935 to enforce the NLRA and reduce interruptions in the economy caused by labor interruptions.

The NLRB has two main jobs. The first is to prevent and correct unfair labor practices regardless of who committed it—labor or employers. The second function is to determine whether employees want to organize their workplaces. The NLRB is organized into two sections:

♦ A five-member governing board, which acts as a quasi-judicial body to decide cases brought to it in administrative proceedings

♦ The Office of the General Counsel, which serves separately from the board and investigates and prosecutes unfair labor practice cases

When a charge is filed with the NLRB that an unfair labor practice has occurred a field office conducts an investigation. The regional office can dismiss the charges at that point, seek a voluntary settlement, or issue a formal complaint that will be heard by an administrative law judge. That decision may be appealed to the board. The board's decision then can be reviewed by a Court of Appeals.

The General Counsel strives to complete investigations and if needed file complaints within 7 to 15 weeks of the complaint being filed if a settlement can't be reached.

Occupational Health and Safety Administration

The Occupational Health and Safety Administration (OSHA) was created in 1970 under the Occupational Safety and Health Act of 1970. The act provides that each employer "shall furnish" a place of employment free from recognized hazards and "shall comply" with the standards, rules, and regulations promulgated under the act.

OSHA's role is to protect the safety and health of American workers by setting and enforcing standards, providing training, and encouraging process improvement in the workplace. OSHA, in combination with state partners, has approximately 1,100 inspectors who conduct on-site inspections of employers. OSHA also creates protective standards, enforces those standards, and helps employers comply with the standards.

Since 1971, OSHA has helped cut workplace fatalities by 62 percent and occupational injury and illness rates by 42 percent. Its inspectors oversee more than 8.9 million worksites. In 2006, less than 1 percent of inspections or 467 came under OSHA's Enhanced Enforcement Program for those employers that repeatedly and willfully violate the law. OSHA offers education and compliance assistance to small businesses.

Consultation _____

OSHA and its state counterparts conduct more than 95,000 on-site inspections a year.

Environmental Regulation Agencies

Since the late 1960s Congress has passed laws that focus on protecting the environment. Two of the agencies that enforce those laws are the Environmental Protection Agency and the Fish and Wildlife Service.

Environmental Protection Agency

In the late 1960s and early 1970s, Congress began aggressively regulating the environment. In order to enforce its new laws, Congress created the Environmental Protection Agency (EPA).

The EPA was established in 1970 as part of a federal government push to provide cleaner water, air, and land. The EPA focuses on pollutants that can damage the environment and harm people. It also tries to find ways to reverse and repair the damage that's already been done. To accomplish this it performs environmental research in laboratories around the country and sponsors research. It also strives to further environmental education.

The EPA administers more than 20 environmental laws through regulations it proposes and adopts. Those acts include the Atomic Energy Act, Energy Policy Act, and Oil Pollution Act. However, the EPA is known more for enforcing the following acts:

- The Clean Air Act regulates air emissions with the purpose of protecting public health by reducing hazardous air pollutants.

- The Clean Water Act provides the structure to regulate pollutants that are released into water.

- CERCLA provides a federal superfund to clean up uncontrolled or abandoned hazardous waste sites as well as accidents, spills, and emergency releases of pollutants.

- The Endangered Species Act provides a program for the conservation and protection of threatened and endangered plants, animals, and their habitats.

One tool that the EPA uses is regulation. It develops new regulations as laws are passed and then enforces those regulations. It also offers financial assistance to state environmental programs and provides grants to educational institutions that research areas that need an influx of scientific knowledge.

Fish and Wildlife Service

Evolving from its earliest beginnings in 1871 as the U.S. Commission on Fish and Fisheries into a 1940 reorganization that created the current agency, the Fish and Wildlife Service (FWS) works with others to conserve, protect, and enhance fish, wildlife, plants, and their habitats. It takes a multipronged approach to fulfilling its mission. From conserving land and resources to achieving recovery and preventing extinction, the agency integrates science, stewardship, and partnerships to administer the Endangered Species Program.

The FWS enforces federal wildlife laws and has been a leader in implementing the Endangered Species Act since it passed in 1973. The FWS works with other agencies to conserve threatened and endangered species by ensuring that their actions do not jeopardize species or habitats. The agency also provides grants to help states and landowners.

Miscellaneous Agencies

While there are several hundred more agencies, we'll look at two more. The Federal Communications Commission and U.S. Patent and Trademark Office regulate important areas of the economy.

Federal Communications Commission

The Federal Communications Commission (FCC) was created by the Communications Act of 1934. The FCC regulates communications in most of its forms: interstate and international communications by radio, television, wire, satellite, and cable.

Five commissioners direct the FCC. The FCC has been organized into seven bureaus. The Consumer and Governmental Affairs Bureau interacts with consumers to educate them about goods and services, as well as receive their input on the commission's work. Its divisions develop consumer policy concerning regulated entities such as common carrier (telephone), broadcast, wireless, satellite, and cable companies. It has the power to resolve complaints about *slamming*, truth-in-billing, telemarketing, and monitoring trends that affect consumers.

def•i•ni•tion

Slamming is the practice of making unauthorized changes in telecommunications providers. It often occurs with long-distance providers.

The Consumer Inquiries and Complaints Division can mediate and attempt to settle unresolved disputes arising from consumer complaints.

The Enforcement Bureau is tasked with enforcing the Communications Act and the commission's rules in order to promote robust competition and innovation in the market. The key areas of enforcement are consumer protection enforcement, local competition enforcement, and public safety enforcement. The FCC has many other bureaus and offices within it. For example, the Media Bureau regulates AM and FM radio, television stations, cable television, and satellite services. Wireless telecommunications regulates the use of radio spectrum.

As with the other agencies, the FCC also regulates under its authorizing legislation. Consumers and businesses can comment on proposed regulations.

U.S. Patent and Trademark Office

While the name has changed during the last 200 years, the U.S. Patent and Trademark Office (USPTO) mission remains the same. As articulated in Article I of the Constitution, it is to secure to inventors for limited times the right to use and profit from their discoveries. The USPTO is fairly unique because it is fully funded by fees. Chapter 21 examines intellectual property and the laws the USPTO enforces.

The USPTO grants patents and trademarks. The staff is highly trained because they must analyze the science behind new inventions and ensure that nobody else made the discovery prior to the applicant. By granting patents and registering trademarks, the USPTO protects valuable products of companies. Unlike other agencies, the USPTO does not enforce the patent and trademark laws. That responsibility rests with the owner of the patent or holder of the trademark.

The Least You Need to Know

- The financial market agencies protect businesses and individuals from antitrust activities of their competitors as well as ensure that information flows to investors before they purchase stock in a company.

- The employment agencies provide protection to employees by regulating discrimination, health and safety in the workplace, wages and benefits, and unionization and labor practices.

- Environmental agencies are an outgrowth of a series of new laws protecting the environment that passed beginning in the late 1960s.

- Agencies play an important role in regulating the activities of businesses and the marketplace.

Part 3

Formation of a Business

Most entrepreneurs start interacting with the law with the foundational question: what kind of business should I start? While this might seem like a straightforward question, there are at least a dozen basic forms to choose from. This part will explain the types of business entities that exist and then evaluate how they differ from each other.

The key players you'll learn are corporations, partnerships, and franchises. But don't forget the limited partnership, limited liability partnership, limited liability company, joint venture, and more. So sit back and let's get ready to learn all about the different options available to those starting a business.

To Incorporate or Not?

In This Chapter

- ◆ Sole proprietorships: going it alone
- ◆ Partnerships, LLPs, and LLCs: working with others
- ◆ Corporations as a separate entity
- ◆ Joint ventures with other companies
- ◆ Franchises: mimicking a process that works

David and Tonya have an idea for the next great invention. They know they need to start a company, but they're not sure which entity will be the best for them. The choices seem endless and confusing.

This chapter provides an overview of the principal forms of business organizations. Chapters 8, 9, and 10 take an in-depth look at corporations, partnerships, limited partnerships, limited liability partnerships, and limited liability companies.

Sole Proprietorship

A sole proprietorship is the simplest structure for a business because it is unincorporated and owned by one person. In fact, some individuals may operate via this structure without realizing it. In our example above, if David takes the lead, he will be operating as a sole proprietor until the business is incorporated. All that is required for a sole proprietorship to exist is that an individual provide goods or services to others. These entities aren't registered with the secretary of state's office and all profits and losses are recorded on the individual's tax returns.

Let's say Bob is a copywriter who works out of his home. He freelances for magazines and companies around the country, but is employed by none. Instead, he works on a contract basis when the companies need his services. Even though he has filed no paperwork with the state, he is operating as a sole proprietorship.

Because a sole proprietorship does not file with the secretary of state or other state entity, it is a simple business to start and maintain. The proprietor does not share management decisions with others. Instead, all control is vested in one person. Because the sole proprietorship is not a separate entity in the eyes of the law, any profits are taxed as personal income, thus avoiding corporate taxation.

The key drawback is personal liability. Since there is no separate legal entity, all liability for any negligence, breach of contract, or other legal problems rests solely with the sole proprietor. The personal assets of the sole proprietor are fully at risk, even when the liability arises from a business action. The law makes no distinction between the person and the business. To avoid liability issues, a corporation or limited liability company (LLC) should be formed (see Chapter 10). Thus, risky business ventures should not be left as sole proprietorships.

Because it is owned by one person, a sole proprietorship is subject to dissolution upon the death of the owner.

Partnerships and Related Forms

Partnerships, which I'll discuss in detail in Chapter 9, are another business form that does not require formality. A true general partnership can exist without the official approval of the state. All that's required is two or more persons or entities that pool resources and talent with the purpose of making a profit. Most often, partnerships take the form of law firms, medical partnerships, accounting firms, and other professional firms. Small retail, service, and manufacturing firms may also choose this form for the flow through taxation of profits and losses. While profits and losses flow to the individual partners, so does liability. And the partnership must be terminated when a partner dies, wishes to leave the partnership, or becomes bankrupt.

Limited partnerships address the unlimited liability that partners in a general partnership share. However, to achieve liability that is limited to their contribution, the limited partners must act as investors and maintain no management in the partnership. For an in-depth look at the structure of limited partnerships, limited liability partnerships, and limited liability companies, turn to Chapter 10.

Limited liability partnerships go a step further by providing *limited liability*—in most states—for innocent partners regardless of their involvement in the day-to-day management.

Limited liability companies provide the most liability protection by adopting the liability standard of corporations while keeping the pass through taxation structure of partnerships. In that sense, this entity is the best of both worlds.

def•i•ni•tion

Limited liability is liability that is limited to the investment in the firm or partnership of the member or innocent partner.

Corporations

A corporation is a separate legal entity that exists to create a profit. In a nutshell, a corporation has shareholders who invest capital in the company. A board of directors oversees managers who run the day-to-day operations of the company. Profits are taxed at the corporate level before passing to the shareholders as dividends and being taxed again. The double taxation that results from profits being taxed at the corporate and shareholder level is the biggest drawback for a corporation.

A corporation has several advantages including it is a separate legal entity that can do anything an individual can, such as own property, enter contracts, and sue others. Because the company is owned through shares, a corporation's ongoing existence is not threatened by the death of a shareholder. Shareholders liability is limited to their investment in the corporation.

In addition to double taxation, the disadvantages include the organizational expenses to launch a corporation. For the detailed examination of corporations, turn to Chapter 8.

Joint Ventures

A joint venture exists when two or more persons or entities combine their labor or property for the purpose of a single business undertaking. The profits or losses are

Consultation

Think of a small pharmaceutical company. It may have created a drug that has made it through FDA approval, but to successfully market that product it will partner with a large pharmaceutical company. That partnership is a joint venture that marries the product of one company with the marketing and sales prowess of another for the limited purpose of marketing that one product.

shared as agreed, and the venture is usually limited in time. It lasts as long as specified in the agreement between the companies. Each participant usually has an equal right to management and control of the project. As with any partnership, a joint venture should not be entered without an exit strategy—a plan for how to end the joint venture.

A joint venture differs from a general partnership in the way it is focused on one particular endeavor, such as marketing a drug or building a mall. Each is a venture that one company cannot do on its own, but also easily defined and limited. Outside the area of the joint venture, the companies do not overlap or work together.

A joint venture can also be a vehicle to help a company enter foreign markets. In that case, the domestic company already has the necessary structure in place and is legally set up to conduct business, while the foreign company brings the new technology or product and business practice to the venture.

Unincorporated Associations and Cooperatives

Two additional forms of business are the unincorporated association and cooperatives. Unincorporated associations exist when two or more people come together for a specific nonprofit purpose. Think community soccer leagues. Because this is an unincorporated entity, it has no legal status on its own. It is a collection of people who each remain liable for their actions. However, if the group begins to act like a corporation, it may be treated as one for tax purposes.

Cooperatives are created when two or more people or entities come together to act through one agent for a specific purpose. Think farmers' co-ops: the farmers all run their farms separately but they come together for the purpose of selling their grain in hopes of obtaining a higher price as a result.

Ace Hardware, Florida's Natural, and Carpet One Floor & Home are examples of cooperatives. Ace Hardware is a dealer-owned cooperative. Florida's Natural was organized in 1933 as a grower's cooperative and now has more than 1,000 members. Carpet One Floor & Home is a purchasing cooperative. In each case, the members banded together to achieve results they could not as individuals.

Cooperatives are owned and controlled by the members. Cooperatives are generally focused on the needs of the members versus the public at large. While farmers may band together to negotiate the best prices and market their products, this is not the only form of cooperative available. Cooperatives can also be consumer cooperatives, worker cooperatives, and purchasing cooperatives. Consumer cooperatives are owned by the people who buy the goods. Worker cooperatives exist where the employees own the company. And purchasing cooperatives are owned by businesses and government entities for the purpose of banding together to enhance purchasing power.

Franchises

Franchises are a method of replicating business. Often the individual franchises are set up as partnerships, corporations, S-corporations, or limited liability companies. The *franchisor* allows the *franchisee* to replicate its business model, methods, and products at a price. Technically, a franchise is the generally exclusive right to engage in an activity in a geographic region. In the business sense, it is usually the right to sell a particular product in a particular area for a certain number of years.

The classic example of a franchise is a restaurant chain. Think McDonalds. Ray Kroc and the other founders of McDonalds did not have the resources to create an international chain and brand at the beginning, so they standardized the process and allowed other people to buy the right to use the products and brand names. Then the explosive growth could occur.

def•i•ni•tion

The Federal Trade Commission defines a **franchise** as an arrangement in which the owner of a trademark, trade name, or copyright licenses others, under specified conditions or limitations, to use the trademark, trade name, or copyright in purveying goods or services. The **franchisor** is the party granting the franchise; the **franchisee** receives the franchise.

Types of Franchises

There are three basic types of franchises:

◆ The **manufacturing or processing franchise** grants the franchisee the right to make and sell the products of the franchisor under its trademark. A great example of this is Coca-Cola. Coca-Cola does not own each bottling plant. Instead, it has divided the country into regions and allows its franchisees to operate their own plants to manufacture and sell the product within that region. Coca-Cola provides a secret ingredient and the process. The franchisee provides the capital, employees, and distribution.

♦ The **service franchise** allows the franchisee to provide a service under the terms of a franchise agreement. This franchise could be a dry-cleaners, a maid service, or a childcare service. Essentially, anything that provides a service rather than a good is franchised this way.

♦ The **distribution franchise** allows the franchisor to sell its products through the franchisees. The franchisees sell the product in a set geographic area to its customers. An oil company like ExxonMobil is a good example. ExxonMobil finds and refines the oil. It then sells that product to franchisees, who distribute it to the public.

Stay Out of Jail

The Federal Trade Commission cautions consumers about franchises that are really pyramid schemes. The difference between a valid franchise and a pyramid scheme? The FTC classifies something as a pyramid scheme based on the number of down-line the franchisee acquires; in other words, the number of people distributing below the franchisee. If commissions are based on that distribution, it's likely an illegal pyramid scheme rather than a legitimate franchise opportunity.

As each franchise type demonstrates, the franchise structure allows the replication and distribution of a product or service beyond the capacity of the franchisor on its own.

Benefits and Responsibilities of Franchise Ownership

A franchise allows the franchisee to operate a business with the benefit of the experience and products or goodwill of the franchisor. Goodwill is the value of a business beyond its tangible assets, and can include items like reputation, strong customer base, desirable location, and name. Often the franchisor has invested large amounts of capital in developing its name and reputation. The franchisee, by paying the franchise fee, gains access to that reputation.

The franchisee also obtains the right to use the trademarks, name, and copyrights of the franchisor. More important, the franchisee gains access to the trade secrets of the franchisor. The franchisor often provides or requires training of the franchisee's employees. For example, potential managers of a restaurant are sent to that franchisor's management school to learn the chain's way of doing things. A car dealership can expect the car manufacturer to train the dealership's service staff in how to care for the manufacturer's vehicles.

The franchisor usually sets up controls to maintain uniformity across franchisees. Those controls may include site approval for franchisees, design and appearance standards, restrictions on the goods and services franchisees can provide, and restrictions on methods of operation and the sales area. Each of these controls leads to greater consistency so consumers know what to expect. For example, a consumer can identify a McDonalds franchise because of the uniform design of the building. Customers also know what to expect on the menu regardless of which corner of the country they find themselves.

In addition to the initial franchise fee, the franchisee may make ongoing royalty payments. These can be in the form of a percentage of gross or net revenue. These royalties are for the ongoing right to use the franchisor's name. The franchisee often also has to contribute to advertising fees. This makes sense as one role of the franchisor is to maintain the goodwill and recognition of the company, which adds to the value of the franchise.

Franchise Agreements

The franchise agreement provides the framework to the relationship between the franchisor and its franchisees. It sets the amount of the fees and the limits of the company's controls on its franchisees. It also provides the terms for termination of the franchise relationship. Termination may usually occur upon some act or inaction on behalf of the parties.

FTC's Franchise Disclosure Document

In an effort to protect investors, the Federal Trade Commission (FTC) requires franchisors to provide a franchise disclosure document to prospective franchisees. Under new rules, this document must be provided to prospective franchisees within 14 days of the first meeting and the franchisee must have the information to review for at least 10 business days before investing.

If a company makes earnings claims, it must have a reasonable basis and substantiating disclosures must be made at the same time as the basic disclosure. A copy of the franchise agreement must be given with the disclosure. The franchisor cannot contradict the claims made in the disclosure.

The disclosures are designed to enable potential investors to protect themselves prior to investing in a franchise by providing key information about the franchise:

- The business experience of the franchisor and its brokers

- Any current and past litigation against the franchisor

- Any previous bankruptcy

- The material terms of the franchise agreement

- Initial and recurring payments

- Restrictions on territories

- Grounds for termination of the franchise

- Actual, average, or projected sales, profits, or earnings

Failure to follow the disclosure requirements can result in stiff fines for the franchisor.

Stay Out of Jail

In theory franchisors are not liable to third parties for the wrongful acts of their franchisees. This is a feature that makes franchisees appealing. However, franchisors can be sued under the theories of actual or apparent authority. To avoid this, franchisors should be careful not to control all areas of a franchisees business.

The Least You Need to Know

- All that is required for a sole proprietorship to exist is that an individual provide goods or services to others.

- Partnerships and corporations are the main forms of business entities.

- A joint venture exists when two or more persons or entities combine their labor or property for the purpose of a single business undertaking.

- A franchise is the generally exclusive right to engage in an activity—like selling a product—in a geographic region for a set period of time.

Chapter 8

Corporations: Separate Legal Entities

In This Chapter

- ◆ The different types of corporations
- ◆ Characteristics and powers of a corporation
- ◆ What's involved in creating a corporation
- ◆ Terminating a corporation
- ◆ Creating a new entity
- ◆ Shareholders and liability

When a group of people decide to start a business together, a likely form is a corporation. While a corporation can be one of several types, all share key benefits that make this entity particularly appealing. There are also weaknesses that need to be carefully evaluated, so the best form can be chosen. So let's dive in and dissect this business form.

Types of Corporations

In its simplest form, a *corporation* is an organization formed under the auspices of a state government for the purpose of operating a business. As a separate legal entity, the corporation can be sued and can do anything under the law that individuals can do.

As a separate legal entity, the corporation has many powers and abilities. For example, a corporation can own property in its own name, unlike a partnership. It can issue stock to shareholders as a vehicle for raising capital. It can continue indefinitely because it is not required to terminate at the death of a shareholder, unlike a partnership.

There are many classes of corporations. The differences stem from the source of the corporation's authority, its relationship to the public, and its activities. Here's a summary of some types:

♦ *Public* corporations are government entities such as cities and counties that are created to perform a governmental function.

def•i•ni•tion

A **corporation** is an artificial person, an entity separate from its owner, created by the government to carry on business or other activities; it is its own legal entity separate and distinct from the people who created and invest in the company.

♦ *Private* corporations can be one organized for charitable purposes or for business purposes. This is the broadest grouping and covers everything from companies that are traded on stock exchanges to charities. A private corporation is often called a public company in the business context. In either case, it's a company that's shares are bought by private investors. In a legal sense it is not a public company, because that designation is reserved for companies performing a quasi-governmental role.

♦ *Quasi-public* corporations exist to carry out a government mandate, but may also have private investors. Sallie Mae is an example. Regardless of who owns stock, the corporation must carry out its government-directed duties.

♦ *Public authorities* are companies owned by the government to provide services. Examples of this type include the Maryland Transit Authority and the Delaware River Port Authority.

♦ *Domestic corporations* are those that are incorporated and that operate in a state.

♦ *Foreign corporations* are those that are incorporated in one state but also operate inside a second state. For example, if you are in Illinois, a company that is incorporated under Illinois law is a domestic corporation. An Indiana corporation that is doing business in Illinois is a foreign corporation.

♦ *Special service corporations* are governed by special laws because of the specialized areas in which the corporations operate. These can include insurance, banking, and savings and loans. Because of the nature of these industries, federal and state governments and agencies heavily regulate them.

♦ *Close corporations* are held by a single or small group of shareholders, and the shares are not traded on a public exchange. These are often mom-and-pop companies that stay in the family. But the pool of investors is always small.

♦ *Subchapter S-corporations* are a type of corporation that grow out of the IRS code. By checking a box on Form 2553, the corporation will be treated as a partnership for tax purposes if it meets the following criteria: it is a domestic corporation with 100 or fewer shareholders; the shareholders are individuals, estates, or exempt organizations; and it has one class of stock. An S-corporation cannot have nonresident alien shareholders. It also cannot be an ineligible corporation such as a bank or thrift institution that uses the reserve method for bad debts, an insurance company subject to take under another section of the code, a professional corporation or a domestic international sales corporation.

♦ *Professional corporations* are those that are organized so that the members can practice a profession. This type of corporation is usually limited to lawyers, doctors, accountants, and architects. This form is similar to a limited liability partnership, in that participants are shielded from liability except for their personal liability for their malpractice or negligence. Professional corporations will have PC or P. C. in the name.

♦ *Nonprofit corporations* are formed for purposes other than making a profit. Most often the purpose is charitable in nature. The most common forms are hospitals, universities and colleges, nursing homes, and organizations that support the arts. In their operating documents, the nonprofit purpose must be clearly stated. It's important to note that a nonprofit corporation is not automatically a 501(c)(3) with all the tax benefits. A nonprofit corporation has to file extensive paperwork with the IRS, and the IRS must approve the application before the corporation can receive a 501(c)(3) designation.

Regardless of the type of corporation, the power to create and regulate the corporation stems from the government. While most corporations are created under state law, it's possible to create one under federal law. While there is a model act, the Revised

Model Business Corporation Act, states have not consistently adopted it. Therefore, each state's law must be carefully reviewed when setting up a corporation.

Citations

When looking for the corporation requirements, each state has a corporation code. That code will list the requirements to create, maintain, and terminate a corporation. The secretary of state, or other authorized government entity, will have the forms and additional information.

Corporate Characteristics and Powers

Once formed, corporations are a separate legal entity, which provides key liability protection to the shareholders. To achieve that protection, the steps necessary for formation must be followed carefully. Because the corporation has a separate identity, it has the same powers as an individual. It can do anything necessary and convenient to conduct its business.

A corporation has the following specific characteristics and powers:

- Unlike other business forms, a corporation has perpetual life. The corporation can continue indefinitely until the owners decide to close the business. There is no automatic termination at death or because one partner wants to leave the business.

- A corporation must have a name to identify it and distinguish it from other companies. It must also have bylaws that guide how the company will conduct its internal affairs. Bylaws are the rules and regulations that shareholders adopt to govern the affairs of the corporation, directors, shareholders, and officers. Corporations can also conduct business in another state.

- The corporation can sell stock and buy back its stock at a later time if it's solvent. Occasionally, you will see a public corporation return to private status through buying back its stock.

- Corporations have the power that individuals have to enter contracts, borrow money, and transfer and acquire property.

- Corporations also have the power to execute negotiable instruments and issue bonds.

Occasionally a corporation will engage in an *ultra vires* act, which is beyond the scope of its authority. *Ultra vires* acts are rarer today than 100 years ago, since states have given corporations such broad powers. The corporation statutes often list every power a business would need to conduct their business. As long as an action is within the stated purposes of the company, the action will not be *ultra vires*. An example: a company cannot operate a bank, even if it's just for employees, unless it has the required charters. If it does so, that would be an *ultra vires* act.

def•i•ni•tion

Ultra vires means beyond powers; that is, the corporation or officers have exceeded the powers granted by law.

Creating a Corporation

Each state's corporation statues provide detailed information on the steps required to create a corporation. While each state's laws may have variations, the following process is common when creating a corporation. The key is to understand the role of the promoter and the liability that person may accept as it acts for the yet-to-be-formed corporation.

The Role and Liability of Promoters

Usually a corporation is created after one or more *promoters* complete the start-up steps. The promoters look for financing, may sign contracts on behalf of the not yet created corporation, and take other steps necessary to create the corporation.

The promoter accepts liability as it promotes the corporation. A corporation is not liable on contracts made by the promoter unless it affirmatively takes steps to adopt the contract. Think of it this way: until the promoter has completed his job, there is no corporation. Thus, the corporation can only accept the liability after the fact by ratifying the contracts or actions of the promoter.

def•i•ni•tion

A **promoter** is the person who creates a corporation including the financing; usually he or she is the principal shareholder or member of the management team.

The promoter is liable. Whoever the promoter contracts with is entering that contract with the promoter and thus can seek damages from the promoter for any breach or negligence. The only time the promoter will not be liable is if the promoter's contract exempt him.

Here's an example. Donovan has been hired to promote a new high-tech venture. As part of his promoting responsibilities he finds a storefront for the company to lease. Sandy, the landlord, knows that Donovan is signing the lease on behalf of this new venture, but there is no agreement between Sandy and Donovan that he will not be liable if there is a problem with the lease. Eighteen months after moving in, the venture folds, and the premises are vacated six months early. Donovan is liable for any unpaid rent.

A promoter is also liable for torts, the negligent acts he commits in connection with promoting (I'll discuss torts in detail in Chapter 25). A promoter also cannot make secret profits on his promoting activities. His role is one of a fiduciary to the corporation and its shareholders. If the promoter makes a secret profit, he must surrender it to the corporation. For example, if Donovan owned land that is perfect for the venture's new plant, he can't sell it to the venture at a profit, because that would be obtaining a secret benefit at the expense of the venture. At the same time, if a landowner offers him a commission bonus for choosing his land for the venture's plant over another, Donovan must also turn over that bonus commission to the venture.

> **Consultation**
>
> A company is often not liable for the expenses of the pro- moter unless the company agrees to pay those expenses or its charter imposes liability on it for those expenses.

The Role and Liability of Incorporators

Anyone can act as an incorporator for a corporation. This role differs from the promoter in that the incorporator signs and files the appropriate paperwork with the state. The incorporator can be the promoter or two very distinct roles. Once the paperwork and filing fee are filed with the appropriate state office—often the secretary of state—that official ensures that the forms comply with statutory requirements. If it does, then the documents are accepted and a stamped copy is returned to the incorporator.

Application for Incorporation

To be incorporated, the incorporators must file articles of incorporation with the appropriate state entity. The articles must state …

1. The name of the corporation.

2. The number of shares that the corporation is authorized to issue.

3. The street address and name of the initial registered agent.

4. The name and address of each incorporator.

If the incorporation steps are properly followed, a *corporation de jure*—by operation of law—is created. If there is a minor defect, it will still be treated as a corporation de jure. Usually, a state will recognize the corporation as valid if the secretary of state has filed the articles of incorporation.

A *de facto corporation* is created when a defect in the incorporation is so substantial that it cannot be ignored. However, because of the actions of the company or board of directors, the corporation will be treated as if it did in fact properly exist. Usually, a court will look to see whether incorporators did three things: acted in good faith to incorporate, had the legal right to incorporate, and acted as if he or she were incorporated.

 **Stay Out of Jail**

States require all corporations to have a registered agent for service of process. By making this information available to the secretary of state or other state entity, there is a public record of who to serve in the event of a lawsuit.

A de facto corporation may also exist when the corporation has dissolved but continues to function as a corporation. The law steps in to treat the corporation as if it were legal to protect people who conducted business with the corporation during that time.

A *corporation by estoppel* arises if third parties thought the business was a corporation that would now profit if the third party was allowed to deny the existence of a corporation.

Dissolving a Corporation

A corporation can be dissolved only after several steps are followed. First, a corporation's board must take formal corporate action to dissolve. That decision must be recorded in minutes and ratified by the shareholders. Then a notice must be filed with the appropriate state office. Statutory notice must also be given to the corporation's creditors. Then all creditors' claims must be processed by the corporation. Any remaining assets must be sold or distributed. Once these steps are completed, the corporation must file articles of dissolution.

Consultation _____

A corporation must give notice to its creditors of its intent to dissolve. That notice should include a mailing address where any claims can be sent, a request for information about the claim, a deadline for submitting a claim, and a statement that the claim will be barred if not received in time. If these steps are followed and creditors fail to respond in time, their claim expires.

A corporation can also be dissolved by judicial action. This is most likely to occur when the board of directors deadlocks, which the shareholders are unable to break. Finally, if the corporation is in serious financial trouble, it may enter bankruptcy and be reorganized.

When Two Corporations Combine

Once corporations are formed, they can pool their resources to create new entities. There are generally two ways companies do this: mergers and acquisitions.

Mergers

Mergers occur when two companies combine. One company offers its stock or cash to the shareholders of the other company. Let's take Company A and Company B. Company A wants to expand into a new geographic region. Rather than create its own distribution system, A purchases B. By merging with A, B ceases to exist while A retains its charter and identity.

Example of a merger, where two companies merge into one.

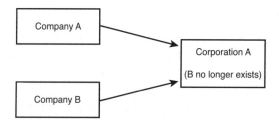

A merger can originate from within one of the merging companies, or the merger can come from outside investors. If outside investors push the merger, it is called a two-step merger. The first step in a two-step merger is for the outside investor to acquire voting control by acquiring stock of the target company. The second step is that the target company and another company already controlled by the outside investor merge. While this process sounds complicated, it can actually be simpler than a one-step merger because the offer time period is shorter and the SEC filings are less burdensome.

The decision to merge is usually made by two companies that are equals. The board and shareholders decide that economies of scales, greater sales revenue and market share, or broadened diversification or increased tax efficiency can be obtained.

A *consolidation* occurs when two companies come together and a third company is born. Each of the original companies ceases to exist. Instead, a new company is created with the assets and property of the original companies.

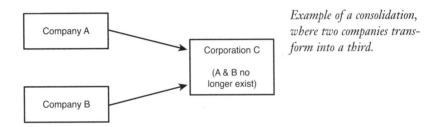

Example of a consolidation, where two companies transform into a third.

Shareholders may object to the proposed mergers and consolidations. If a shareholder chooses that route, she can ask a court to determine the value of her stock. If anybody does not cooperate with the appraisal process, the courts can penalize that party by assessing attorney fees and court costs.

Acquisitions

An *acquisition* occurs when a much larger company takes over a smaller one. There is an inherent inequality in the balance of power between the two companies. The larger company purchases the other—and while these can be friendly, the takeover can also be hostile.

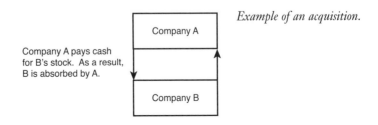

Example of an acquisition.

Conglomerates

A *conglomerate* defines a parent company's relationship with its subsidiary corporations, when the subsidiaries are not engaged in the core business of the parent.

Example of a conglomerate.

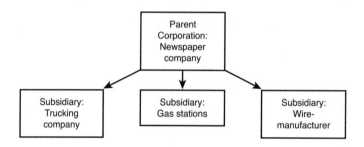

If the subsidiaries are related to the parent's business, it is called an *integrated industry* rather than a conglomerate.

Example of an integrated industry.

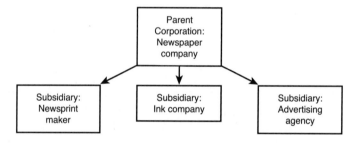

If the parent is not engaged in production or services, it is a *holding company*. The parent exists only as a vehicle to manage the various subsidiaries.

Regardless of the type, each subsidiary is a distinct corporation. That means each will have its own board of directors and bylaws. Antitrust laws may step in to prevent a merger or acquisitions that will have anticompetitive impacts on the economy. See Chapter 4 for more on antitrust law.

Liability of Successor Corporations

Successor corporations, the corporations that remain after a merger, acquisition, or other consolidation, can be liable for the debts and obligations of its predecessors. With mergers and consolidations, typically the corporation that continues the business of the merged or consolidated corporation obtains all the rights and liabilities of the prior corporation. The reason is that someone must be responsible if something goes wrong with the merged company's products after the merger. The law will not allow a vacuum to develop regarding that liability.

If the assets of the prior corporation were obtained through an asset sale, the purchaser is not liable for the obligations of the predecessor. However, if a corporation tries to hide a merger or consolidation as an asset sale, the courts will not allow liability to be avoided.

Shareholder Liability

One of the great benefits of the corporate entity is that the shareholders are shielded from personal liability for the acts of the corporation. There are exceptions to this general rule, the main exceptions being piercing the corporate veil and the corporation as alter ego.

Piercing the Corporate Veil

In rare circumstances, a court may pierce the corporate veil if the corporate form has been ignored by the shareholders or managers. By piercing the corporate veil, the court determines that the shareholders or directors of a corporation should be liable for the acts or debts of the company. To determine whether the veil has been pierced, the court will look at the following factors:

♦ The owners failed to maintain adequate corporate records or commingled corporate and personal funds.

♦ The corporation is inadequately capitalized.

♦ The shareholders have diverted corporate funds or assets.

♦ The corporation was formed to evade an obligation.

♦ The corporation was formed to commit fraud or conceal illegality.

♦ If the corporate entity were recognized, injustice or inequity would result.

Consultation

While a shareholder is generally not personally liable for the corporation's debts and liabilities, the shareholder's investment of capital may be consumed by creditor's claims.

The Corporation as Alter Ego

Sometimes the court will find that the corporation is merely the alter ego of a wrong-doer. As such, there is no liability protection for the shareholder or owner. In this case, the corporation is so dominated by the board, owner(s), or shareholder(s) that the distinction between individuals and company evaporates. Even here, the courts will require a high degree of fraud or injustice, because it is important that shareholders have certainty of limited liability absent wrong doing.

The Least You Need to Know

◆ When properly formed, corporations are a separate legal entity that can do anything a person can do.

◆ Corporate shareholders are shielded from personal liability for the bad acts of the corporation beyond the shareholders investment in stock.

◆ Two companies can merge into one, or another corporation can take over another company through an acquisition.

◆ If the corporate structure has been abused and the court finds the corporation is merely the alter ego for the shareholders or that the corporate veil has been pierced, liability extends beyond the capital investment.

9

Partnerships: Teaming Up

In This Chapter

- A partnership's characteristics and formalities
- Partners' authority inside the partnership
- A partner's duties, rights, and liabilities
- How to dissolve and terminate a partnership
- Distributing the partnership's assets
- Why a partnership might not be the best entity

Partnerships appeal to many as a way to join with one or more people to create a business without all the formalities of a corporation. However, like with many real-life partnerships, this should be considered only with your eyes wide open. There are many challenges that offset the benefits of this form. Think of it as marriage, only with a business partner.

Let's say two college buddies, Frank and Don, want to launch a business together, called F&D Partnership. Frank is the brains behind the invention, but Don has the marketing know-how to get the invention in stores and homes. Each brings something unique to the business. Together, they have the skills to make the company work. A partnership could be a good vehicle for them, though it also has its challenges. We'll discuss both in this chapter.

This chapter will highlight the requirements of a partnership as well as the duties, rights, and liabilities of each partner. Finally, we'll examine the requirements to successfully dissolve or terminate a partnership.

Anatomy of a Partnership

While partnership law is governed at the state level, 49 states have adopted either the Uniform Partnership Act (UPA) or the Revised Uniform Partnership Act (RUPA). These acts, as adopted by the states, determine the rights of partners and what a partnership can and cannot do. In many ways this creates a certain baseline that you can anticipate regardless of the state.

Citations
A partnership exists when there is a voluntary agreement between co-owners who contribute capital, services, or both for profit.

Let's go back to Frank and Don. They have decided after talking to an attorney that a partnership might work for them. They frankly don't have the money or time to invest in getting a corporation started. Especially at this stage in the business, it doesn't seem worth it to them. But do they qualify as a partnership?

The Internal Revenue Service defines a partnership as the relationship existing between two or more persons who join to carry on a trade or business. "Each person contributes money, property, labor or skill, and expects to share in the profits and losses of the business." In this case, Frank is bringing the invention or property, and Don is bringing the marketing ability or skill. Since each will contribute something to the entity, the basic ingredients for a partnership exist.

For tax purposes the profits and losses flow through the business to the partners and are reported on their individual tax returns. This avoids the double taxation to which corporation profits are subject. This can make a partnership very appealing—especially when the business is young.

In addition, there is no requirement for formalized documents or filing with the state; you can form a partnership with a handshake. The name for the partnership should be reserved with the state to protect it from use by another entity. And for future protection, it's a good idea to have an attorney draft a buy-sell agreement and a formalized partnership agreement that outline shares, responsibilities, and expectations.

Frank and Don are sure an attorney can take care of any formalizing documents for them when they need them. In fact, they aren't concerned at all since they've known each other for several years. For now a handshake will work for them. They're ready to set the world on fire with their fantastic product.

They both took a business law class in college, but the details are a bit hazy. What they'll wish they'd remembered is that the rights of partners flow from their agreement, whether it's in writing, by implication, or from their practice. Anything left out is filled in by the Uniform Partnership Act.

Consultation

While a partnership can be formed without any paperwork, it's in the best interest of the partners and the partnership to put the working terms of the partnership in writing in a partnership agreement. The name of the partnership should also be reserved with the appropriate state entity.

So what are those rights? Good question. The rights flow in part out of the role the individual partner accepts. Those roles include:

- **General partners:** These partners are visible to the public and take an active role in the partnership. There must always be at least one in a general partnership.

- **Nominal partners:** Held out as partners to the public because of something he or she can add to the partnership, usually status or goodwill; may be liable as partners.

- **Silent partners:** These are not active participants in the partnership on a day-to-day basis; usually he or she adds something like money to the partnership and may be known to the public as partners, but sometimes are hidden from the public.

- **Secret partners:** May be active in the partnership, but are not visible to the public as partners.

- **Dormant partners:** As the name suggests, these partners share no active role in the partnership and are unknown to the public as partners. The dormant partner may have played an active role at the beginning but that has since changed.

Because Frank and Don are not minors, don't have any mental incapacity, nor any other restriction under contract law to prevent them from entering a contract, they can form a partnership. Both will likely be general partners, though they will need to find at least one other participant who can provide money to get their venture off the ground.

Authority of Partners

Authority is a broad concept that basically means someone has been given permission to act on behalf of a partnership. Partners receive authority just by being a partner. In very general terms a decision made by the majority of the partners prevails in a dispute unless it conflicts with the partnership agreement.

The problem doesn't usually come from situations where the partners vote, but don't agree; those can always be resolved by the court if there's a true deadlock. The question becomes whether the partner had the authority from the other partners to act on behalf of the partnership.

Express Authority: The Right to Act

The first kind involves *express authority*. An individual partner may have express authority to do something because the partnership agreement gives it to him or because the partners have voted to give it to him. For example, in a law firm, one partner may have authority to handle payroll, another advertising, and a third technology. The responsibilities are broken down among the partners to share the burden. But the partner with authority to order payroll does not have the authority to buy the computers as well.

def•i•ni•tion

Express authority is the authority to take an action because the partnership agreement gives the authority to a partner or because the partners have voted to delegate that authority.

In addition, a partner has the authority to do acts that are customary to the partnership. For example, if the partnership is an accounting firm, all partners have authority to seek and accept accounting work for the firm. However, they would not have authority to seek new lines of business, like computer consulting, for the firm.

Here are some other authorized powers:

◆ A partner can enter contracts necessary for the partnership to conduct business.

◆ A partner can sell the firm's goods in the normal course of business.

◆ A partner can make purchases within the scope of business.

◆ A partner may borrow money for the firm's purposes.

◆ A partner can hire employees, buy insurance, and take other steps necessary for the firm to remain in business.

While a partner has all these powers, the partners can agree to limit any of the traditional powers. If there is such a limitation—say, one partner is prohibited from hiring employees, but the third party, the prospective employee, has no knowledge of the limitation—then the action will be enforced and the employee will be hired.

Stay Out of Jail

Both the Uniform Partnership Act and the Revised Partnership Act provide more detail on what partners can and cannot do. While these laws are intended to be uniform, be sure to check the code in your state for any deviations.

Unauthorized Actions of a Partner

While a third party can assume a partner has authority to act in many situations, there are instances where the partner can never have authority. The first is if the third party should be aware of a limitation on a partner's authority, then the third party is bound by that limitation. A third party also cannot enter prohibited transactions with a partner. Other unauthorized actions include the following:

♦ A partner cannot bind a partnership to a contract that would force the closing of the business.

♦ A partner cannot bind the partnership to a contract that is outside the scope of that firm's normal business.

♦ A partner cannot submit the partnership to arbitration without the consent of the other partners.

♦ A partner cannot on his own consent to a judgment against the partnership. There must be agreement among the partners for it to be binding.

♦ A partner cannot assign partnership property to a creditor without approval from the other partners.

♦ A partner cannot discharge personal obligations at the expense of the firm.

Each of these prohibited transactions is designed to protect the innocent partners from acts that will bind them or harm the partnership as a whole.

The Duties and Rights of Partners

Each partner has several duties to fulfill to the other partners and the partnership. These include …

- **Loyalty and good faith:** A partner cannot take advantage of the partnership. A partner must not hide or misrepresent information to the partnership that is relevant to the partnership's business. The partner must put the partnership's interests and business above his own. It also means partners cannot make a secret profit at the expense of the firm. For example, Don could not start promoting or marketing a company that has a product that is in direct competition with that produced by F&D Partnership.

- **Obedience:** Each partner must perform the duties assigned to him and obey any restrictions imposed by the partnership agreement. If that agreement clearly stipulates that a partner may not go to work for a competitor, he is restricted from carrying on outside work.

- **Reasonable care:** Partners must exercise the same level of care that would be reasonable to expect another person with the same training to take when performing a job.

- **Information sharing:** A partner cannot withhold information from the partnership that would benefit or harm the partnership, especially if the partner intends to use that information for his benefit. For example, a partner must share with the other partners information that the city plans to zone the area around their building for a strip mall if that will increase the value of the building and the partners are trying to determine what to do with the property.

- **Accounting of the finances of the partnership:** Each partner is entitled to review the financial books of the partnership. It's common for partnership agreements to require the request be made in writing, but this requirement exists to protect partners—especially silent or nonmanagement partners.

Partners also have many rights that are designed to protect their interests. Those include …

- **Management:** Each partner has the right (and responsibility) to share in the management of the firm. Often, the management will be divided among the partners in an attempt to prevent any one partner from carrying that burden alone.

- **Share of profits:** Each partner has a right to a share of the profits. The amount can be tied to contributions or any other arrangement that the partners agree to in writing. For the protection of each partner, how profits and losses will be divided should be explained in writing in the partnership agreement.

- **Compensation:** Normally, a partner is not entitled to compensation for any work he does for the partnership. The profits alone serve as compensation. If the partners plan to be paid a salary or other form of compensation, then that must be stated in a written agreement. The only exception occurs when a surviving partner wraps up the business. Then he is entitled to reasonable compensation for that service.

- **Repayment of loans:** If a partner makes a loan to the partnership that is above and beyond the initial contribution, that partner is entitled to repayment of the loan. If the capital is part of the original contribution, the partner is only entitled to payment if the other partners are also being reimbursed.

- **Payment of interest:** Unless otherwise stated in a written agreement, the partners are not entitled to interest on their contributions of capital to the partnership. Advances that are loans and not initial contributions can receive interest as if made by a nonpartner.

- **Contribution and indemnity:** If a partner finds himself paying more than his share of the debts of the partnership, he is entitled to contribution from the other partners in amounts equal to their ownership interest in the partnership. The partnership must indemnify, or make whole and protect from losses, individual partners when the partner acts reasonably in the ordinary conduct of the business. However, if the partner acts in bad faith, negligently caused the need for payment, or previously agreed to bear the expense alone, he cannot be reimbursed.

- **Distribution of capital:** After creditors and loans from partners have been repaid, then if any money remains, the partners are entitled to a return of their capital investment.

That's quite a list of rights and obligations. This is why as many of the details as possible should be in writing, to avoid future problems among the partners or provide a clear list of expectations if the dispute finds its way to court. After sitting down with their attorney again, Frank and Don decide it is in their best interests as well as those of the partnership to get their agreement and expectations down in writing.

def•i•ni•tion

In **joint liability,** two or more people are liable for a debt; the plaintiff can sue both and a defendant can demand that any person who shares joint liability is brought into the lawsuit. In **joint and several liability,** each debtor or defendant is responsible for the entire debt or amount awarded.

This brings up another sticking point: the liabilities of partners for the partnership contracts and any breaches of duty. Founding partners are *jointly liable* on all partnership contracts and *jointly and severally liable* for torts of partners or employees. Frank and Don gulp as the attorney explains that an injured party could sue either of them or the partnership. Whichever partner is sued and pays can seek contribution from the other partners. Contribution often arises when one person is sued on a debt or judgment that has joint and several liability. The defendant who pays more than his share can demand contribution from the other liable parties. If $9,000 is owed from two partners, but only Don is sued, he can sue Frank to pay the balance.

New partners are liable to the extent of their capital contributions for obligations in existence at the time of their admission to the partnership and have full liability for any obligations incurred after admission. For example, if Frank and Don take on a new partner, but are sued for a product malfunction that occurred prior to that partner joining the firm, the new partner's personal assets will be protected. Judgment can only be taken from his contribution to the partnership.

The partnership is also protected from suits against a partner individually. The personal creditor must first seek fulfillment of the judgment from the partner's individual assets. Once those are exhausted, the creditor can obtain a court order that partnership profits be paid to it until the debt is satisfied.

Partnership property consists of all property contributed by the partners or acquired for the firm or with its funds. Title to partnership property may be carried in the name of the partnership or one or more of the partner's individual names. Title to partnership property is held in tenancy in partnership which is similar to joint tenancy for passage of title upon the death of one of the partners.

Dissolution and Termination

Eventually, most partnerships will dissolve or be terminated. Dissolution occurs when the partnership ceases to exist as a going concern, either by agreement of the partners that they no longer wish to conduct business together or by operation of law. The law steps in when any of the following occur: death of a partner; bankruptcy of the partnership or any partner; illegality on the part of the partnership; or by decree of a court.

Dissolution essentially signals a "change in the relationship of the partners caused by any partner ceasing to be associated in the carrying on as distinguished from the winding-up of the business." If the partnership agreement allows, innocent partners can buy the interest of another partner and continue the business.

If the remaining partners cannot buy the shares of the former partner, the partnership will enter a period called winding up. Essentially, the remaining partners are winding up the firm's remaining obligations. This could mean fulfilling contracts, providing ordered services, and any other necessary steps to let the rest of the world know that the partnership has ceased to exist.

During the winding-up period, the remaining partners only have authority to finish work in progress and cannot accept new work on behalf of the partnership.

Citations
RUPA requires creditors and tort victims to seek satisfaction of claims from the partnership first before proceeding against a partner's personal assets.

Dissolution by Partners' Acts

There are several ways that partners can dissolve the partnership by their acts. Those include …

- ◆ **Agreement:** Partners can agree that the time has come to end the partnership. It may mean that an agreed term has expired or the reason the partnership was formed has ended.

- ◆ **Expulsion:** A partnership can be dissolved when a partner is expelled for any reason.

- ◆ **Withdrawal:** A partner can withdraw at any time from a partnership. The partnership agreement should stipulate any limitations on the partners' ability to withdraw at will. If professionally drafted, the agreement may include a covenant restricting where the partner can seek employment after leaving the partnership— a covenant not to compete.

In each of these cases, the partners agree that the partnership should be dissolved. An expulsion or withdrawal can force the issue where the partners' agreement can't be reached.

Dissolution by Law

In addition to dissolution by the partners' acts, the law requires a partnership to be dissolved in certain circumstances:

- ◆ **Death:** The death of a partner dissolves the partnership immediately.

- ◆ **Bankruptcy:** Insolvency alone is not enough to end the partnership, but once the partnership or a partner is declared bankrupt, the partnership is dissolved.

- ◆ **Illegality:** If the partnership is engaged in unlawful business, that will dissolve the partnership.

A partner can ask a court to determine that any of these three situations exists and the partnership should be dissolved, or the partners can agree to dissolve at that time.

Dissolution by Court Order

On occasion, a court will become involved and dissolve a partnership by court order. There are many reasons that a court may step in and order the dissolution of a partnership. Those reasons include …

- ◆ A partner being declared insane by a court.

- ◆ One partner becoming incapable of performing his role in the partnership.

- ◆ A partner acting in a way that harms the partnership's reputation or ability to continue to conduct business.

- ◆ The inability of the partners to cooperate and work together or when their confidence in each other is destroyed.

- ◆ Lack of success of the partnership.

- ◆ Any other reason that calls for an equitable dissolution of the partnership.

Upon dissolution, the parties may continue in certain circumstances or wind up the firm's obligation, liquidate, and terminate. Distribution of partnership assets upon liquidation is controlled by the UPA.

When a partnership is to be dissolved, notice must be given to all partners and third parties. Partners must receive notice unless the acts of the dissolving partner make it clear that he intended to leave. Third parties must receive notice that expressly states the partnership has been dissolved. This is best accomplished by a letter to all people and firms with which the partnership has conducted business. For all others, publication in the newspaper is sufficient notice.

Winding up occurs once the partnership is dissolved. The sole purpose of this period is to wrap up the affairs of the partnership. New business cannot be accepted.

Distribution of Assets

When a partnership is being dissolved, the assets are distributed in the following manner. Firm creditors get the first chance to be paid. After that, individual creditors—that is, partners—may step into line for repayment of their advances. After that, partners may be repaid for capital contributions to the firm. Any remaining assets are distributed as profits to the partners. If there is a loss, the partners assume it in equal portions unless the partnership agreement states differently.

The Downside of a Partnership

There are several advantages to a general partnership over a corporation. Partners can share the financial commitment for the business. Resources, expertise, and strengths can also be pooled by the partners. And startup costs are limited because there are few formalities beyond applicable licenses.

However, as with any business relationship, there's always the possibility that the partnership will sour. In a corporation this isn't a large issue because the stock can be sold according to the terms of a buy-sell agreement or other mechanism established in the formation documents. Or the stock can be sold on the open market.

With a partnership, however, this is not the case. Partnership shares cannot be freely traded on the open market. Instead, the partnership shares must be purchased by a remaining partner or the partnership must be dissolved.

There is also the likelihood that partners may have or develop different visions or goals for the business over time. On the other hand, the partners may develop over time an unequal commitment to the partnership in terms of time and finances. Partners may also have disputes that are not easily resolved considering the way partners are tied to each other for the duration of the partnership.

Stay Out of Jail

A large concern is that partners are personally liable for business debts and liabilities. There is no corporate protection to provide a shield for debts and torts of the partnership.

Another disadvantage, which makes partner trust crucial: each partner may be liable for debts incurred, decisions made, and actions taken by another partner. Even if he knew nothing about the decisions! There can develop disagreements in management plans, operational procedures, and future vision for the business and there are few ways to address those outside of dissolving the partnership if they cannot be resolved. Finally, the uncertainty of the partnership form can make it difficult to attract investors.

The Least You Need to Know

- A partnership is created when two or more individuals join to share a trade or business.

- Profits and losses must be split between the partners either in equal shares or according to the partnership agreement.

- Partners have duties toward each other including loyalty and good faith, obedience, and the rights to review the books and management.

- Partners are liable personally for the debts and torts of the partnership.

- Partnerships are terminated by agreement, bankruptcy, court order, death, or illegality.

- A partnership should only be entered if the benefits outweigh the possible costs; however, no amount of planning can completely eliminate the risk of a partnership souring.

Chapter 10

Variations on Partnerships

In This Chapter

- The variation of limited partnerships
- Limited liability partnerships (LLPs) and how they differ
- Characteristics of the limited liability companies (LLCs)
- Comparing the different partnerships

While partnerships (see Chapter 9) are the oldest form of business, there are many drawbacks from liability to raising capital to duration. Several variations on partnerships have developed as a way to address those concerns. Those variations are limited partnerships, limited liability partnerships, and limited liability companies.

Limited Partnerships

Limited partnerships were created in an effort to address some of the liability issues of general partnerships. Since 1916 the Uniform Limited Partnership Act (ULPA), in one of its three versions, has provided consistency in this area to all states but Louisiana, which has not adopted it.

Characteristics and Requirements

The goal of a limited partnership is to shield some partners from liability. To accomplish this, those partners desiring limited liability contribute capital to the endeavor but do not participate in the management of the firm. If the *limited partners* walk that line, the most they will be liable for is their capital contribution. The partners who manage the firm are called general partners and are open to full liability beyond their capital contribution. A limited partnership can have more than one general partner and more than one limited partner.

To maintain the limited liability protection of the limited partnership, it's critical that the limited partners avoid any role in the management of the firm. If they begin to act as managers, the limited liability protection disappears.

def•i•ni•tion

Limited partners are those who do not participate in the management of the partnership and do not appear to the public as general partners.

To form a limited partnership, a certificate of limited partnership must be filed with the state, usually the secretary of state. This filing is necessary to provide notice to the public of some partners' limited liability. Otherwise, the public would interact with the partnership with the assumption that it is a general partnership and all partners are liable in the event there is a problem that creates liability.

Under the 1985 amendments to the Revised ULPA, the certificate must contain five items:

1. The limited partnership's name

2. The limited partnership's registered office address and name and business address for its agent

3. The name and business address for each general partner

4. The partnership's mailing address

5. The latest date on which the limited partnership must dissolve

As with general partnerships, the partners in a limited partnership should draft and adopt a limited partnership agreement. When there is conflict, the courts will resolve it against the drafting partners.

Let's say Alice, Betty, and Carrie decide to form a limited partnership. Alice as the general partner drafts the agreement. If there's a dispute later, the court will read the

agreement and construe it in favor of the
limited partners, Betty and Carrie, when
there is a dispute about the meaning of the
agreement. This lines up with general contract principles. Essentially, the drafter was
in the best position to draft the agreement
without ambiguity, so any mistakes or ambi-
guities will be interpreted in favor of the
nondrafting party.

Consultation

Remember that unlike corporations, partnerships do not
exist for an indefinite period
of time, but are dissolved at a
certain date or by death, bankruptcy, and other means including court action.

Formalities

To be a limited partnership, the partnership must have the following elements:

♦ Capital contributions of a limited partner will be in cash or property but not services. The Revised ULPA allows the contribution of services.

♦ The firm name should contain the words *limited partnership*. This is to alert the
public to the nature of the partnership.

♦ The management and control of the firm must be exercised by the general partners alone. If a limited partner moves into active management of the limited
partnership, he or she will lose the limited liability protection inherent in this
form of business. The best way to think of a limited partner is as an investor. He
or she provides capital to the partnership but nothing else.

The Revised ULPA provides several activities or roles that limited partners can have
in the firm without moving into management that will remove them from the limited
liability protection. Those actions include
being a contractor or employee of the firm,
consulting with a general partner on the
firm's business, acting as a *surety*, or voting
on partnership matters. Moving beyond
those activities can be dangerous for a limited partner.

The limited partner retains the right to sue
in a derivative action. By doing that, the
limited partner is protecting the partnership by enforcing its right when the general

def•i•ni•tion

Acting as a **surety** means you
are primarily liable for the debt
or obligation of the principal
debtor. In partnership law, the
principal debtor would be the
general partner or firm, and the
limited partner is accepting an
obligation that is not otherwise
his or hers.

partners refuse to do so. Thus, the limited partner is enforcing rights that belong to the partnership. That's why they're called derivative rights. Again, think of the limited partner as an investor. As such, he or she has rights similar to shareholders to bring derivative lawsuits. The limited partner sues the partnership as well as any other parties that are refusing to act. The limited partners can also sue general partners to protect limited partners interests.

Winding up a limited partnership operates under the same principles as a general partnership. See Chapter 9 for more on that process.

Limited Liability Partnerships

Limited liability partnerships (LLPs) have developed almost as a response to the success of limited liability companies (LLCs). LLPs maintain the pass-through taxation of partnerships, but enjoy more of the limited liability of LLCs.

Citations

Some groups are not allowed to form entities like LLCs. For example, attorneys are often prohibited by their governing organizations from incorporating as LLCs. Thus, the LLP provides an entity that holds many of the same benefits of an LLC, but works for professionals who may otherwise be prohibited from forming an entity with the limited liability protection of an LLC or other corporate form.

Characteristics and Requirements

All states provide that in a limited liability partnership, innocent partners are not liable for vicarious negligence or malpractice of other partners. Some states provide no liability for innocent partners from the acts of other partners. This is an added layer of liability protection that is not available from other partnership forms.

For example, let's say Alice, Betty, and Carrie form a limited liability partnership in a full shield state, one that provides full protection for limited partners. Two years into the LLP, Carrie embezzles money from the partnership and enters into fraudulent transactions in an attempt to hide her fraud. If the partnership were a general partnership, all partners would be jointly and severally liable for that fraud and jointly liable on the contracts. With an LLP, only Carrie is liable, because Alice and Betty are innocent partners.

Formalities

As with the limited partnership, LLPs must register with the state and the firm name must contain the words *limited liability partnership* or *LLP*. This requirement provides a clear signal to the marketplace that liability is limited, unlike general partnerships where there is joint liability for contracts and joint and several liability for torts.

As with all partnerships, a written partnership agreement is a good idea. General rules of contract law will apply. A general partnership agreement can also be transformed into a limited liability partnership agreement.

Limited Liability Companies

Limited liability companies (LLCs) are a relatively new form of business that started in Wyoming in the early 1990s and are now available in every state and the District of Columbia. LLCs merge the best of corporate and partnership structures.

Characteristics and Requirements

LLCs gained their unique status through a revenue ruling that allows LLCs to be treated for tax purposes as a partnership. Thus, LLC profits are taxed as income to the individual members rather than being taxed at the corporate level and again as income once the profits are distributed as dividends.

LLCs also provide the liability protection of corporations. Thus, as long as a member fulfills its common law duties to the company, members cannot be personally liable for the debts or torts of the company. (*Members* refer to the owners of the LLC, who have an ownership interest in proportion to their capital contribution and the operating agreement or articles of organization.) The most a member can lose is the amount of capital contributed to the company. Members can avoid the uncertainty of how much he or she will be liable for in a partnership.

Members contribute property, services, and cash to obtain an ownership interest in the LLC. They manage the LLC according to the terms set forth in the operating agreement, an LLC's equivalent to a corporation's bylaws. An operating agreement can be oral or in writing, but any amendments must be agreed to by all members. Unless stated differently in the operating agreement, all members have an equal right to share in the management of the LLC.

Members may manage the LLC. Or they can delegate the management to employees. For example, let's say Alice, Betty, and Carrie have decided they prefer the LLC for their company. Management of the LLC can take several forms. All three can manage the LLC. The three can decide that Alice has the management skills, so they delegate the day-to-day management to her. Or the three can choose a manager to run the company for them. However they choose to run the firm, a member may not be compensated for managing the LLC unless the operating agreement provides for compensation.

Stay Out of Jail

As with any contract, the best way to avoid future problems and disputes is to put all terms in writing. That provides for the least ambiguity. While an operating agreement may be amended by oral terms if the agreement allows, the safest course is to have all amendments made in writing and signed by all parties.

Distributions of profits and losses are shared according to the terms of the operating agreement. In the event of the liquidation of the LLC, distributions must first be to members in a return of contributions not previously returned. Any balance is distributed to members in a per capita fashion or according to the terms of the operating agreement. If Alice, Betty, and Carrie's operating agreement calls for Alice to get 50 percent and the other two to receive 25 percent each, that would trump a per capita distribution of 33.34 percent to each.

An LLC owns and holds property in its name because it is a legal entity separate and apart from the members. Thus, interests in the LLC property can usually be assigned. A member's right to participate in the management of the LLC cannot be assigned without the agreement of the other members. A member's creditor can only take rights to the member's interest through a charging order.

Formalities

To form an LLC, articles of organization must be filed with the secretary of state. The articles of organization are similar to the articles of incorporation filed by a corporation. The articles of organization must include the name, purpose, duration, registered agent, and principal office of the LLC. If this is done, LLCs exist independently of the members as a separate legal entity.

To be taxed as a partnership, an LLC simply needs to make the correct election on the appropriate IRS form. Once this is done, the profits and losses of the LLC will flow through the entity to the members in proportion to their ownership interest in the business.

Dissolution of the LLC occurs when the members consent, or the death, retirement, expulsion, resignation, or bankruptcy of a member. Some state statutes provide that the LLC can continue with the agreement of remaining members. In cases where it is not reasonable for the LLC to continue carrying on business, a court can decree that the LLC dissolve.

Partnership Forms

The following table compares the various partnership formats.

	Creation	Liability	Management	Dissolution
General partnership	By the act of the parties; no formal document required	Each partner has unlimited liability	All partners share in management according to partnership agreement or UPA/RUPA	By terms of partnership agreement or UPA/RUPA
Limited partnership	Created by filing a certificate with the state	General partners have unlimited liability; limited partners' liability restricted to contribution as long as not involved in management	General partners per terms of partnership agreement or ULPA/RULPA Limited partners cannot participate in management	By terms of partnership agreement or ULPA/RULPA
Limited liability partnership	Registration with the state	Liability limited to amount of investment, except full liability for their wrongful acts	All partners per terms of partnership agreement or UPA/RUPA	By terms of partnership agreement or UPA/RUPA

continues

continued

	Creation	Liability	Management	Dissolution
Limited liability company	File articles of organization with the secretary of state	Liability limited to amount of members capital contribution	Members manage but may delegate to managers	By terms of articles of organization or the LLC statute

LLC Versus an S-Corporation

An LLC and S-corporation share many characteristics. In both cases, the owners have elected to have profits and losses taxed as if the company was a partnership. Both retain the limited liability protection of the corporate form, meaning the liability of the members or shareholders is limited to the amount of their contribution to the company as long as they fulfill their common law duties and disclose they are agents of the LLC.

There are a couple key distinctions. An S-corporation is limited to 100 shareholders, while an LLC can have unlimited members. Ownership in an S-corporation is limited to U.S. citizens and resident aliens, while foreign shareholders can invest in an LLC. The managing member of an LLC will pay self-employment taxes, while S-corporation shareholders do not.

LLC Versus Limited Partnership

While both an LLC and a limited partnership provide limited liability, a limited partnership must have at least one general partner who accepts full liability. That is not the case with an LLC. Instead, all members of an LLC have their liability limited to their investment as long as they fulfill their common law duties and disclose they are agents of the LLC.

The Least You Need to Know

- ◆ Limited partnerships provide limited liability protection to limited partners who are not involved in the management of the partnership; there must be at least one general partner who is fully liable.

- ◆ Limited liability partnerships provide limited liability to innocent partners.

- ◆ Limited liability companies provide the best of partnerships (pass-through taxation) and corporations (limited liability).

Part 4

Contracts and Sales

Contracts are the foundational legal documents that direct interactions between the signers. Don't nod off yet. This part will give you the keys you need to understand this key area of the law.

While contracts are often a document, they can also be oral. They can cover any subject matter as long as it is not illegal or unconscionable. But to be valid, a contract must have key items like meeting of the minds, offer and acceptance, exchange of consideration. By the end of this part, you'll know exactly the concepts those terms represent.

And sales are merely a variation on contract law. Easy enough once you know the key distinctions.

Elements of a Contract

In This Chapter

- ◆ Defining a contract
- ◆ Offer requirements
- ◆ Terminating the offer
- ◆ Accepting the offer

The contract is the building block of transactions. The contract's language sets the terms between two or more parties and determines how the relationship will be handled if a problem develops. This chapter will evaluate the key elements of a contract including what an offer must contain, terminating an offer, and accepting an offer.

A Contract Defined

Contracts in their simplest forms are agreements containing specific terms between two parties that will govern the relationship of those parties. There is a promise by a party to do something in exchange for valuable consideration. Contracts can cover practically any subject matter and take any form, but all contracts must contain a promise exchanged for valuable consideration.

Let's say you go to a car dealership to buy a car. You are willing to part with your hard-earned cash in exchange for receiving a car that day. The cash is your promise in exchange for a vehicle, the consideration. The dealership is willing to sell you a car in exchange for cash.

Every contract must have these elements: 1) An agreement, 2) between two or more parties, 3) an offer to perform with, 4) an acceptance of that offer. There must also be 5) a set time period, 6) terms for performance, and 7) valuable consideration exchanged for that performance. Once performance has occurred, the contract is complete. Without each element being present, there is no valid contract.

def•i•ni•tion

A **meeting of the minds** is when the parties to a contract have the same understanding of the terms of the contract. This must occur for a contract to be valid.

The example of buying a car also demonstrates the key terms of a contract. You offered to pay cash. The dealership accepted your offer. There was a *meeting of the minds* regarding the terms of the contract. Valuable consideration is exchanged. There is a deadline for performance, and both sides must perform their promises. And there are terms and conditions to performance. With each of those elements in place, a valid contract has been created.

A contract can cover most subject matters. It could be for services such as employment or for goods. It can cover real estate or intellectual property. It cannot cover illegal subject matter. (I'll discuss illegal contracts in Chapter 12.)

Key Terminology

As with other areas of the law, contracts have a unique vocabulary. Here are a few of the key terms you'll need to know:

- A *promisor* is the person who makes the promise. The person to whom the promisor makes the promise is the *promisee*. If the promise is binding with an obligation to perform, the promisor may be called an *obligor*, and the promisee who benefits from that obligation is called the *obligee*.

- *Privity of contract* is required between parties to a contract in order to enforce the terms of the contract. Privity means that the person enforcing the contract was a party to the contract. For example, if Acme contracts with Beta's sales agent to purchase 20 cases of widgets, Acme can enforce the contract against Beta. It isn't limited to proceeding against the sales agent, because Acme is in privity of contract with Beta.

- *Agency law* deems the contract as being entered by the principal and the company. See Chapter 16 for a detailed explanation of agency law.

Types of Contracts

There are several categories of contracts, as summarized in the following table. Express contracts are formed by written or oral communication. (I'll discuss written contracts in detail in Chapter 12.) Implied contracts arise from the conduct of the parties. Quasi-contracts are enforced by courts when a contract didn't exist but should have to avoid inequities between the parties.

Let's say Jillian wants to get her house painted. She enters a written contract with a painter. In that case she has an express contract with the painter. If she doesn't sign a contract, but allows the painter to paint her house, an implied contract is created because of the actions of the parties. Jillian did nothing to stop the painter, so her inaction is acceptance of his offer to paint. She will be required to pay the painter the fair market value of his services. If Jillian refuses to pay and the painter takes her to court, the judge could impose a quasi-contract. Anything less would be inequitable, because Jillian is *unjustly enriched* by the service the painter provided.

def•i•ni•tion

Unjust enrichment is a benefit that is incurred to one person either by mistake, chance, or someone's misfortune, yet that person refused to pay.

In a bilateral contract, both parties exchange promises. It's a promise for a promise. A unilateral contract exists when the offer requires performance rather than a promise. Modern law favors bilateral contracts, and the Uniform Commercial Code and Restatement (Second) of Contracts allow a bilateral contract to be formed by starting performance. In other words, a contract can be accepted by exchanging promises or by action. At the same time, unilateral contracts are limited to two categories. First, a unilateral contract is created if the offeror clearly indicates that performance is the only way that the contract can be accepted. Second, a unilateral contract is formed if the offer is made to the public at large, like a reward, which can only be accepted by performance.

Some contracts are entered solely to allow one of the parties an opportunity to enter a second contract at a later date. An option contract gives one party the absolute right to enter a second contract. A right of first refusal provides a party with the right to enter a contract with someone to purchase something before the item can be offered to a third party.

Let's say Felicia and Mike have fallen in love with an old Victorian home. The owner, Oscar, is unwilling to sell it at this time. If Felicia and Mike enter an option contract with Oscar, they will be the only party that can purchase the home if Oscar decides to sell during the option period. Within the option contract they can set all kinds of terms like price, closing, etc. Or Felicia and Mike could enter a contract with Oscar for the right of first refusal. Under a right of first refusal Oscar would have to offer Felicia and Mike the opportunity to purchase the home before he sold it to anyone else.

Not every contract is a valid contract. Invalid contracts generally fall into three categories:

◆ Void contracts fail to have any legal effect. An example of a void contract is when two people agree to commit a crime. The contract is void because the content of the contract is illegal.

def•i•ni•tion

Capacity is the ability to know a contract is being entered and its general intent.

◆ Voidable contracts are those that either party can elect to avoid. Generally, voidable contracts are made with minors, the mentally ill, or someone who is being forced to sign a contract against their will. Neither minors or those with a mental illness have *capacity* to enter a contract. (There's more on capacity in Chapter 12.)

◆ Unenforceable contracts can't be enforced because of a legal failing. For example, the contract should be in writing to satisfy the Statute of Frauds, but it isn't.

An additional classification of contracts is executed vs. executory. Executed contracts have been completed by both parties. Each has done what they promised. In an executory contract, either or both parties still have an action to complete.

Type of Contract	Definition	Example
Express	Formed by written or oral communication	Written contract to buy a home; oral contract to paint a house.

Type of Contract	Definition	Example
Implied	Arise from the conduct of the parties	Jillian doesn't enter a contract with the painter but allows him to paint her home anyway.
Quasi	Enforced by courts when a contract didn't exist but should have to avoid inequities between the parties	Jillian lets the painter paint, but refuses to pay him. The court will create a contract.
Bilateral	Both parties traditionally exchanged promises; can also form by starting performance	Elizabeth agrees to purchase a car, and Tom's Dealership agrees to sell the car for $5,000.
Unilateral	The offer requires performance rather than a promise for acceptance	A reward is offered for the finder of a lost puppy. It can only be claimed by the one who finds the puppy.
Option	One party obtains the absolute right to enter a second contract	Felicia and Mike contract with Oscar to buy his home when he decides to sell.
Right of first refusal	Provides one with the right to enter a contract with someone to purchase something before the item can be offered to third party	Oscar must offer Felicia and Mike the opportunity to purchase his home before offering it to someone else.
Voidable	Either party can elect to void or cancel the contract	Contract entered with a minor or mentally ill party.

continues

continued

Type of Contract	Definition	Example
Void	Have no legal effect; treated as if the contract was never formed	Contract to engage in crime. A contract between two parties to murder someone.
Unenforceable	Can't be enforced because of a legal failing in the contract	Statute of Frauds requires a contract to be in writing, but it isn't.

Requirements of an Offer

An offer is the cornerstone of contract law. Without an offer and acceptance, there is no contract. Therefore, it's important that the parties properly handle the offer. An offer must create a reasonable expectation in the offeree that the offeror is willing to enter a contract that contains the expressed terms. To meet this expectation, the offer must express a promise to enter a contract, create certainty about the key terms, and clearly communicate those items.

Contractual Intent

The communication from the offeror must clearly convey that the offer is more than an invitation to negotiate. Courts will consider the language used. Using the words "I offer" or "I promise" can show contractual intent. Language like "I would consider" or "I would like to pay" is not strong enough to show more than an interest in negotiating. However, there are no hard and fast rules about exact words that have to appear to show contractual intent. Courts will also look at the context of the statement and the prior practice and relationship of the parties. For example, if Oscar tells Mike, a virtual stranger, he'll sell Mike his home for $25,000 but he's drunk and the home is worth $250,000, the court will likely find no contractual intent.

Courts will also consider what is customary in an industry. The terms of the communication are also important. If the terms are specific and won't require additional rounds of negotiation, a court is more likely to view the communication as an offer. If more negotiation is required, the communication is likely an invitation to negotiate.

Citations

The broader the communication, the less likely a court will find it a definite offer to contract. If an advertisement identifies low prices or specials, the law treats the advertisement as an invitation to negotiate rather than an offer to contract. The offer is made when the customer walks the item to the cash register with the intent to purchase it. Price quotes are also treated as invitations to negotiate.

Definite Terms

An offer must contain certain and definite terms. Accordingly, an offer should be evaluated on whether there are sufficient terms to actually enforce the contract. The parties should determine the content of their contract, since courts don't want to insert terms.

It's in the best interests of the parties to ensure that the terms of the contract are clear and definite. If they fail to do that, a court or jury will need to insert terms into the contract. Any time that happens, the parties risk having terms added that were not their original intent.

The Uniform Commercial Code will insert missing terms if the contract involves the sale of goods of $500 or more. Even then, the parties are better off drafting their own terms. The key terms a contract should contain include: the identity of the parties, the item being contracted, price, time of payment, delivery and performance, the quantity of goods, and nature of the work to be done.

If the contract is for real estate, the contract must list the exact location of the land and the price. The exact location must be included since land is unique. There is only one of each plat of land. In an employment contract, the duration of the employment period must be stated.

If the contract is for the sale of goods, the quantity must be stated. The Uniform Commercial Code will not supply that term. The exceptions to a specific amount are for requirements and output contracts. In a requirements contract the buyer promises to purchase all of a product that it needs from the seller, and the seller promises to provide that quantity to the buyer. In an output contract, the seller promises to sell to the buyer all the goods of a kind that it makes, and the buyer agrees to purchase those goods.

Let's say Acme Corporation needs to buy uniforms for its employees. It decides to purchase those from Uniforms, Inc. If the parties enter a requirements contract, Acme will agree to purchase all the uniforms that it needs from Uniforms, Inc. So if it needs 10 uniforms this month and 15 next month, it will purchase all of them from Uniforms, Inc. If Acme goes to a different firm for some of the uniforms, it will violate the contract. If the parties opt for an outputs contract, then Uniforms will agree to sell all of the uniforms that it makes to Acme, and Acme will agree to purchase them all. Even if Uniforms makes more uniforms than Acme needed one month, Acme will be obligated to purchase the excess uniforms.

If the parties fail to supply all of the terms, reasonable terms may be added in some cases. Case law or the Uniform Commercial Code (UCC) may supply what is reasonable. However, the court will have to determine what the intent of the parties was and how to satisfy that.

Consultation

Article 2 of the Uniform Commercial Code supplies the missing terms for sales of goods of $500 or more. Chapter 14 will take a closer look at sales of goods contracts.

However, if the term in question is a vague term, contract law and the UCC will not provide the term. There are a couple ways to cure vagueness. First, if one party has started to perform under the contract, that part performance will indicate the true intent of the vague term. If the uncertainty stems from the offeror giving the offeree two options, acceptance of one option will cure the vagueness. A term can also be made more definite if another document is incorporated into the contract. This may occur when a contract refers to a price list or other separate document.

A contract may be divisible if it contains two or more parts that can be performed separately. If one section is vague, the other may still be definite and performable. In that case, the court will blue-line or alter the contract to enforce the definite sections.

Communicating the Offer

It may seem like common sense, but an offer must be communicated to the offeree. Without definite communication, the offer fails. This communication can be made orally or in writing, but it must be communicated by the offeror. Even if the offeree somehow stumbles into performing (think turning in a criminal without knowledge of the reward), that performance won't be sufficient to constitute acceptance since the offeree did not know of the offer.

Termination of the Offer

Offers do not usually exist for perpetuity. Instead, an offer will terminate at some point in time. Once it's terminated, the offeree cannot accept the offer. Instead, if the offeree tries to accept, the offeree becomes the offeror proposing that the former offer come under consideration again. There are four basic ways that an offer is terminated:

♦ The offer is revoked by the offeror.

♦ The offeree counteroffers.

♦ The offeree rejects the offer.

♦ The offer is terminated from lapse of time or by law.

Revocation of Offer

Revocation terminates the offer by retracting it. The revocation is binding if the offeree receives it before accepting the offer. Revocation can be communicated in the manner the offer was made. The revocation can also be communicated indirectly if the offeree receives information from a reliable source that the offeror has acted in a manner that would cause any reasonable third person to assume the offer was off the table. For example, if John negotiates with Stan to buy his farm, but Stan sells the farm to someone else before John accepts his offer, then the offer has been revoked. Stan can't sell what he no longer owns.

A revocation can usually be made at any time if the offer is not supported by consideration or *detrimental reliance*. However, since this is law, there are exceptions. If the offer was an option, then the offer cannot be revoked because the offeree gave consideration for the option. If it is a firm offer made by a merchant in writing, under the UCC it must stay open for a reasonable time not to exceed three months. If the offeree has detrimentally relied on the offer, the offer may not be revoked.

If the contract is unilateral requiring performance for acceptance, then part performance by a party prevents termination of the offer. In other words, once a party begins performance, that party has signaled to the other that it accepts the offer. That acceptance is a bar to revocation. Once the

def•i•ni•tion

Detrimental reliance is a substitute for consideration that arises when one party relies on the acts or representations of another party to the first party's detriment.

offer is accepted by part performance, the offeree has a reasonable time to complete the contract by complete performance.

So how do you know what constitutes part performance? The offeree must start performing. Preparations to perform are not sufficient. Even if the offeror refuses to accept performance, once the offeree has partially performed the offer cannot be terminated.

Counteroffers

A counteroffer by the offeree terminates the offer and puts in place a new offer. A counteroffer will be on the same basic subject matter as the original offer, but will alter one or more terms. This can occur by rejection combined with counteroffer or by acceptance conditioned on additional terms. For example, Lois offers to sell James her car for $5,000. James could counteroffer by offering to pay $4,000 for the car. The subject matter is the same (Lois's car), but a material term has changed (the price). In that case, James has extended acceptance conditioned on additional terms. Or James could say, "I won't buy the car at that price, but would for $4,000." Then he has counteroffered combined with rejection.

> **Citations**
>
> If the offeree asks about additional terms, that is not an express rejection unless the offeree uses the language of rejection. The test is whether a reasonable person would interpret the communication as a rejection of the offer.

Rejection of Offer

In addition to terminating an offer by counteroffer, the offeree can expressly reject an offer. If the offeree rejects, the rejection is effective when the offeror receives it. If the offeror chooses, he or she can revive the offer by restating the offer. Then the offeree has an additional opportunity to accept the offer.

Termination from Lapse of Time

If the offer states it can only be accepted by a set time, failing to do so terminates the offer. If no time is specified within the offer for acceptance, the offeree has a reasonable time to respond. If the offer will expire at the end of a certain time, that time commences when the offeree receives the offer. If there was an obvious delay in the offer reaching the offeree, the offeree is supposed to take that delay into account. Evidence of an obvious delay includes a postmark or the date on an offer letter.

Terminated by Law

An offer may also be terminated by law. If one of the parties dies or becomes mentally incompetent, the offer terminates. If the subject matter is destroyed, then the offer terminates. For example, if the Monet painting that is the subject of the contract is stolen, the contract may be revoked. Finally, if the subject matter of the contract becomes illegal, the offer will terminate. If the offeror has offered to sell a drug to the offeree, but the drug subsequently becomes illegal, then the offer is terminated.

Acceptance of the Offer

To accept an offer the offeree must manifest acceptance according to the terms of the offer. The offeree is also the only person or firm who can accept the offer. Only with an option contract is there the right to assign acceptance, because an option is a contract. Once an offer is accepted, the contract is formed and binding on the parties. Remember that acceptance is a critical half of creating a contract. Without acceptance there is no contract. And it doesn't matter how often the offeror and offeree have contracted in the past. Unless the offeror accepts the terms of the contract this time, there is a failure of acceptance.

Differing Terms in Acceptance

If any term of the contract is not accepted, then there is no acceptance of the contract as a whole. Instead, under the common law, the offeree has just rejected the offer and made a counteroffer. Under the UCC, the rules change dramatically. Those differences will be addressed in Chapter 14. At this point understand that if two merchants contract, the contract will be accepted with additional terms unless the terms materially alter the offer, the offer limits acceptance to the original terms, or the offeror objects to the additional terms. If one party is a nonmerchant, the original terms govern and the additional terms are merely proposals.

When Acceptance Is Effective

Acceptance is generally effective when received by the offeror. However, under the mailbox rule, an acceptance is effective when put in the mailbox unless the offer states acceptance is only effective when received. Let's say Ruth wants to accept Sam's written offer to paint her house. When she puts her acceptance in the mailbox and it's no longer under her control, she has accepted the offer even if Sam doesn't receive the letter for four days. This is important because if an acceptance is mailed before the offeree receives a revocation, then a contract is formed. Let's say Sam decides to revoke his offer to paint Ruth's house. If Ruth puts her acceptance in the mail prior to receiving his letter revoking, then a contract exists. Ruth accepted before getting knowledge of the revocation, and that's enough under the law.

An options contract is a little different because its acceptance is only effective when received.

What if the offeree mails a rejection and then an acceptance? Which wins? If an offeree sends a rejection and then an acceptance, whichever is received first wins. However, if the offeree sends an acceptance and then the rejection, the mailbox rule applies. A contract is created when the acceptance is mailed. However, if the offeror received the rejection first and relied on it, the offeree can't enforce the contract.

Citations

At this time, most courts apply the mailbox rule to telephone transactions. Telephone acceptances are valid at the time of the call. Some courts have found faxes will satisfy the mailbox rule. As of this writing, courts have not addressed the mailbox rule as applied to e-mail. The key seems to be whether the communication of the acceptance is instantaneous.

The Exceptions

There are a few exceptions to these rules—this is the law, after all. Occasionally, a contract can be accepted without communication. This can happen if the offer expressly waives communicating acceptance. Or the offer may allow acceptance by performing an act. This is not a unilateral contract, but a bilateral contract allowing acceptance via action. Rarely, silence may show acceptance, particularly if there's a history of prior dealings between the offeror and offeree.

At an auction, a bid is merely an offer. The offer is accepted when the auctioneer selects the winning bid. Because the bid is an offer, the bidder can withdraw their bid at any time prior to the auctioneer's hammer falling.

The Least You Need to Know

♦ Contracts are an agreement containing specific terms between two parties that will govern the relationship of those parties.

♦ Every contract must contain: 1) An agreement, 2) between two or more parties, 3) an offer to perform with, 4) an acceptance of that offer. There must also be 5) a set time period, 6) terms for performance, and 7) valuable consideration exchanged for that performance.

♦ An offer must express a promise to enter a contract, create certainty about the key terms, and clearly communicate those items.

♦ An offer is terminated in one of four basic ways: 1) the offer is revoked by the offeror; 2) the offeree counteroffers; 3) the offeree rejects the offer; or 4) the offer is terminated from lapse of time or by law.

♦ To accept an offer, the offeree must manifest acceptance according to the terms of the offer.

Going Deeper with Contracts

In This Chapter

- ◆ The importance of putting it in writing
- ◆ Determining the parties' intent
- ◆ Consideration: do the parties have it?
- ◆ Contractual capacity required for contracts
- ◆ Mistakes, deception, and other contract problems
- ◆ The impact of illegalities on contracts

In addition to the contract requirements covered in Chapter 11, several other items must be present in an effective contract. Most, but not all, contracts should be in writing. The parties to the contract must also have contractual capacity. Consideration must be exchanged by the parties. And how should parties handle contracts when mistakes have been made, deception has occurred, or other problems arise? Finally, what happens if a contract is illegal? This chapter will examine each of those areas.

A Contract Should Be in Writing

In general, a contract can be either in writing or oral. However, there is a strong bias in the law for contracts to be written. In the event of a dispute about the terms of a contract, the courts don't want to decipher the parties' intent without some kind of contemporaneous memorialization. There are also circumstances in which the contract must be in writing to be valid.

Statute of Frauds

The Statute of Frauds (SOF) requires the parties to put certain classes of contracts in writing to be valid and enforceable. On occasion oral contracts will satisfy the SOF if enough of the terms are in writing to memorialize the intent of the parties. The following must be in writing:

♦ **Agreements that cannot be performed within one year of the contract.**
The year runs from the time the contract is made rather than when performance begins. If a contract may be terminated by either party at will, it cannot be performed within one year. Employment contracts cannot usually be completed within one year because the term of employment can extend beyond a year, even though it may end prior to that. If the contract is possible to be performed within a year, an oral contract is enforceable. This includes oral contracts for the lifetime of someone because his or her life could end within one year.

♦ **Contracts regarding real estate.** Because land is a unique commodity, contracts regarding real estate must be in writing. That way it is easy to trace the title to the land. This requirement also covers leases, easements, fixtures, mortgages, and minerals or structures that are to be severed from the land.

♦ **Promises in consideration of marriage.** This includes prenuptial agreements and any contract used to induce someone to marry.

♦ **Promises of an executor or administrator of a will to personally pay estate debts.** This covers promises that the executor or administrator are not obligated to accept. It is not their responsibility to personally pay these debts. Therefore, the contract must be in writing.

♦ **Promise to pay the debt of another (suretyship).** Again, this occurs when a person is accepting a responsibility that is not theirs. For a court to enforce it, it must in writing.

◆ **Sale of goods of $500 or more.** The Uniform Commercial Code (UCC) allows oral contracts if the contracted goods are specially manufactured for the buyer, there is a written confirmation of the oral contract between merchants, there is an admission of the oral contract in legal pleadings or court, or there is partial payment or delivery of the contracted goods. All other sales of goods of $500 or more must be in writing.

Under the SOF any writing will work as long as it contains the essential terms of the agreement. Those essential terms are the identity of the party, the contract's subject matter, the terms and conditions of the agreement, inclusion of the consideration, and signature of the party the contract is used against.

Parol Evidence Rule

The *parol evidence rule* must be followed when there is disagreement about whether the contract represents the full and final agreement of the parties. The general rule is where parties have a writing with the intent it serve as the complete agreement, any prior written or oral expressions along with those made at the time the contract was signed are inadmissible. The theory is the parties had the opportunity to integrate anything contained in those oral or written communications into the written contract but decided not to. A court will not step in later to insert those items into the contract.

def•i•ni•tion

The **parol evidence rule** states that evidence cannot be admitted in court if it would add to, vary, or contradict a written contract.

There are two questions to ask. Is the writing the final expression of the parties? Is the writing a complete or partial integration of the intent of the parties? The more complete the contract, the more likely it encompasses the full intent of the parties. If the finished contract contains a merger clause that states the contract is the complete contract, that creates a strong presumption the contract integrates the negotiations.

The parol evidence rule does not apply in the following situations: If a contract is ambiguous as to certain terms, parol evidence may be admitted to determine the meaning of the ambiguous term. Parol evidence may also be submitted if a contract that looks valid on its face is missing terms due to fraud, duress, or mistake. The rule also does not apply to exclude evidence that a contract was modified or terminated.

Determining the Intent of the Parties

So if the court can't use parol evidence to determine the true intent of the parties, what can it do? Anytime a contract is brought before it, the court's purpose is to determine and give effect to the intent of the parties. There are several principles it will use to reach that determination:

◆ Ordinary words will be given their ordinary meaning. Technical or trade terms will be used according to that technical meaning.

◆ Missing terms can be supplied if the contract incorporates them by reference. They will be incorporated from a second document that must be clearly identified in the contract.

◆ The court will construe the terms of the contract as a whole.

◆ If a term is ambiguous or contradictory, the court will determine what the parties meant by looking at evidence outside the contract.

When a term is ambiguous or contradictory, the court may apply the following rules. If a contract is partially printed, typed, and/or handwritten, the written part prevails over the other parts. When the printed and typed part conflict, the typed part prevails. The reason is the typed or handwritten part was inserted by the parties, and therefore, demonstrate the most recent intent of the parties. If there is a conflict between a number expressed in words and numbers, the written version prevails. Finally, the court will construe any ambiguous or contradictory terms against the drafter, since that party was in the best position to avoid the problem.

Consultation

Courts will not protect the parties to a contract from a bad decision. However, the court may interpret the contract in a way that avoids an undue hardship on one party. If necessary, the court may imply a term to avoid hardship.

In addition, if the court must determine the meaning of a contract, it may insert implied terms if the parties failed to cover a situation. The court will also look at the conduct of the parties and the custom and usage of the trade.

No Contracts Without Consideration

To make a bilateral contract enforceable in court, both parties must change their legal status by giving up valuable consideration. If either side fails to give consideration, a contract was not formed. Consideration has two parts: 1) it must be a bargained-for exchange between the parties and 2) it must have legal value. The promisor must give up something that will benefit the promisee.

In Chapter 11, I used the example of going to a car dealership to buy a car. You are willing to part with your hard-earned cash in exchange for receiving a car that day. The cash is your promise in exchange for a vehicle, the consideration. The dealership is willing to sell you a car in exchange for cash. The detriment to the dealership is losing a car. The detriment to you is parting with the cash. Consideration would support this contract.

Gifts

A gift does not have consideration to support it, so the giver is not contractually obligated to make the gift. There are rare circumstances where a gift induces the promisee to act in a way that benefits the promisor. If that occurs, there is consideration.

Stay Out of Jail

Gifts that are made as pledges for charitable institutions can be enforced in court if the charity acted in reliance on the pledged gift. Usually this will arise in a capital campaign where the university or other organization begins constructing a building in reliance on pledged funds. While a charity could enforce the gift in court, it rarely will due to the negative publicity that can arise.

Adequacy of Consideration

When it comes to the adequacy of consideration, the courts leave that to the parties. At the time of bargaining, the parties determine they are each receiving a fair deal. Forbearance may also serve as consideration. Legal forbearance occurs when one party to the contract gives up the right to do something they have a legal right to do. For example, if an employee over the age of 40 is terminated, he or she will often be asked to sign a document stating he or she waives the right to sue under the Age Discrimination in Employment Act (ADEA). In exchange, he or she will be paid a sum of money. While that employee would ordinarily have the right to sue for a violation of the ADEA, by accepting the payment, the court will accept the forbearance of that right as consideration.

Illusory Promises Are Not Consideration

Illusory promises will not be enforced by a court. If it appears that both parties have agreed to give valuable consideration, but one party's promise is not an obligation or only an apparent obligation, then it is illusory and will fail. If Archie's Accounting promises to buy all the carpet cleaning services it may need from Annie's Carpets, that is illusory. Archie's Accounting is free to purchase the services from anybody or not at all.

Outputs and requirement contracts have sufficient consideration because the buyer has parted with the legal right to purchase the items from anyone else. However, the output and requirements contract must not become unreasonable in the number of goods that are required. It must be in line with estimates or reasonable expectations.

Preexisting Legal Duty

Normally a preexisting legal duty cannot be used as consideration. My favorite example is that a police officer cannot be paid by a company to take extra patrols past its location if the building is within the officer's normal patrol area. The police officer already has a preexisting legal duty to patrol as a requirement of his or her job. Also, a contractor cannot refuse to complete a project that is already contracted for unless the contractor receives additional funds. Even if the owner agrees, he or she can later refuse to pay because the contractor had a preexisting legal duty to complete the project. This is why change orders are routine on construction projects.

> **Consultation**
>
> Past consideration is similar to a preexisting legal duty. It cannot be used to support a contract. The reason is the past consideration was used for a prior contract. New consideration must be used for the current contract.

Exceptions to the Requirement for Consideration

We've already discussed the fact that if a pledge is made to a charity, consideration is not needed for the charity to enforce the pledge. There are two additional exceptions to consideration:

◆ Promissory estoppel will prevent a contract from being voided for lack of consideration, especially where one party has detrimentally relied on the contract. Promissory estoppel is a false statement that the court will treat as a contract when the person making the statement benefits at the expense of the person who relied on the statement. It is the attempt of the courts to prevent the person from benefiting from their lie. Justice requires the contract to be enforced without consideration if the promisee relied on the contract and will be harmed if the contract is nullified.

◆ The UCC also creates several exceptions to consideration. If the merchant's firm offer is irrevocable, consideration is not needed. If the party affected by the lack of consideration waives that in writing, no consideration is needed. And an agreement to modify a contract for the sale of goods does not require fresh consideration.

Contractual Capacity

As I mentioned in Chapter 11, for a contract to be valid, the parties must have the capacity to enter a contract. Capacity became a factor in contract law to protect some individuals from being harmed in contracts. Those classes are minors, the mentally incompetent, and to a lesser extent, the intoxicated.

Minors

While minors can enter contracts, the law treats them as lacking mental capacity. Generally, a minor is anyone who is under 18 years old. A minor may enter a contract and later disaffirm that contract because of his or her incapacity.

Let's say Billy goes to a car dealership to buy a Ferrari on his sixteenth birthday with money given to him by his grandparents. He can enter the contract with Sean's Hot Rods. He can take the car home and drive it around. At some time in the future he can decide he doesn't want the car and return it, disaffirming the contract. There is nothing the car dealership can do because he lacked the capacity to enter a contract. However, if Billy misrepresented his age, Sean's Hot Rods can enforce the contract because it had no knowledge of his minority. If Billy damages the car and then disaffirms the contract, he only has to return what he has to Sean's Hot Rods. He does not have to make additional restitution for the damage.

Once a minor reaches majority—18 years old—he or she must act quickly to disaffirm the contract. If the minor does not disaffirm, the contract will be ratified. To ratify, the individual may communicate acceptance or by conduct, letting the contract stand.

Mental Incapacity

The law also protects those who are unable to understand the contract and implications of what they are signing because their mental capacity is diminished. The contract may be disaffirmed when that individual regains mental capacity or by his or her legal representative.

Intoxicated Persons

If someone becomes so intoxicated that he or she no longer understands the significance of the legal promise made, then the contract is voidable if the other party to the contract had reason to know the first was intoxicated.

Citations
Whether someone is a minor, mentally incapacitated, or intoxicated, contracts for necessities like food, clothing, and shelter cannot be disaffirmed. While the common law did not, now every state often includes medical care and education as necessities.

Mistakes, Deception, and Other Problems

In addition to lack of capacity, there are other reasons a contract may not be enforced. Those include when a mistake has been made in the contract, when one party intentionally misrepresented a material fact or term, if the contract is fraudulently obtained, one party negligently misrepresents a fact or term, or one party exercises undue influence or inflicts duress on the other party.

Unilateral and Mutual Mistakes

A unilateral mistake is one that is made by one party. A unilateral mistake will not affect the contract when the nonmistaken party is unaware of the mistake. Let's say the parties agree to a price that was reached by a mistake of the offeror. If the offeree did not know of the mistake, then the contract stands with the mistake. If the offeree knew or should have known, then that term in the contract may be avoided by the offeror. If it's a computational error on the part of the offeror, then it will stand unless the error is so noticeable that the offeree should have recognized it as an error.

A mutual mistake occurs when both parties misunderstand the other party's intent about a material term of the contract. The classic example here involves two different ships, both called the *Peerless*. In that case, the parties entered a contract for cotton to be delivered to England from Bombay on the *Peerless*. The only problem is one party meant the *Peerless* sailing in October, the other meant the *Peerless* sailing in December. Because each party was thinking of a different ship when the contract was formed, the contract was voidable. If the difference had been one of judgment rather than fact or law, the contract would not be voidable.

If a mistake is made in the transcribing of the contract, the contract can be reformed to match the intention of the parties.

Intentional Misrepresentation

Intentional misrepresentation is otherwise known as fraud. It occurs when someone deliberately misleads a party about a material fact in order to gain an advantage over the other party. Fraud requires that the party making the misrepresentation do it with knowledge that the information is false or a reckless indifference to its truth, with the intent that the listener rely on that information, that the listener does rely on it, and as a result the listener is harmed.

To be a material misrepresentation of fact, that fact must be likely to induce a reasonable person to agree to the contract. However, opinions about the value or future events are rarely fraudulent. Instead, the law allows for a little *puffing* of a product. Statements about a product that are merely matters of opinion are not fraud. A reasonable person should recognize the statements for what they are: opinion. However, if the person stating the opinion knows of facts that make the opinion false, it is fraud.

To be important, someone must rely on the fraudulent statement. If the relying party should have known that the statements were fraudulent, he or she cannot rely on those false statements because a reasonable person wouldn't have. To recover under fraud, the injured party must have proof of the harm. The injured party can recover actual damages as well as punitive damages when the fraud is oppressive. The court can rescind or cancel the contract.

def•i•ni•tion

Puffing is a nonspecific, unmeasurable statement about a product; this statement cannot be interpreted by a reasonable person as a benchmark about the truth of the statement.

Negligent Misrepresentation

Negligent misrepresentation is similar to fraud in its elements only it does not require known false statements. Instead, for negligent misrepresentation the negligent party has to fail to exercise due care regarding material information. There is no intent to deceive, but carelessness. This is an easier standard to prove, so it is often alleged along with fraud.

Consultation

Nondisclosure can result in a contract being voided. In a normal situation a party has no duty to volunteer information to a party. However, in the following cases a party does have a duty: 1) duty to disclose an unknown defect or condition, 2) duty to disclose a confidential relationship between the parties, and 3) active concealment of information (this can be physical concealment of harmful evidence or hiding information).

Undue Influence and Duress

Another area where someone may not be able to give actual consent is if they are being unduly influenced by someone or are under duress. Many people rely on others to assist them with their financial and legal affairs. An elderly parent may rely on an adult child, a patient on a nurse, a client on a trusted advisor. In those cases, the person relied on can exert *undue influence*. Essentially, the weaker party loses the ability to exercise independent judgment and is unduly influenced by the other party. When that occurs, the contract can be voided. Courts will normally default to a position that the weaker party was persuaded rather than unduly influenced. The inability to exercise free will becomes the key in these disputes.

def•i•ni•tion

Undue influence is the unfair or improper persuasion of one person by another who has a dominant position in the relationship. **Duress** is the threat of harm used to compel another to do an act against his or her will or judgment.

A related issue is *duress*. A party can argue that they only entered the contract because of duress. Physical duress occurs when someone is threatened with physical harm unless he or she acts in a desired way. Emotional duress occurs when someone enters a contract under circumstances which require him or her to sacrifice free will. If a contract is made under duress, it is voidable at the victim's choice.

Illegal Contracts

Not surprisingly in normal circumstances, an illegal contract is void. To be illegal, the contract must cover illegal actions or subject matter. The subject might be a contract on someone's life—these are always illegal, because you can't contract to kill someone. Drug transactions also can't be enforced in court if the product is an illegal drug.

There are a couple of rare exceptions. The first occurs when the law at issue is designed to protect one party to the contract. The other is when the parties are not *in pari delicto* (a Latin phrase meaning "equally guilty"). When the parties are not equally guilty, the court may protect the weaker party if the law allows.

Partial Illegality

If a contract is severable into legal and illegal sections, then the legal sections will be enforced. However, if the contract is illegal through one interpretation, but legal under another, the court will determine which interpretation is correct. If the contract is interpreted by the court as illegal, the entire contract will fail.

Unconscionable Clauses

Occasionally, a court will find that a clause in a contract is unconscionable. When this happens, that clause is unenforceable. Unconscionability is one of the longer legal terms, but it essentially means if a contract or term gives one party a significant advantage over another the court can void that contract or term.

Procedural unconscionability looks at the inequity of negotiating power between the parties. It can come in hidden terms, relative freedom of a party to choose whether to contract, and the inability to actively negotiate. Substantive unconscionability refers to the terms themselves. A contract of adhesion arises when a dominant party offers a contract to a weaker one on a take it or leave it basis. The weaker party has no choice but to accept the contract.

> ### Consultation
>
> Contracts for a civil wrong are invalid. You can't contract to defraud someone or slander them. Contracts are supposed to adhere to underlying principles of good faith and fairness. Good faith is the absence of the knowledge of defects or problems. Thus, a party cannot do anything that will injure or destroy the rights of the other party.

For example, a contract that calls for the buyer to purchase a $300 freezer for more than $1,400 after all the fees are added in is substantively unconscionable as to price. If the buyer had no other options—no other places to purchase the freezer—and it was offered in a take-it-or-leave-it manner, it could also be procedurally unconscionable.

Agreements Affecting Public Policy

Agreements that will harm public welfare are not binding. Generally, public welfare and policy relate to the areas of health, morals, and integrity of the government. The law steps in to declare invalid any contracts that would conflict with these greater goods. Some agreements that fall into this area include contracts for illicit sex or gambling.

The Least You Need to Know

◆ A contract can be either written or oral; however, some contracts are required to be in writing by the Statue of Frauds, and if it is written, the parol evidence will exclude evidence regarding earlier or contemporaneous conversations.

◆ Consideration is a necessary element for a valid contract and requires a bargained-for exchange between the parties and that item has legal value.

◆ Capacity is the ability to know one is entering a contract, and without both parties having capacity the contract fails.

◆ Contracts are unenforceable when a mistake has been made in the contract, when one party intentionally misrepresented a material fact or term, if the contract is fraudulently obtained, one party negligently misrepresents a fact or term, or one party exercises undue influence or inflicts duress on the other party.

◆ Contracts that contain illegal subject matter will not be enforced.

Chapter 13

Discharge of Contracts, Breach of Contracts, and Remedies

In This Chapter

◆ How to terminate contracts

◆ Evaluating breach of contract

◆ Resolving breach of contract problems

◆ Contract provisions affecting remedies and damages

In a perfect world once a contract is signed, all dealings between the parties would proceed smoothly. There would be no problems with compliance. No contracts would go unfulfilled. The contract would be perfectly discharged. Instead, things go wrong. This chapter will examine how a contract is discharged as well as the rights of the party when a contract is broken or—to use the legal term—breached.

Discharging a Contract

Discharging a contract occurs when a party satisfies an obligation it has under the contract. There are several ways a contract can be discharged. This section will examine those as well as the conditions that must be met before the contract is discharged.

Conditions to Discharging a Contract

The terms of the contract will outline any conditions—those stipulations or prerequisites contained in a contract, will, or other legal document—that must be satisfied before a contract is discharged. Those conditions fall into two categories:

♦ *Conditions precedent* are those that must be satisfied before rights can arise under the contract. Let's say parties have entered a contract that the buyer will purchase the items on a ship when the ship reaches port. If the ship never makes it to port, the buyer is not required to pay for the goods it never received.

♦ *Conditions subsequent* terminate rights to a contract. For example, if a business closes, any obligation to continue to fulfill a supply contract with that company terminates.

Concurrent conditions are the normal conditions in a bilateral contract. The parties must each perform an action concurrently.

Time and Adequacy of Performance

Normally a contract is discharged when the terms of the contract are satisfied. On occasion, the contract will be discharged when the time allotted by its terms expires. Performance of a contract is generally done by performing an act or *tendering* payment.

def•i•ni•tion

To **tender** payment is to present payment to another or delivery under terms of contract; tender ends a party's obligations under the contract.

If a time period for performance is outlined in the contract, performance must be made by or on that date. If there is no specified time, performance must be made within a reasonable time. If it's vital that performance is made in the timeframe specified, time is of the essence. Usually, this is the case when perishable goods or items that have volatile pricing are the subject matter of the contract. If the contract is not completed by the stated time, the nonbreaching party is entitled to damages.

In addition to being timely, performance must be adequate. That means the performance must satisfy the terms of the contract. Problems arise when there is partial performance of the terms—and this usually arises in construction cases. If performance is substantial, the performing party can sue for payment, but the other party can countersue for the unfinished performance. For example, if the owner has to repair defective work, the contractor is liable for that cost. Usually, the damages are cost of completion, but if that is disproportionate, the measure of damages will be the reduction in value of the building from the defective performance.

A party cannot complain about performance when it was according to the contract. So, if there's a problem with the framing of a home, but the contractor framed it according to the provided plans, the homeowner can't sue for improper performance. Occasionally, a contract will state that performance must satisfy the other party. If that's the case, the court will enforce that as long as the dissatisfaction of a party is made in good faith. This personal satisfaction usually occurs when an opinion is involved such as interior design work or for-hire art.

Ways to Discharge a Contract

For a bilateral contract to be discharged, both parties must perform their obligations. For a unilateral contract, only one party has to perform. (See Chapter 11 for a review of these and other types of contracts.)

Consumer protection laws have created unilateral methods for a consumer to rescind a contract. For example, homeowners have three days to rescind a mortgage for any reason. If someone purchases an item worth more than $25 through a home-based sale, he or she has three days to rescind.

There are several ways that a contract can be discharged by the agreement of the parties:

- The contracts can be discharged by its terms, meaning both parties have completed their obligations.

- The parties can execute a release or waive their rights under the contract.

- The parties can mutually cancel or substitute a new contract for the original one.

- The parties can agree to accord and satisfaction (see the following sidebar).

- The parties can mutually agree to cancel the contract.

Consultation _____

With accord and satisfaction, the parties substitute a new form of payment for the original contract amount. For accord and satisfaction to work, the parties must have a dispute under the original contract, negotiate a settlement, and then perform the new agreement. For example, if two businesses dispute the amount that is owed under the contract, they can negotiate a new amount, which serves as full satisfaction of the claims between them.

Discharge by Impossibility

External causes can also discharge a contract, usually because the contract has now become impossible. The Restatement of Contracts defines impossibility as "not only strict impossibility, but impracticability because of extreme and unreasonable difficulty, expense, injury or loss involved."

After Hurricane Katrina swept through New Orleans and part of Mississippi in 2005, thousands of contracts became impossible because the companies no longer had inventory, buildings, and so forth. If the inability to perform had been due to shortages of material, that in and of itself is not sufficient for impossibility unless a specific source for that material was listed in the contract. Without a specifically designated supplier, the law assumes material can be found from another supplier.

If the parties have contracted for a particular item or subject matter and that is destroyed, the contract is discharged for impossibility. For example, if a rice farmer and a buyer contracted for the buyer to purchase the rice from his fields, the contract would be impossible after Hurricane Katrina flooded the fields and destroyed that crop. If, however, the contract was for rice without specification as to what field, the rice farmer would still be obligated to perform the contract since he could obtain the rice to sell from any source.

Similarly, if the subject matter of the contract becomes illegal after the contract is in effect, it is discharged for impossibility. If one party to a personal services contract dies or becomes ill or otherwise incapacitated, the contract is discharged if it called for a specialized service. If a party refuses to perform in a manner that makes the contract impossible, the other party is discharged from performing. For example, if a contractor refuses to provide needed material or payment to a subcontractor, the subcontractor is released from his obligation under the contract. However, the subcontractor may have to show that he or she could not find similar goods from another source.

When determining which party should bear the risk of the contract impossibility, the court will ask two questions:

◆ Which party had the greater expertise in the subject area of the contract?

◆ Which party took initiative in drawing up the contract?

A developing and related theory to impossibility is commercial impracticability. Under that theory, a contract may be discharged because fulfilling the contract is unreasonable and carries an excessive cost. To prevail, the discharging party must show that something unexpected occurred, the risk of that occurrence was not assigned to one of the parties by contract or custom, and that unexpected event rendered performance of the contract commercially impracticable.

Temporary impossibilities may arise that frustrate the ability to perform a contract for a period of time. Usually these are related to events like the 9/11 terrorist attack or extreme weather. The event is out of the control of the parties and requires a temporary suspension of the contract. Eventually, the parties will be able to honor the contract.

> **Stay Out of Jail**
>
> The Frustration of Purpose doctrine allows a party to be discharged from performing a contract if that contract had a purpose that has ceased to have value. However, both parties must be aware of that frustrated purpose and that frustrating event must have been unforeseeable.

Discharge by Law

The law will discharge a contract in several situations. If the court discharges claims in bankruptcy, they are discharged regardless of whether the contracting party received full compensation. Statutes of limitations can also bar contract claims if the injured party allows too much time to pass. In addition, the contract may contain a clause that limits how long a party can wait to file suit. Once that time expires, the aggrieved party cannot sue. There may be a similar provision requiring notice of the intent to sue.

Understanding Breach of Contract

Breach is the failure to perform or act in the manner called for by the terms of the contract. While parties do not sign a contract anticipating one of them will breach the contract, the question of how a breach occurs is important.

A breach of contract occurs when a promisor is under an absolute duty to perform and fails to discharge that duty. Sometimes that breach will be anticipatory, occurring when the promisor announces its intent before the duty to perform. The promisee can accept that as a contract breach.

If the breach is minor, the promisee has received the benefit of a substantial portion of the contract despite the promisor's defective performance. The promisee may be compensated for any costs of the minor breach, but must still complete its portion of the contract. If the breach is major, the promisee did not receive the substantial benefit intended by the contract. In that case, the promisee can treat the contract as discharged and immediately seek remedies for the breach. In certain cases the promisee can treat a minor breach when it's paired with anticipatory repudiation as a major breach.

Repudiation

Contracts are repudiated when a party to the contract indicates by words or deeds that it has no intention of performing its obligations under the contract. In other words, repudiation is a threatened breach of contract. Anticipatory repudiation occurs when a party who has an obligation to perform under a contract repudiates before the time of performance. Then the injured party has the right to damages for total breach as well as discharges any remaining duty to perform that party has.

Anticipatory repudiation also occurs when one party becomes insecure that the other party will actually perform its portion of the contract. The insecure party can contact the other party demanding assurances. If it does not receive satisfactory assurances, it can consider the contract anticipatorily breached.

To determine which level of breach is involved, courts will examine several factors. They look at the amount of the benefit received by the promisee. The adequacy of damages to substitute for performance will also be considered. Then the courts consider the extent of the promisor's part performance and the hardship the breach imposes on the promisee. Finally, the courts determine whether any negligent or willful behavior led to the breach as well as the likelihood the breaching party can fully perform the contract.

The breaching party can retract its repudiation if the other party has not changed its position in reliance on that repudiation. Let's say Acme Inc. is purchasing widgets from Brown & Co. Brown tells Acme it will be unable to fulfill the contract because its supplier for a scarce commodity has gone bankrupt. Acme acknowledges the repudiation but takes no action to mitigate the damage. Before Acme signs a contract with another firm, Brown locates a new supplier and announces it intends to fulfill the original contract. Brown has successfully revoked its repudiation, and Acme must allow Brown to fulfill the contract. If Acme had already signed with another company, Brown would be liable for any damages Acme incurs as a result of the breach.

Consultation

One challenge with anticipatory repudiation is what constitutes sufficient evidence the questioned party can indeed fulfill its portion of the contract. Can promisees claim insecurity as a way to avoid contracts? This area, like so many in the law, is fact sensitive and left to judges and juries to wade through with guidance from the Uniform Commercial Code and case law.

Waiver

A party may waive the other party's breach. There may be business reasons the non-breaching party will waive the breach. Maybe the promisee has found a source of materials cheaper than the promisor and is happy to allow the promisor to breach. If the promisee later decides to sue the promisor for breach, the question of whether it waived the breach is one of fact for the judge or jury to determine.

Waiver can be expressly stated or it can be inferred from the actions of the party. A contract could state that payment must be on time or the contract is breached, but a payment is late and the promisee says nothing and continues to accept payments. The continuing acceptance of payments constitutes waiver of breach for the late payment. Sometimes a party will be willing to waive breach without waiving its right to damages. In that case, that party should make what's called a *reservation of rights*.

def•i•ni•tion

A **reservation of rights** is the assertion by a party that it is not waiving its right to damages for potential nonconformity even though it accepted performance that does not comply with the terms of the contract.

Remedies for Breach

Before a promisee can sue for the promisor's breach, the promisee must show that he or she is willing and able to perform the contract. The only thing stopping the promisee's performance is the promisor's breach. Once the promisee makes that showing, the issue of remedies rises to the surface. (See Chapter 14 for a discussion of remedies for breach of contracts that deal with sales of goods.)

Remedies for Anticipatory Repudiation

If a party has been harmed by the anticipatory repudiation of another party, he or she has three options:

- ◆ The aggrieved party can do nothing other than require performance as called for in the contract.

- ◆ He or she can consider the contract broken and bring immediate suit to enforce it.

- ◆ The party can consider the repudiation an offer to cancel the contract.

General Remedies

The court will impose quasi-contractual damages if the contract is defective but one party performed and the other party benefited. The courts will attempt to balance the outcome so that neither party receives an undue benefit. Let's say Bob and Jane enter a contract for Bob to paint Jane's house. Jane gives Bob a down payment and then decides to hire someone else. Because Bob has not performed any work on Jane's home, he must reimburse her for the down payment. Otherwise, he is unjustly enriched at Jane's expense.

> **Citations**
>
> Monetary damages in a breach of contract case will be the amount sufficient to place the injured party in the position he would have been in before the breach. Courts will not normally allow money damages to place a party in a better position than it would have been under the terms of the contract.

Sometimes restitution of money is insufficient to remedy the breach. This often arises in circumstances where the subject matter of the contract is a unique item or land. Because each parcel of land is unique, money may not be a sufficient substitute for performance of the contract. In cases like that, the courts can impose specific performance. In other words, the breaching party must perform the actual terms of the contract because merely suing for damages is not adequate to compensate the aggrieved party.

Monetary Damages

Monetary damages for breach fall into several categories, as summarized in the following table. *Compensatory damages* will compensate the injured party for the injuries from the result of the breach. Again, the idea is to place the injured party in the position they would have been in if the contract had been honored by the breaching party. *Punitive damages* are used by a court to punish the breaching party for its bad acts. Punitive damages are rarely awarded in contract cases. Normally, the contract will not allow the use of punitives, but will limit damages to compensatory or liquidated damages.

Direct damages are those that flow directly from the breach of contract. Direct damages may include *incidental damages,* which are those extra expenses the injured party had to pay as a consequence of the breach or to mitigate damages. *Consequential damages* are those that can't necessarily be anticipated before the breach but flow from special circumstances of the injured party. However, the damages must have been reasonably foreseeable to the parties because of the special circumstances. For example, if a company contracted to have hotels built in Beijing in anticipation of the Olympics, it would be reasonably foreseeable to both parties that the failure of the contractor to have the hotels ready for occupancy in time would result in extra damages to the company.

Nominal damages are token damages. The amount can be as little as $1 and is awarded simply to show the contract was breached. However, the injured party suffered no real harm from the breach. *Liquidated damages* are agreed to by the parties in the contract. These are often used in construction contracts where a specific amount of damage for delay is hard to ascertain ahead of time, yet the parties want to quantify the damage if there is delay.

Regardless of the damages, the nonbreaching party has an obligation to mitigate—or limit—the damages. This may require the nonbreacher to buy goods from someone else. For example, a landlord will be required to attempt to release an apartment if the tenant moves out prior to the expiration of the lease instead of waiting for the end of the lease. Then any rent received from releasing the apartment will be applied to the rent the former tenant owes. The former tenant will also be required to pay the difference between the new rent and the rent under his or her lease if the new rent is lower. The landlord must receive the full rent amount owed under the terms of the lease, but must take steps to mitigate the harm by renting the apartment if possible and applying that rent to the balance.

Type of Damage	Definition
Compensatory	Compensate the injured party for the injuries from the result of the breach
Punitive	Punish or make an example of the breaching party for its bad acts
Direct	Flow directly from the breach of contract
Incidental	Extra expenses the injured party had to pay as a consequence of the breach or to mitigate damages
Consequential	Can't be anticipated before the breach yet reasonably foreseeable damages that flow from special circumstances
Nominal	Token damages, usually for $1, that show the contract was breached but with no actual loss
Liquidated	Agreed to by the parties in the contract and will be enforceable by the courts

Additional Remedies

The remedies I've just discussed are not the only ones available to contract parties. Parties can also consider using the following remedies when a contract is breached:

- **Rescission:** If one party commits a material breach of the contract, the remaining party may rescind the contract. If the nonbreaching party has already performed services prior to the breach and rescission, it can recover the reasonable value of those services.

- **Injunction:** The nonbreaching party can seek an injunction against the breaching party continuing to act in a way that does not comply with the contract. For example, this remedy is effective for noncompete covenants as applied to an employee. An employer can ask the court to enjoin or prevent the former employee from violating the terms.

◆ **Court reformation:** A court can reform the contract to better reflect the intent of the parties. However, the party seeking reformation must prove that the agreement was supposed to be what he or she seeks through reformation.

Contract Terms that Address Breach and Remedies

Contracts can be drafted to remove the mystery from how a breach will be treated as well as the measure of damages. Contracts often have terms that expressly limit damages. For example, if you buy electronic equipment, the damages in the warranty are often limited to repair or replacement.

A contract may also limit damages through a liquidated damages clause. This is often used in construction contracts as well as noncompete covenants. The parties agree that damages in the event of breach are too hard to determine, so they set a specific amount in advance. To be effective, liquidated damages provisions can only be used in situations where it's difficult or impossible to determine actual damages, and the amount stated must not be excessive.

Contracts may also contain clauses that limit liability. These are called either an exculpatory clause or limitation-of-liability clause. Courts will generally allow parties to allocate the risk between them as they choose. Thus, the clause can leave the risk unbalanced, but courts will rarely enforce a clause that leaves one party free from any liability. Releases signed when participating in risky outdoor events are one example of a limitation-of-liability clause.

The Least You Need to Know

◆ Contracts are discharged when both parties have completed their obligations under the contract.

◆ A contract is discharged by impossibility if it's no longer possible for one or all parties to perform their obligations.

◆ Breach is the failure to perform or act in the manner called for by the terms of the contract.

◆ If a contract is breached, money damages are the usual remedy, but parties can ask a court for other remedies including specific performance, rescission, and reformation of the contract.

◆ A contract should be drafted to make clear what will happen in the event of a breach.

Sales of Goods

In This Chapter

- ◆ What is a sale of goods?

- ◆ Modifying the contract

- ◆ Performing the contract

- ◆ How to allocate interest and risk of loss

- ◆ Breach of contract and remedies

The Uniform Commercial Code (UCC) Article 2 is the model legislations for the sale of goods. As of July 2008, the 2003 revision to Article 2 had not been adopted by any state, though 49 states and the District of Columbia have adopted some portion of the earlier version of Article 2. This chapter will examine key provisions of Article 2. Keep in mind that while it is called the Uniform Commercial Code, its adoption has not been uniform.

Nature of Sale of Goods

Article 2 covers the *sale of goods*, which is defined as personal property and commodities. As with other contracts there must be an exchange of goods for payment. That payment can be money, services, or other goods. Sale of

def•i•ni•tion

Sale of goods refers to the sale of personal property—anything that isn't real property or a service. So sales of goods rules cover when you purchase a car, a big-screen TV, a DVD, or groceries, for example.

goods does not cover contracts for services and real property. It also does not cover insurance contracts, commercial paper, and investment securities. Those are covered by other sections of the UCC.

The sale of goods is distinct from other transactions. A bailment is not a sale but merely a transfer of possession of a good (see Chapter 20 for more on bailments). A gift is not a sale because it is the free transfer of goods. The title is transferred without an exchange of money. A contract for services is not covered by Article 2, but by common law principles.

Mixed Contracts for Goods and Services

If a contract covers both sales and goods, the court must consider which element is predominant in determining whether to apply UCC Article 2 or common law. The general rule is that whichever dominates the contract wins. For example, a contract is formed between a homeowner and a painter for the painter to paint the outside of the homeowner's home. The painter purchased the paint, valued at $200, and included it on the invoice for the painting, valued at $1,000. Painting is a service, and the paint is a good. Because the value of the painting service is higher than the paint, the contract will be governed by common law principles.

Consultation

Is computer software classified as a good or information? If it's information, Article 2 does not apply. If it's a good, the software companies are making warranties through Article 2 about the nature of the good. During the 2003 revisions, where computer software should fall was heavily debated. The final position in Revised Article 2 was that information is not covered. So the courts will be left to determine which element dominates: information or good?

Formation of Contracts

Article 2 provides missing terms in contracts for the sale of goods, so the requirements to form a contract are not as stringent as the common law. Under Article 2, the parties must set the subject matter (what is purchased) and the quantity. Article 2 can supply everything else including price, delivery, time for performance, and payment.

Thus, a contract can be formed at a much lower threshold than under common law. It also means the terms supplied by Article 2 may not be what the parties envisioned. As always, it's much better for the parties to fully draft the contract themselves than to rely on a court to supply missing terms from Article 2.

Merchants Versus Nonmerchants

In general, Article 2 treats all parties the same. However, there are provisions that create a distinction between merchants and nonmerchants in applying terms to the contract. Article 2 makes a conscious decision to apply a higher standard to merchants in transactions between merchants and nonmerchants. This attempts to balance the power between the two groups, since merchants usually negotiate from a position of greater power than nonmerchants.

Citations
Why would the Uniform Commercial Code recognize a difference between merchants and nonmerchants? In part it's a recognition that merchants have more experience than nonmerchants and at times must act quickly without all the terms completed. It's also an acknowledgment that nonmerchants are generally in a weaker bargaining position than the merchant.

The following table highlights the differences between merchants and nonmerchants under the UCC.

	Representative Distinctions Between Merchants and Nonmerchants in the UCC
Risk of loss in nonshipment contracts	If seller is merchant, risk of loss transfers to buyer on actual receipt of goods from the merchant.
	If seller is nonmerchant, risk of loss occurs when seller makes the goods available to the buyer or on tender.
Acceptance	If a party to the contract is a nonmerchant, the terms of the offer govern.

continues

continued

	Representative Distinctions Between Merchants and Nonmerchants in the UCC
Acceptance (continued)	If both parties are merchants, additional acceptance terms are usually included in the contract unless they materially alter the contract, the offer is expressly limited to the original terms, or the offeror objects to the new terms within a reasonable time.
	If both parties are merchants and there are opposing terms in the acceptance and offer, some states knock out the conflicting terms and the UCC fills the gaps.
Offers	Offers made by merchants that state the offer will remain open for a set period of time cannot be revoked during that time period.
Confirmatory memo	If the agreement is between merchants, one party can draft and send a confirmatory memo in a reasonable time after the oral agreement and the terms of that memo will bind the parties.

Making an Offer

If a merchant makes a firm offer that states the offer will remain open for a set period of time, the merchant cannot revoke the contract prior to the expiration of that time. This set period cannot extend beyond three months. No consideration is required for this firm offer if it is a firm offer in writing from a merchant. Other offers operate as under common law: they remain available for a reasonable time or until accepted or revoked. If the buyer purchases the right to have the offer remain open for a set time, then it is an option contract. See Chapter 11 for more on option contracts and acceptance under the common law.

Acceptance of an Offer

Under Article 2, an offer may be accepted in several ways. The buyer can use any reasonable method such as phone call, letter, or fax. The offer can be accepted by shipping or promising to ship the goods. A party can also accept an offer by beginning performance of his or her portion of the contract and notifying the seller of that acceptance in a reasonable time.

In addition, a party can accept the offer to contract by shipping nonconforming goods. However, if the party does this, not only have they accepted the contract—they've also breached it. If the seller notifies the buyer that the goods will be nonconforming goods as an accommodation to the buyer, the shipment is a counteroffer.

The UCC abandons the mirror image rule and institutes what's called a battle of the forms. Any acceptance is acceptable under the UCC even if it has different terms than the offer. If the acceptance is conditioned on the different terms being incorporated into the offer, the acceptance is really a counteroffer.

Who wins the battle of the forms depends on if the parties are both merchants or a merchant and nonmerchant. If the contract involves a nonmerchant, the offer stands. The only way the additional terms will be incorporated is if assent is expressly given. If both parties are merchants, the *additional* terms will be included unless one of the following occurs:

- They materially alter the contract.
- The offer expressly limits acceptance to the offer's terms.
- The offeror has already objected or objects within a reasonable time to the additional terms.

Let's say the seller sends an offer, and the buyer responds using its purchase order. The purchase order contains terms that differ from the offer. In that case, if both are merchants, the different terms will normally be incorporated unless one of the three conditions listed above exists.

Now say two merchants contract but the acceptance contains *different* terms from the offer. Some courts will treat the different terms as additional terms while others will follow the knockout rule. Under the knockout rule conflicting terms in the offer and acceptance are stricken from the contract because the court assumes each party objected to the inclusion of the differing terms. The UCC fills the gap in any necessary terms.

If there are open terms yet the parties intended to enter a contract, the court can supply reasonable terms to fill the gaps. Price can be left open, and the court will fill in a price that was reasonable at the time of delivery. The contract can also leave it to one party to fix the price at a later time. That party has a duty to set the price in good faith. While price does not have to be set, quantity does unless the parties enter an output or requirements contract.

Citations

UCC Article 2 section 328 contains special rules for auctions that include the following: Lots are sold separately. A sale is complete when the hammer falls—at that point the auctioneer has accepted the bidder's offer. If an auction is "with reserve" the auctioneer can withdraw the item if the reserve is not met. The seller may not drive up the price of the item by bidding unless the buyers have received notice to that effect.

Defenses to Contract Formation

As with non-UCC contracts, there are defenses to the formation of a contract. The statute of frauds requires that all contracts for the sale of goods of $500 or more be in writing and signed by the party to the contract All other rules apply: quantity must be stated, price can be filled in, and so on. If the parties are merchants, the confirmation memo will satisfy the statute of frauds. The recipient of the memo will be bound if he or she knows the contents of the memo and does not object in writing within 10 days of receipt.

A written contract is not required if the goods are specially manufactured, and the seller has made a substantial beginning on the manufacture or made commitments for their purchase before notice or repudiation is received. If a party has made an admission in legal pleadings that the contract existed, a writing is not required. Also, if a party has performed by receiving the goods, accepting the goods, or paid for the goods, then a written contract is not required.

Citations

As with the Statute of Frauds, the parol evidence rule (see Chapter 12) applies under the UCC. Therefore, no prior agreement or contemporaneous oral agreements can be offered into evidence. Only subsequent modifications can be offered as evidence of the intent of the parties.

Under the UCC, unconscionability of a contract is determined by whether the contract or one of its terms at the time of execution could result in unfair surprise or be oppressive to the injured party. If a court finds that the contract was unconscionable at

:fuse to enforce the contract, enforce the con-
, or limit the application of the clause so it is no

; not require new consideration for a contract
odification is sought in good faith, the modifi-
equirement is that the parties put the modifica-
1uds if required. If the original contract has a
:ovision must be followed. For example, if the
ions are not allowed, the parties can't attempt
ting. However, if the parties attempt to modify
iver of the original contract if one party relied

ies, the contract may be modified by the UCC.
the contract are totally destroyed before the
avoided. If the goods are damaged, the con-
:s to accept the damaged goods at a lower price.
nsportation will not work, then the parties can
rtation.

The UCC also allows for impracticability. When the contract becomes truly impracticable, the seller is discharged from the contract. Unless it rises to the level of
impracticability, the seller must bear the added costs and continue to perform. To be
impractical, the parties must not have anticipated the potential occurrence. A shortage
of the raw materials necessary for the contract or crop failure can also discharge the
contract.

Performance of the Contract

The seller can perform the contract by tender and delivery of the goods. If a carrier
is used, the seller performs by placing the goods under the control of a carrier and
making a contract for the goods to be delivered to the buyer. Then the seller needs
to give the buyer any title or other documents he or she will need to claim the goods,
and notify the buyer that the goods have shipped. If the seller has agreed to deliver
the goods to a specific location, the seller must deposit the goods there along with any

documentation the buyer needs to obtain title. If a carrier is not used, the seller must make the goods available for the buyer for a reasonable period of time and give the buyer notice that the goods are available. Without a carrier, the place of delivery is assumed to be the seller's place of business unless the contract calls for another location.

The buyer performs by paying cash and taking delivery of the goods when a carrier is not used. If a carrier is used, the buyer pays when the goods are delivered by the carrier. The buyer has a right to inspect the goods on delivery prior to payment.

Allocation of Interest and Risk of Loss

Under the UCC several concepts were instituted to provide buyers and sellers with certainty regarding their interests in the goods and the *risk of loss* while the goods were in transit.

Identification and Insurable Interest

Identification of specific goods in the contract gives the buyer an insurable interest in the goods. It may also give the buyer the right to obtain the goods from the seller as well as sue third parties. Identification occurs at the time of the contract if specific, ascertained, and existing goods are the subject of the contract. The interest in a crop can occur at planting if the crop will be harvested within 12 months of the contract. Similarly, the interest in livestock can occur at conception if the animals will be born within 12 months of the contract. The identification can also take place when the goods are shipped, marked, or otherwise designated by the seller to pass to the buyer under the contract.

def•i•ni•tion

Risk of loss is the liability of a carrier, borrower, or user of property or goods if there is damage or loss; it determines whether the buyer or seller is financially responsible for the loss.

Identification is important because the buyer can obtain insurance on the goods once the goods have been identified. Otherwise, the buyer can't obtain insurance until the risk of loss has passed to him or her. The seller has an insurable interest as long as he or she has a security interest in or title to them.

What Happens When Goods Are Destroyed?

The risk of loss determines who will pay if the goods are lost, stolen, damaged, or destroyed. This risk always starts with the seller. The question is when it transfers to the buyer. If the seller is a merchant and the goods are not shipped by carrier, the risk of loss passes to the buyer when he or she takes possession of the goods. If the seller is a nonmerchant, the risk of loss transfers when possession is tendered. For example, if the nonmerchant tenders delivery of the goods at 3 P.M., and the goods are destroyed in a fire at 5 P.M. before the buyer picks up the goods, the buyer bears the loss. The right to possession transferred to the buyer at 3 P.M. with the tender.

If the contract is a carrier contract, the risk of loss transfers from the seller to the buyer at the time the goods are delivered to the carrier. If the contract requires the delivery to be at a particular location, then the risk of loss transfers to the buyer when the goods are delivered to that location. If the goods are to be delivered to a third party without being moved, the risk passes to the buyer when one of the following occurs: 1) the buyer receives the negotiated title to the goods, 2) the third party acknowledges the buyer's right to the goods, or 3) the third party receives a nonnegotiable document of title or other written direction to deliver the goods to him.

If the goods are defective when the buyer receives them, the risk of loss does not pass to the buyer until the defects are cured or the buyer accepts the goods despite the defects. If the buyer revokes acceptance but fails to have sufficient insurance to cover any loss, he may treat the risk of loss as having rested with the seller from the beginning. And if the buyer repudiates or breaches the contract before the risk of loss passed to him or her, any risk of loss that is not covered by the seller's insurance is charged to the buyer. However, the loss must occur within a commercially reasonable time.

While title is not a central theme under the UCC, there are rules for how title will flow in sales. The general rule is that title passes on delivery of the goods. At that point the seller has generally completed his or her duties under the contract. That means if a carrier is used, the title passes when the goods are entrusted to the carrier.

If a particular destination is identified in the contract, the title passes when the goods are delivered there. In noncarrier cases, the title passes when the document is delivered. If the goods are not to be moved, the title passes at the time of the contract.

> **Citations**
>
> Sections 509 and 510 of the UCC address risk of loss.

Breach of Contract Remedies

When a sales contract is breached there are several remedies available to buyers and sellers. A buyer's remedies are broadest prior to acceptance of goods (See Chapter 13 for remedies for breach of nongoods contracts). Thus a dispute will often arise on when acceptance actually occurred. Under the UCC, acceptance occurs when …

◆ The buyer after a reasonable opportunity to inspect the goods indicates to the seller that either the goods conform or the buyer will keep them anyway.

◆ The buyer fails to reject the goods in a reasonable period of time after tender of the goods or fails to notify the seller the goods are rejected.

◆ The buyer acts as if it does not own the goods.

Buyer's Remedies

If the contract is for the sale of goods and the seller is the breaching party, the buyer has several options available. The buyer may reject the goods if they don't conform to the terms of the contract. If delivery of the defective goods is in a single delivery, the default rule, the buyer can accept or reject all or any combination of commercial units he or she chooses. The buyer may also reject if the seller failed to contract with a carrier for delivery of the goods where the contract required delivery or the seller failed to notify the buyer that the goods had shipped. The buyer can only reject in those two instances if a material loss or delay results.

A buyer may reject an installment of goods under an installment contract if that installment does not match the contract and lowers the value of the goods.

The buyer must tell the seller of his rejection in a reasonable time after delivery or tender and before acceptance. And if there is a particular defect, the buyer must tell the seller what it is so the seller has the opportunity to cure the defect. After rejecting the goods, the buyer must hold the goods with reasonable care until the seller can remove the goods. The buyer can reship the goods to the seller, store them for the seller, or resell them for the seller if the seller fails to give the buyer instructions on what to do with the goods.

While the buyer may usually reject the goods for any reason, the seller has a right to cure if the goods are rejected because of a defect. To cure within the time for performance, the seller must give reasonable notice of intent to cure and make a new tender of conforming goods. If the seller offered goods that he or she thought conformed and then learns that the buyer rejected the goods, the seller will have a reasonable period of time—even if it extends beyond the contracted time for performance—to submit conforming goods. This will generally arise if the seller believed based on prior dealings with the buyer that the goods conformed or the defect was not obvious.

Remember that once the buyer accepts the goods, he or she is unable to reject the goods. At that point the buyer must pay for the goods minus an amount for the damages resulting from the seller's breach, if any. In rare circumstances, the buyer may revoke after acceptance. The goods must have a defect that substantially harms their value and the buyer accepts them on the reasonable belief that the defect would be cured or the buyer accepts them because the defect was difficult to discover or because the seller assured the buyer that the goods conformed to the contract. Even with those elements, the buyer must revoke acceptance in a reasonable time and before there is any substantial change to the goods.

Another limited option for the buyer who has made partial payment prior to receiving goods identified that the seller refuses to deliver is *replevin*. To pursue replevin, the seller must become insolvent within 10 days after receiving the buyer's first payment. The buyer may also seek replevin if he or she is unable to obtain adequate substitute goods from an alternative source. In fact the buyer can exercise this option before obtaining title to the goods.

The buyer can obtain specific performance if the goods are such that the remedy is available. The UCC states specific performance is available where the goods are unique or in other proper circumstances. The "proper circumstances" language gives the courts limited flexibility to apply this option.

def•i•ni•tion

Replevin refers to the court action for the repossession of personal property wrongfully taken or detained by the defendant; the plaintiff gives security for the goods and holds them until the court can decide who actually owns them.

Buyer's Damages

If the seller does not deliver the goods or the buyer rejects or revokes his or her acceptance of the tendered goods, the buyer's remedy is the difference between the contract price and either the market price or the cost of replacement goods. Market price will be measured on the day that the buyer learned of the breach and at the location the goods are tendered. If the rejection occurs after delivery, the market price will be that at the location of delivery. This contrasts with the seller's damages that are always set to the date of delivery.

If the breach is an anticipatory repudiation by the buyer, the seller's damages are linked to the actual time for performance, unless the trial somehow occurs before that time. Then damages are set to the time the seller learned of the breach. The buyer's damages in anticipatory repudiation are linked to the time she learned of the seller's breach.

Consultation _____

Let's say the buyer is forced to buy substitute goods on the open market after the seller refuses to deliver the agreed upon goods. This action is called cover. Under the UCC cover is also the term used to describe the difference between the contract price and the cost of the substituted goods. The cover must be a reasonable contract for substitute goods in good faith and without unreasonable delay.

For these cases, the buyer is entitled to incidental and consequential damages. If the accepted goods breach a seller's warranty, the buyer's damages are measured by the loss resulting in the normal course of events from the breach. To receive damages, the buyer must notify the seller in a reasonable time of the defect. Then the buyer may recover damages for the value of the goods as delivered as opposed to if they'd been delivered without a defect as well as consequential and incidental damages.

Seller's Remedies

If the contract is for the sale of goods, the seller has several options available when breach occurs. A buyer could wrongly revoke acceptance or reject the goods, fail to pay for the goods, or repudiate the contract. If that occurs the seller could withhold delivery of the goods or resell the goods in an effort to mitigate the damages. The seller could also stop delivery by the carrier. Or the seller could cancel the contract. The seller can also recover the price of the goods if the buyer accepted the goods or the risk of loss had passed to the buyer and the goods were lost or damaged. The seller can also recover the price if the goods are identified in a contract and the seller cannot resell the goods. The seller can also recover the damages listed in the prior section.

If the buyer becomes insolvent, the seller can reclaim the goods as long as he or she does so within 10 days. He or she may also reclaim them if they are with a third party at the time of the buyer's insolvency. The seller also has a limited right to force the buyer to purchase the goods if the seller has been unable to resell them at a reasonable price or the goods were lost or damaged within a reasonable time after the title to the goods passed to the buyer.

Seller's Damages

Generally the seller may recover incidental damages as well as the difference between the contract price and the amount the seller is able to sell the goods. If that is not sufficient to restore the seller to the position he should have been in, he may recover lost profits as well.

Lost profits are most useful when the seller is a volume seller. A volume seller has an unlimited supply of a good available to a limited number of buyers. In those cases, the loss of the sale is the loss of volume, and lost profits are a necessary part of the damage equation to make the seller whole.

Let's say the Acme Corporation makes gears and agrees to sell 1,000 gears for $2 each to Beta Incorporated. Beta revokes the contract, and Acme sells the same 1,000 gears for $2 each to Camna Corporation instead. Without lost profits, Acme appears to have suffered no damage. It sold the 1,000 gears for $2,000. Why should the law care that there might be more damages? Because, what Acme lost was the ability to sell 2,000 gears: 1,000 to Beta and 1,000 to Camna. To truly be made whole, Acme must be compensated for the lost profits.

The seller is always entitled to incidental damages.

Remedies Available to the Seller and the Buyer

Under the UCC, if a party fears anticipatory repudiation, he can demand assurances from the other party. This allows the party who fears the contract will not be honored but is unsure the other party will actually repudiate, to receive assurances that the contract will be honored rather than be left wondering. And if the other party admits he or she will have to repudiate, it provides more time for the nonbreaching party to mitigate the damages.

If the party demands assurances, he may suspend his own performance. And if the assurance does not arrive in a timely reasonable manner—usually 30 days—the party seeking assurances can treat the contract as if it were repudiated. The problem with this approach is that it depends on the facts of each contract, leaving a lot of discretion to the trial judge or jury to determine what is reasonable.

If it's clear from the words or actions of the other party that she will not honor the contract, the nonbreaching party may 1) await performance for a commercially reasonable time, 2) rely on any remedy for breach, or 3) suspend his own performance. Remember also that a repudiating party may retract that repudiation unless the other party has materially changed her position based on that repudiation or indicated she considers the repudiation to be final.

The parties may both have liquidated damages available for breach under the terms of the contract. The liquidated damages may not be unreasonably large or they will be void.

Regardless of the theory used, the statue of limitations for breach of a sales contract is four years under the UCC. The parties may limit the statute of limitations to a period between one and four years. However, the parties may not extend it beyond four years.

The Least You Need to Know

- Article 2 covers the sale of goods, defined as personal property and commodities.

- If a contract covers both sales and goods, the court must consider which element is predominant in determining whether to apply UCC Article 2 or common law. The general rule is that whichever dominates the contract wins.

- In general, Article 2 treats all parties the same. However, there are provisions that create a distinction between merchants and nonmerchants in applying terms to the contract.

- Unlike the common law, Article 2 does not require new consideration for a contract modification. Instead, as long as the modification is sought in good faith, the modification will bind the parties.

- The seller can perform the contract by tender and delivery of the goods. The buyer performs by paying cash and taking delivery of the goods.

- There are multiple remedies for breach of contract available under the UCC.

Supply Chain Management and Title to Personal Property

In This Chapter

- ◆ What is supply chain management?
- ◆ Challenges with title and risk of loss
- ◆ How to identify goods
- ◆ How title passes between the buyer and seller
- ◆ Special circumstances with supply chain management

Now that you understand the basics of contracts and sales, the next step is to grapple with supply chain management, title, and the risk of loss. Supply chain management addresses the flow of goods from the seller to the buyer. The allocation of interest and risk of loss concerns arise when the property covered by a contract is damaged or destroyed during transition. In those situations who bears the risk of the damaged or destroyed property? Title issues arise when someone questions who owns the property.

Supply Chain Management

Supply chain management focuses on the *bailment* of goods. Bailment, which I'll discuss in detail in Chapter 20, is the relationship that exists when personal property is delivered to another under an agreement that the same property will be delivered to another in accordance with the agreement. Often warehouses are used in the management process.

What to Expect from a Warehouse

A warehouse holds itself out to the public for the purpose of holding goods for a fee. Because a warehouse is a bailee, the rights and duties overlap between the two.

To leave items with the warehouser, the depositor (*bailor*) should get a receipt from the warehouse (*bailee*). The warehouse receipt can become the title to the goods, and should contain the following items:

- The location of the warehouse where the goods are stored
- Date of receipt
- The number of the receipt
- Negotiability of the receipt
- Charge for storage
- Description of the goods
- Statement of any liabilities

The warehouse receipt is considered a document of title. This becomes very important when there's a question about whether the goods were delivered to the right person or entity. Negotiability of that receipt is a key concept (see Chapter 23 for more on negotiability).

def•i•ni•tion

A **bailment** is the relationship that exists between owner of personal property who delivers possession of those goods to another without transferring ownership. The **bailor** is the owner who delivers personal property to another for purposes of a bailment. The **bailee** is the one who accepts possession of personal property without becoming the owner of the property.

Warehousers have a lien against the goods that they hold. The lien arises if the bill for storage isn't paid. Thus the specific lien attaches against those goods only—the warehouser can't seize other goods the seller has stored with it. The exception is if the warehouser notes on the receipt that the lien will extend to other products.

Rights of Warehouse Receipt Holders

The warehouse receipt holder has rights that flow from holding that document. Non-negotiable warehouse receipts are those that can't be transferred to someone. Only the designated person on the receipt can collect the goods. A negotiable warehouse receipt can be transferred according to the bearer or order paper rules articulated in Chapter 23.

While you'll learn the ins and outs of negotiability in Chapter 23, here's what you need to know now. Let's say Baker and Sons deposits 20 cases of widgets with Public Warehouse Company. On the warehouse receipt, Baker and Sons's agent states the cases shall be delivered to Hanson Company. If Warehouse Company delivers the cases to anyone else, it has violated the receipt because it is not negotiable. However, if the receipt has language of negotiability, if it's bearer paper, whoever brings in the receipt can collect the boxes. If it's order paper, the cases can be delivered to the person identified on the receipt or whoever that person has identified through negotiation.

Types of Warehouses

Warehouses can be traditional. Think of storage places where you can leave furniture and items that don't fit in your home or apartment. That's one type of warehouse. Another is field warehousing. This is where a plant has a place on site to store the goods, and doesn't want to pay the expense of transporting the goods to an off-site warehouse.

For example, where I live, there's a car manufacturer and truck trailer manufacturer. Both have acres of parking lots where finished product is stored. If these are field warehouses, the warehouse has exclusive control of that area. The purpose of field warehousing is to create receipts that can be used as collateral or security for loans.

Stay Out of Jail

Warehousers can limit their liability for any damage by the terms of the receipt. Consider taking a package to the local shipping store. When you drop the package off, the shipper asks whether you want extra insurance. If you opt not to purchase more, you are limited to the amount the shipper states. Warehousers can do this as long as they give you the opportunity to purchase more insurance and tell you the limits they place on the insurance.

Common Carriers

Think of *common carriers* as warehouses on wheels.

def•i•ni•tion

A **common carrier** is an individual or organization that transports goods and is available to the general public for the purpose of shipping at a cost. A **contract carrier** is an individual or organization that transports goods and is available to those that contract with it. Finally, a **private carrier** is an individual or organization that transports goods for its owner.

There are three basic types of carriers:

♦ A true common carrier is one that can be used by anyone. The best examples are United Parcel Service (UPS), Federal Express, and the United States Postal Service (USPS). Anyone can walk into one of these companies' offices and ship a package.

♦ A contract carrier is one that will transport goods only under a contract. Railroads and long-haul trucking fill this role. A moving company is another example. They make their routes based on the contracts that customers sign.

♦ A private carrier is one that is owned by the company. Next time you're running up and down the interstate, notice the Wal-Mart and McDonald's trucks—both are examples of private carriers, since they only carry products to the company's stores.

Bills of Lading and Airbills

Bills of lading and airbills are the warehouse receipts of carriers. Both have the same purpose: serving as a document of title with rights like a warehouse receipt. The bill of lading covers ground and water transportation, while the airbill covers air transportation.

The bill of lading will contain language that identifies it as negotiable or nonnegotiable. If the bill is to a specific person and without words of order, it is nonnegotiable. If the bill contains order or bearer language, it is negotiable.

Common Carrier's Duties, Rights, and Liabilities

The carrier can charge the rates it needs to make a profit. It also has a lien on the goods that are deposited with it that includes demurrage, the cost of preserving the goods, and selling them. The carrier has a duty to receive and carry the goods as long as it has space. It must provide the proper storage space for the goods and follow the directions it receives from the shipper. If requested, it has the duty to load and unload the goods. It also has the duty to deliver the goods as ordered in the shipping contract.

The common carrier's basic duty is to deliver the goods as instructed in the shipping contract. Once it accepts that duty, it has absolute liability for not completing the duty. The only way it can avoid liability is to show that the loss or damage arose because of an act of God, a public enemy, a public health authority, or the shipper, or the inherent nature of the goods—such as spoilage because the goods deteriorate. The carrier can also be liable for any loss caused by its delay in delivering the goods.

As with the other warehousers, the carrier can limit its liability by the terms of the shipping contract. The shipper must have the opportunity to purchase additional liability coverage.

Citations
Factors and hotelkeepers are bailees with special obligations. Factors, also known as consignees, hold and attempt to sell the property on behalf of the owner (consignor). Title to the property does not change while the consignee holds the property. Hotelkeepers have a bailee's responsibilities toward property specifically entrusted to their care.

Potential Problems with Title and Risk of Loss

There are several problems that can arise during a sales transaction. What if the goods are destroyed in transit? Who bears that loss? The buyer? The seller? The carrier who transported the goods?

Prior to the Uniform Commercial Code (UCC), title was critical to determining how loss would be allocated between the buyer and seller in the event of the destruction of contracted goods. With the wide passage of the UCC, the importance of title in allocation situations has been replaced in large part by the concepts of identification, insurable interest, and risk of loss.

So let's look at a few of the problems before turning to how to determine allocation issues.

Damaged Goods

Goods can be damaged as the result of one party's actions. In those situations it's clear who is responsible for making the other party whole. But what happens when neither party is to blame? What if the goods are destroyed en route when a semi-truck hits the truck transporting the goods at no negligence of the driver? Even if all parties have insurance, whose insurance must pay? In these situations, the law has to step in to provide guidance on who will bear the loss of the goods.

Insurance

A key question when the goods are damaged or destroyed is who has an insurable interest in the goods. Once the required steps have occurred to obtain an insurable interest, the buyer can obtain insurance protection. This is always a good idea, because then their insurance policy will cover any damage or destruction of the goods.

Creditor's Claims

Another problem arises when either the buyer or seller's creditor asserts a claim to the goods. Is the claim valid? Should it be honored or ignored? How should the courts determine which claim is valid if multiple creditors vie for the goods? What happens if the buyer's creditor takes the goods? Similar issues extend to the question of who should pay property tax on the goods. The claims against the goods can be unlimited, so it is important to be able to determine who owns them.

For more on determining whether someone is liable to another, see Chapter 25. The key is to determine who had the duty and then breached it. Then, you must decide whether the breach is the cause of the damages and the amount of damages.

Identifying Goods

Identification of specific goods is a key element of the allocation issue. Once the goods are specifically identified in the contract, the buyer has an insurable interest in the goods. It may also give the buyer the right to obtain the goods from the seller as well as sue third parties.

Identification occurs at the time of the contract if specific, ascertained, and existing goods are the subject of the contract. The interest in a crop can occur at planting if the crop will be harvested within 12 months of the contract. Similarly, the interest in livestock can occur at conception if the animals will be born within 12 months of the contract. The identification can also take place when goods are shipped, marked, or otherwise designated by the seller to pass to the buyer under the contract.

Consultation

Section 2-501 of the Uniform Commercial Code gives three examples of when identification occurs absent an explicit agreement. The specific examples relate to specific, ascertained, and existing goods; crops and unborn animals; and when the goods are shipped, marked, or otherwise designated by the seller.

Some sources refer to these categories of goods as existing goods that physically exist at the time of the contract; future goods that the seller does not own yet and don't actually exist yet; and fungible goods that are indistinguishable from each other like a crop.

Identification is important because the buyer can obtain insurance on the goods once the goods have been identified. Otherwise, the buyer can't obtain insurance until the risk of loss has passed to him or her. The seller has an insurable interest as long as he or she has a security interest in or title to them.

Passage of Title

Even though title is not a central issue with the UCC, it provides rules for the passage of title. It also contains exceptions: for example, title cannot pass before the goods are identified. This makes sense, because if no one knows which goods are selected in the contract, there's no title to pass.

Before we go any farther, remember that the document of title is key. It provides a simple way of knowing when title passes. When control of the document shifts, title passes between the seller and buyer. Documents of title also allow ownership to be easily transferred and creditors to take an interest in the goods. Now let's look at some specifics.

The general rule of passage of title is that title passes when the seller has completed his or her performance by physically delivering the goods. If delivery is made by carrier, delivery occurs when the seller entrusts the goods to the carrier unless the contract calls for delivery at a specific location. If a specific location is required for delivery, delivery occurs when the goods are transferred at that location.

If a carrier is not involved, the title passes when the document of title is transmitted if the goods don't have to be moved. If no document of title is required, the title passes at the time and place called for by the contract.

Goods Held by a Warehouser

The title to the goods passes when the buyer receives the documents it needs to obtain the goods from the warehouse. This may be an actual document of title, or the warehouser may require different documents. The key is that the buyer has obtained those documents.

UCC Provision

Under UCC section 2-401, the parties can agree to any manner to transmit title. They can set the provisions and requirements that they chose on the transfer. In addition, if the buyer should for some reason reject the goods, the title reverts to the seller.

There are a few circumstances that can raise questions about title. If the goods are stolen, the thief or finder of the stolen goods does not have title. If someone purchases the goods, even unknowingly, they must return them to the proper owner. If the seller in any way misleads the buyer, the seller is stopped from continuing to assert ownership. In some cases, the holder of the goods can sell them because of a lien or other permission from the seller.

Delivery and Shipment Terms

If delivery is required under the contract, the seller's obligation is usually complete when it ships the goods. If the contract contains the following terms they control the delivery and shipment of the goods:

◆ **Free on Board (FOB) place of shipment:** The seller's obligation is to deliver the goods to the carrier.

◆ **Free on Board (FOB) place of destination:** The seller's obligation is to deliver the goods to the buyer.

◆ **Free alongside ship (FAS):** The seller delivers the goods to a boat for transportation.

◆ **Cost and Freight (CF):** The seller delivers the goods to the carrier and the contract includes the cost of shipping.

◆ **Cost, Insurance, and Freight (CIF):** The seller delivers the goods to the carrier and purchases insurance to cover the goods while they are in transit.

◆ **Cash on Delivery (COD):** This is purely a payment term, requiring the buyer to pay prior to obtaining the goods.

If the contract is FOB, then the title transfers when the seller delivers the goods to the carrier. In destination contracts, the title passes to the buyer when the goods are tendered to the buyer. That can be at the buyer's location, the seller's location, or wherever the parties agree the goods are to be tendered.

Special Circumstances

There are certain situations that do not follow these rules precisely because they are considered special situations. Sometimes the parties agree that the goods are returnable as in a sale on approval or with a sale or return.

In a sale on approval the sale does not occur until the buyer actually approves the goods. Until that approval is given, the title and risk of loss remain with the seller even if the buyer has possession of the goods. The contract can set up approval to occur after a set number of days, with verbal or written communication, or by conduct. In either case, once that approval is given, the title and risk of loss transfer.

In a sale or return, the sale is completed with the buyer retaining the option to return the goods. The title and risk of loss are the buyer's unless and until he or she actually returns the goods. At that point, they revert to the seller.

If the goods are placed on consignment, the consignee has the ability to sell them and pass the title to those goods. If goods are sold at an auction, the title to each lot passes when the auctioneer announces the lot has sold to a bidder.

The Least You Need to Know

- When goods are deposited with a warehouse, a warehouse receipt is issued and can become the title to the goods.

- If warehouse receipts are negotiable, they can be transferred according to the rules for bearer or order paper.

- Carriers are individuals or organizations that transport goods and serve as a type of warehouser.

- The general rule for how title passes is that the buyer acquires title when the seller has completed his or her performance by physically delivering the goods.

Part 5

Employment and Agency Law

This part will explore employment and agency law. This is one of my favorite areas of the law because at some point in time we'll all be employees or employers. So you can't get much more practical. Add that it will be on your tests, and it's an important area to understand.

So we'll start this part by examining the agency relationship, which includes employment. Then we'll hone in on how employment relationships are created and terminated before examining some of the key federal laws that apply.

Chapter 16

Agency Law

In This Chapter

◆ A look at the agency relationship and the different types of agents

◆ Launching the agency relationship

◆ Understanding the agent's authority

◆ The agent and principal's duties

◆ Ending the agency relationship

◆ The liability of agents and principals to third parties

Whether you are aware of it, agency relationships exist all around you. From an employee who acts as an agent for his employer to your mother who acts as your agent when she picks up your dry-cleaning, agents have varying responsibilities and authority.

In this chapter we'll examine the important role agents play, what distinguishes them from employees, and key steps to protect the principal. No matter what you do in life, you will utilize agents and serve as an agent.

The Agency Relationship

First, let's look at some key definitions:

♦ *Agency* is the relationship that exists between a principal and an agent because of an express or implied agreement.

♦ An *agent* is the person or firm authorized by the principal or by law to make contracts with third parties on behalf of the principal.

♦ The *principal* is the person or firm who employs an agent.

♦ A *third party* is anyone who is not either an agent or a principal.

The following figure illustrates the basic agency relationship. As shown, the principal authorizes the agent to act on its behalf. The principal could be a business that authorizes an employee to sign a contract. The agent then signs the contract on behalf of the principal. The agent is not a party to the contract. Only the principal and third party are parties.

The agency relationship.

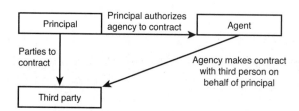

When the law is concerned about the agency relationship, it usually focuses on the relationship the principal and third party are thrust into by the agent. The agent can obligate the principal by making contracts or acting on the principal's behalf with third parties.

def•i•ni•tion

An **independent contractor** is a person or business who works for another according to the terms of a contract, but not given specific instructions and guidelines on how to complete that job.

Confusion often comes in determining whether someone is acting as an employee or an *independent contractor*. There is a simple test that usually helps determine that status. An employee is directed in his action and efforts by the employer. An independent contractor is hired to do a job, but not told how to do it. Keep in mind that in general, an employee is not authorized to obligate his employer to contracts—unless he has specific authority to do that.

For example, an employee who works for a company may be sent to a foreign country to enter into negotiations with the government there because of special language skills he has. In general, this employee has no authority to commit his employer to a contract. However, in this instance he does for the specific intent of contracting with this government. Once that purpose is accomplished, he no longer has authority to enter contracts. And he never has authority to enter alternative contracts.

In contrast, an independent contractor is bound by contract to produce a certain result. But the actual performance of how that result is achieved is left to the discretion of the independent contractor.

Let's say Marcia wants to build a house. She could hire an independent contractor to serve as the general contractor for the home. Marcia knows she needs an electrician, plumber, drywaller, and so on, but she expects the general contractor to hire the right firms at the right time to complete construction. She does not tell him how and when to do it, but hires him for his expertise.

Classes of Agents

In its simplest form an agent is one who is authorized to act on behalf of another. But, as with many things in the law, there are multiple subsets of agents. Those include ...

- ◆ **Special agents.** These agents are authorized to handle only a specific project or transaction, such as the earlier example of the employee sent to another country to negotiate one contract only.

- ◆ **General agents.** These agents have authority to transact any kinds of business that can be lawfully delegated—for example, the manager of a business for the owner. Generally, third parties can expect a manager to be authorized to do anything the owner can unless told otherwise.

- ◆ **Universal agents.** The principal has delegated to these agents everything that can be lawfully delegated. Think of someone who has been given power of attorney. That person can act on behalf of the principal to the extent allowed by law and incorporated into the power of attorney. All he or she has to do is present the document to the people or companies he or she transacts business with on behalf of the principal.

Stay Out of Jail

It's important to understand the differences between the agents since each has different levels of authority. Trouble occurs when the third party doesn't understand the limits of an agent's authority.

Creating an Agency Relationship

There are four basic ways to create an agency relationship: appointment, conduct, ratification, and operation of law. Let's take a closer look at each.

Agency by Appointment

Agency by appointment usually involves an express appointment. That means the principal expressly authorizes the agent to act in a specific manner for the principal. Most often, the principal gives the agent oral authorization. If the authority is in writing, it is called a power of attorney, and the agent is called an agent in fact.

Agency by Conduct

Agency by conduct develops when a third party is led to believe the agent has authority to act based on the actions of the principal. This form of authority is also called apparent authority. The principal can't contradict the appearance of authority it created. For there to be apparent authority, the third party must "reasonably" believe that such authority actually exists.

For example, if a principal has allowed an agent to sign contracts for services with a third party for months and has honored each of those contracts, it cannot suddenly stop honoring those contracts without advance notice to the third party.

Agency by Ratification

If an agent acts in a way that he is not authorized to, the principal can choose to ratify the agent's action and follow through on the contract. Or he can deny the contract. But once the principal takes steps to fulfill the unauthorized contract, he can't later change his mind.

In addition to an intent to ratify, these three elements must be present on the part of the principal:

- The agent must have stated he or she acted on behalf of the principal.

- The principal must have had the ability to complete the action at the time the agent entered the contract.

- The principal must know all material facts. Knowledge may be imputed by what a prudent person would be expected to know or learn.

Once a principal has ratified an authorized act, it's as if the agent had the authority to act from the beginning.

In the case of each type of agency, the third party is the person with the burden to show the agent was in fact an agent.

Agency by Operation of Law

In rare instances the law may enforce an agency relationship. This usually occurs if there is an emergency and the agent must act without first receiving approval. For example, if an employee hits a motorist with a company truck, the employee can contact 911 without permission of the employer.

The Agent's Authority

The fact that someone is an agent with authority is the first step in the analysis. The courts will look at the express words of the principal or what its words and conduct imply when determining the scope of the agent's authority:

Express authority is given orally or in writing to do a specific task.

Incidental authority is the authority to perform any reasonable act necessary to execute the express authority given to the agent. For example, if an agent is authorized to hire someone, he is also authorized to take any steps necessary to complete the employment process.

Customary authority is the authority to do anything that is customary in the community to complete the authorized act. For example, if the agent is authorized to sign a contract, then he is authorized to make arrangements for payment.

Apparent authority is the authority an agent has when the principal's act or words lead a third party to believe that the authority exists. Thus, it is critical for principals to clear up any misconceptions immediately.

When an agent acts within its authority to enter a contract, the principal is bound by that contract. If for any reason, the principal fails to honor the contract, the third party can seek to have it enforced in court.

If the agent does not have authority to act, the court will place the burden to determine the level of authority on the third party. Thus, if the agent had no authority and the third party had no reasonable belief that the agent had authority, the alleged contract will be voided. The courts will also require a third party to exercise due diligence to ensure that he or she contracted with an authorized party. Third parties must also discover the limits of the agent's authority.

Finally, if the agent is acting in a manner adverse to the principal, the third party is on notice that there are problems with the agency. The best way for a third party to determine the authority of the agent is to ask the principal. Once the principal admits there is authority, she can't change her mind.

Duties of the Agent and Principal During the Relationship

During the agency relationship, the agent and principal owe certain duties to each other. These duties provide limitations on how the agent can act while in that role.

The Agent's Duties

While the agent is acting on behalf of the principal, he has certain duties to the principal. Those include …

◆ **Loyalty.** An agent must act for the best interests of the principal. The agent also may not act for his or her secret benefit. While an agent for the principal, the agent must put the principal's interests first. For example, the agent cannot sell property he or she owns to the principal without disclosing that he or she owns the property.

An agent cannot act for both parties to a transaction unless both know of the relationships and agree. Think of a real-estate transaction. The realtor cannot represent both the buyer and seller unless both parties know and agree to the dual representation. Otherwise, a conflict of interest will be assumed.

An agent cannot accept secret commissions or gifts from third persons because of his role as agent. An agent also cannot knowingly deceive the principal or aid the principal's competitors.

◆ **Obedience and performance.** An agent has a duty to obey all lawful instructions. Lawful is the key here. If the principal asks the agent to act in a way that is against the law, the agent can refuse. Otherwise, the principal can expect the agent to obey and perform as instructed. If the agent doesn't, the agent is liable to the principal for failing to obey and perform its responsibilities.

♦ **Reasonable care.** An agent must use the care a reasonable person would use. If the agent fails to, the agent is liable to the principal for any damages. The agent must utilize any special skills he has on behalf of his principal. "Reasonable care" in this instance is similar to the standard for torts as discussed in Chapter 25.

♦ **Accounting.** An agent must account to the principal for all property or money the principal entrusts to her. Toward this end, the agent must keep the principal's money separate from her own. This is why attorneys are required to have trust accounts for client funds and not intermingle client funds with firm assets.

♦ **Information.** An agent must keep the principal informed of all facts related to the agency.

The duties and liabilities of the agent continue after the termination of the agency. At that point the agent continues to owe a duty until he has completed the tasks he was assigned during the agency.

The Principal's Duties

The principal also owes duties to the agent. Those include …

♦ **Honoring any employment contract.** If there is a contract, the agent is allowed to work for the principal for the duration of the contract terms. The only exception occurs if the contract provides an early termination procedure.

♦ **Compensation.** The agent is entitled to payment for the services rendered. This amount can either be set in a written contract or determined by the reasonable value of the services. There are two variations on compensation:

♦ Repeating transactions: Often if a third party will make repeated purchases from the principal after the agent contracts the original business, the agent will receive a stream of income from those secondary purchases.

♦ Post-agency transactions: While an agent is not entitled to payment for post-agency transactions, if the parties' employment agreement calls for such compensation, the agent will receive ongoing compensation.

Terminating the Agency Relationship

An agency relationship can be terminated in many ways. The two primary ways are by act of the parties and operation of law.

Termination by Act of the Parties

Usually, either party can terminate the agency relationship at any time. However, if there is a written contract between the agent and principal, the terms of that contract will govern how the agency can be terminated.

> **Stay Out of Jail** _____
>
> It's critical to provide notice to third parties that the agency relationship has ended. The agent can continue to bind the principal until third parties receive that notice. This rule is designed to protect principals and third parties when the third parties have worked with the agent.

Termination by Operation of Law

The agency relationship can be terminated by law if any of the following happens to either the agent or principal: death, insanity, bankruptcy, or impossibility of performance of the agency. An agent can also be released if war erupts between the countries of the agent and principal.

Liability of Agents and Principals to Third Parties

If there is an agency relationship, the question turns to who is liable to a third party if the relationship between the third party and the principal sours. The answer, as with many things in the law, is "it depends." It depends on whether the third party knows the principal and whether the principal authorized the agent's action.

Let's explore the nuances of liability.

The Agent Can be Liable to the Third Party

If the agent acts within his or her authority, the third party knows who the principal is, and the contract is ratified, the agent will not be liable for the contract. Remember, authorized agency actions can include those that were originally unauthorized, but the principal chose to ratify anyway.

However, if the agent acts outside his or her authority and that action is not ratified by the principal, the agent is liable to the third party. The third party can then proceed against the agent for any losses she has suffered. An agent who acts beyond the scope of his or her authority is always treading in dangerous waters.

An agent's liability also depends on the amount of disclosure regarding the principal:

♦ **Disclosed principal.** If the agent tells the third party who the principal is, that principal is disclosed. The agent is not liable for any contracts a third party enters with a disclosed principal.

♦ **Partially disclosed principal.** In this case, the agent tells the third party there is a principal, but does not reveal the principal's identity. In that instance the agent is the party to the contract with the third party and is liable.

♦ **Undisclosed principal.** Here the principal remains hidden from the third party. As with the partially disclosed principal, the agent is the one entering the contract with the third party and is liable. This would occur in situations where there is an economic advantage to the principal if others don't know its identity. Think a company that wants to come in and buy hundreds of acres for a new plant. It can likely get a better price if the fact a company is purchasing the land remains hidden. In that case, the real estate agent or another will act as the purchaser.

Regardless of whether the principal is disclosed, the agent can choose to assume liability on a contract. The easiest way to think of this is when the principal is from outside the area and the agent is a broker or other agent from the local area. If the third party expresses concern about being paid by the principal, and the agent says "Don't worry about it," the agent has assumed liability for payment.

If an agent commits a tort, a civil wrong that harms another, while in his agency role, that agent is still liable for his negligence. For example, if Bob is a driver for a company and is involved in a car accident, he can be sued for his negligence that led to the accident. The same holds true if the agent commits a crime. He will be responsible personally for that criminal act. (See Chapter 25 for more on torts.)

Citations
The safest way for an agent to sign a contract is to sign the principal's name and either *by* or *for* then the agent's name. Then it is clear on the face of the contract that the agent is acting as an agent and not offering a personal guarantee on the contract.

The Principal's Liability

The principal is always liable for properly executed and authorized contracts made between an agent and third party. The question comes when the agent acts *without* authorization.

If the principal is disclosed, the principal is liable on the contract. If the principal is partially disclosed, the third party can sue either the agent or the principal if the agent acted with authorization. If the principal is undisclosed but the agent is authorized, the principal is liable on the contract. Again, the third party can sue either the principal or agent. In this last case, the agent and principal share joint and several liability once the third party learns of the undisclosed principal.

If the third party has made a payment to the agent for a debt owed to the principal, that payment is deemed made to the principal. It is the responsibility of the principal to collect payment from his or her agent.

A principal is also bound by statements made by the agent to the third party on his or her behalf. It doesn't matter that the agent misspoke or had bad information. The third party can rely on the information.

A principal is deemed to know whatever information the agent has. So, for example, if an agent enters a contract to buy a retail location knowing there is mold on the premises, the principal is deemed to know that fact and cannot void the contract later based on the mold.

The Principal's Liability for the Agent's Torts and Crimes

The principal may be held liable for the torts or crimes of the agent if certain criteria are met. The innocent employer or principal is guilty of the agent's or employee's wrongdoing under *vicarious liability* or the doctrine of *respondeat superior.*

def•i•ni•tion _____

> **Vicarious liability** is imposing liability for the fault of another. **Respondeat superior** means that the principal or employer is vicariously liable for the unauthorized tort of an agent or employee while acting within the scope of the agency or employment.

The theory is that the business should pay for the harm caused by its agents or employees in the course of conducting business. The hope is the employer or principal will be more careful when it hires employees in the future and will maintain the necessary liability insurance for its protection. Generally, these theories apply when an agent was negligent, committed an intentional tort, engaged in a fraudulent act, or violated a government regulation during the course of their employment or agency.

Principal's Liability for Negligently Hiring or Retaining Employees

The principal can also be liable if a court determines it negligently hired or retained employees. This is raised when the third party believes the employer should have known the employee would be incompetent, violent, dangerous, or criminal. This is why many employers now require background checks before completing the hiring process. All the third party needs to show to prevail is that the employer knew, or would have known if he or she had exercised ordinary care, that the applicant would create a risk of harm to others in the job. The employer must have also been able to foresee the injury to the third party.

For example, if the employer learns through a background check the potential employee has a violent drinking problem, it may be reasonably foreseeable that the employee would assault a customer at some point in the future. Conducting checks on the potential hire's work experience, background, character, and qualifications can provide protection to the employer. The fact that the potential employee has a criminal background is not sufficient on its own to create the tort of negligent hiring.

Negligent retention is similar to negligent hiring. For negligent retention, the third party must show the principal continued to employ the agent once it knew of the problems with that agent.

Negligent supervision and training alleges that the principal did not properly train or oversee the agent/employee.

Usually, a principal is only liable for the crimes of the agent that occur at its direction. If the principal is an owner who has employed an independent contractor, the principal is generally not liable for contracts signed by the independent contractor, torts of the employees of the independent contractor, or damage caused by the independent contractor. An exception occurs when the work the independent contractor engages in is inherently dangerous or the independent contractor is not disclosed. For example, if James hires an independent contractor to demolish with dynamite a building he owns, James will be liable for any damage. If the independent contractor is undisclosed, James is liable for the torts and contracts.

The Least You Need to Know

- An agency relationship exists between a principal and an agent because of an express or implied agreement that the agent do something on behalf of the principal.

- An agent is always liable for his acts of negligence; however, the third party can sue the principal as well.

- The amount of liability the agent carries for contracts depends in part on whether the principal is disclosed.

- A prudent principal will give notice to third parties when an agency relationship terminates to avoid ongoing liability for the acts of the agent.

Chapter 17

Employment Relationships and Laws

In This Chapter

◆ Does an employment relationship exist?

◆ Duties and rights of employees

◆ State laws that apply to employment relationships

◆ Federal laws that apply to employment relationships

◆ Employees' right to privacy

Employment law is a key cornerstone of business law, because most businesses employ people. This area also touches most people's lives because most people work. Employment law is a complex area that strives to balance the needs of the employers and employees.

In this chapter we'll examine several items starting with how to determine when there's an employment relationship. Then we'll look at the basic state and federal laws that govern employment relationships. Finally, we'll take a look at what privacy rights, if any, employees have.

Defining the Employment Relationship

When determining whether an employment relationship exists, the first question you have to consider is whether someone is an employee or an independent contractor. In general, an employee is one who works or provides a service for another at that employer's direction. There may be a written contract between the employee and employer, or their agreement may be implied through conduct or words.

The key distinction between an employee and an independent contractor is who controls the actions. An employer tells an employee what to do, how to do it, and when to do it. The employer exercises control over the employee's actions while on the clock.

On the other hand, as discussed in Chapter 16, an independent contractor retains control over how it completes a job. For example, if James wants to have a home built, he will usually hire a general contractor to complete the job. James will give the general contractor a set of plans to follow, tell it which plot of land to build the home on, and give it a timeline for completion of the project. Other than that, the general contractor controls how the home will be built. Usually, it can determine which subcontractors it wants to hire to do the dry-walling, plumbing, electrical work, etc. It also determines when each stage of the construction will be completed and how. The general contractor is thus an independent contractor.

James could choose to fill the role of general contractor. Then depending on how he structures the agreements with the subcontractors, they could be deemed to be his employees, hired specifically to complete a job and given detailed instructions on how and when to do their jobs. Or James could treat them as independent contractors by giving them the plans, telling them when to show up, but allowing them to complete their portion of the job without his supervision.

Creating an Employment Contract

An employment contract requires both parties to consent to the agreement. It can arise by an express agreement between the parties. This agreement can be verbal or written. Occasionally, the employment relationship grows out of the employer accepting the acts of the "employee" after the fact. In a sense the employer has ratified the efforts of another, which makes that other party an employee.

Regardless of how the contract arose, the parties must agree to terms. Usually any terms will work as long as those terms don't violate the law. A unique form of contract is collective bargaining, in which the employer negotiates with employee representatives on terms such as wages, hours, and benefits. The collective bargain will also outline a grievance procedure for use if the contract breaks down.

Terms of the Employment Contract

All states follow the employment-at-will doctrine. That doctrine basically allows either the employer or employee to walk away from the employment relationship whenever either party chooses without a reason. There are three basic exceptions to this rule:

- ◆ **Violation of Public Policy.** Some examples include hiring a child under the age of 16 to work more hours than allowed by law, hiring someone to work for less than minimum wage, or firing someone in retaliation for that employee filing a workers' compensation claim.

- ◆ **Breach of Implied Contract.** This arises whenever an employee is told one thing about his or her potential employment, but then given something different after he or she starts. For example, Monica is promised $50,000 a year as a salary, but finds out after she's started the job that she will only be paid $35,000.

> **Consultation**
>
> Congress passed the National Labor Relations Act (NLRA) in 1935 to govern collective bargaining and provide some protections to employers and the employees. Read more about it later in this chapter.

- ◆ **Breach of Covenant of Good Faith and Fair Dealing.** This requires each party to deal with the other in a way that does not deny the other party of the benefit of their agreement. Simply put, it's the expectation that parties will deal fairly with each other. Some states interpret this to mean that an employee cannot be fired without just cause, or without a good reason.

> **Citations**
>
> Employee handbooks are often construed as part of the employment contract. If an employee handbook establishes a pretermination procedure, employers must follow that policy. If a written handbook exists, employers need to follow those policies. Otherwise, the employer is better off having no handbook at all, because the courts will enforce the policy included in the handbook that the employers have ignored.

An employer has just cause to fire an employee if the employee fails to perform assigned duties, commits fraud to obtain employment, disobeys instructions, is disloyal, commits theft or other acts of dishonesty, possesses or uses drugs or alcohol on the job, or is incompetent.

An Employee's Duties and Rights

An employee has several duties that he or she is expected to meet while working for an employer. In exchange, he or she can expect fair compensation from the employer.

First, an employee should provide the contracted services for the employer. The employer can expect the employee to complete the requirements of the job.

Second, an employer can expect the employee to protect its trade secrets. Sophisticated employers will require employees to sign covenants regarding trade secrets, but even if the employees didn't, there is usually a state law to provide protection. Trade secrets can include client lists, policies, procedures (think design and manufacturing), and similar items essential to the ongoing success of a business. To receive trade secret protection, a company needs to take steps to protect those secrets. Thus, a client list should be password protected if stored on a computer or kept in a locked file cabinet with limited access.

Finally, inventions created while working for the employer are the employer's property. This is because the inventions are created with employer resources on the employer's dime. If an employee creates an invention off the clock and without employer resources, that invention is the employee's. The employer and employee can also reach an agreement that would allow the employee to have an ownership interest in any inventions created on the clock, but that should be in writing.

The employee has the right to compensation for his labor and that the wage complies with the regulations of the Fair Labor Standards Act.

State Laws Applied to Employment

States regulate many areas of employment law from the type of contract between the employer and employee as just discussed to workers' compensation and hours and wages laws.

When it comes to hours and wages, the state provides regulations that supplement those of the federal government. Where the Fair Labor Standards Act does not apply, the state may step in and provide additional regulations. States have departments of labor that administer those regulations.

Covenants Not to Compete

One area where state law applies is covenants not to compete, an agreement between the employer and employee that the employee may not directly compete against the employer for a set time in a set geographic area. These covenants must be in writing and contain restrictions on an employee's future work when the employee leaves the current employer. When examining a covenant not to compete, the courts generally look at three items:

 ♦ The geographic scope of the restriction

 ♦ The time the covenant will be enforced

 ♦ The activities that are limited

In general, a covenant not to compete is against public policy, because it restricts the future employment options of the employee. That is why courts closely examine them to determine whether the covenant is narrowly constructed. Each state will have its own set of specific guidelines based on case law. In general, though, the geographic scope should be related to the actual area the employee worked. Think a sales region. The covenant should cover that actual area and not more. The time of the restriction should usually be limited to less than three years. The activities that are limited should relate to the actual job the person did and not foreclose them from working in the general field.

Workers' Compensation

Workers' compensation was designed to protect workers who are injured on the job. Each state has its own law, and that law provides a detailed scheme for providing benefits to injured or killed employees and their families. The benefits usually include partial payment for time off work, payment of medical expenses, and a specific payout for permanent injuries or death. Disputes often arise regarding how injured an employee is and whether that injury is permanent or temporary.

Federal Laws Applied to Employment

There are a host of federal laws that impact employment relationships. I'll review those that relate to employment discrimination in the next chapter. Here the focus is on the National Labor Relations Act, ERISA, unemployment benefits, family leave, and social security. These laws are complex, often with hundreds of pages of regulations each, so keep in mind this is an overview of the laws and not comprehensive.

The National Labor Relations Act

The National Labor Relations Act (NLRA) was enacted in 1935 to "protect the rights of employees and employers, to encourage collective bargaining, and to curtail certain private sector labor and management practices, which can harm the general welfare of workers, businesses and the U.S. economy." The law was a reaction to the violent strikes and union elections that rocked the United States in the early twentieth century. The National Labor Relations Board (NLRB) and its General Counsel enforce the law and oversee disputes growing out of the effort to unionize, union elections, and strikes.

Citations
Twenty-two states have enacted Right-to-Work Laws, which state that workers cannot be required to join a union as a condition of employment.

The Act applies to employers with gross incomes of $500,000 or greater. The General Counsel investigates unfair labor practices and then prosecutes those in front of the NLRB. The NLRB also oversees union elections through 32 regional offices. The NLRB has generated preelection rules that govern the actions of employers, employees, and unions, like prohibiting the making of speeches to captive audiences, like employees over a public address system, the 24 hours prior to an election.

The NLRA balances the rights of employees and employers. While employees have the right to unionize, employers have the right to maintain discipline. As a result, employers can generally prohibit unionization activities while employees are on the clock. However, during breaks and other nonworking times, employees can actively engage in unionization unless there exist legitimate safety and efficiency concerns. An employer can also prohibit the distribution of union materials on its property if there are other viable means for the union to distribute the material to the employees.

One thing an employer cannot do is fire an employee for being active in a union or the effort to unionize employees. An employee can even be a *salt*—a worker that the union plants at the employer for the purpose of encouraging unionization—as long as he is working. The exception to this rule is if the salt lied during the interview about qualifications that are a requirement of the job. The employer is required to bargain collectively once the employees have voted for unionization.

Union employees have the right to participate in picketing and strikes, with limitations. If employees strike to highlight economic actions of the employer, the employer is not required to rehire the striking employees. However, if the employees strike because of unfair labor practices of the employer, the employer must give the strikers their jobs back at the end of the strike.

Consultation

With picketing and strikes, it helps to remember why Congress passed the NLRA in response to the violent strikes and picketing of the early twentieth century. Legal strikes and pickets tend to be those that highlight a labor dispute at the site, but don't involve large groups of union members.

There are three types of picketing:

- *Primary picketing*, the only type that's legal, occurs when employers picket a business to alert the public to a labor dispute.

- *Mass picketing* is illegal and occurs when employees mass in great numbers to shut down the employer. Think a mob blocking the gate to the employer prohibiting replacement workers and deliveries from entering a plant.

- *Secondary picketing* is also illegal and occurs when union members picket a retailer like a grocery store for carrying a product made by the company with the labor issues.

ERISA

Congress passed the Employment Retirement Income Security Act (ERISA) in 1974 to protect employee pension plans. Essentially, ERISA requires pension fund administrators to follow fiduciary standards and requirements for administration, vesting of funds, funding of the plans, and termination insurance. The law prohibits an employer from using the funds in a pension plan as its own, even if it contributed 100 percent of the money in the account. Once the money is contributed to the plan, it belongs to the employee. In addition, ERISA requires that the employee's right to the money must vest within five to seven years, and the employee may earn a right to a percentage of that money prior to fully vesting. The Secretary of Labor enforces ERISA.

Unemployment Benefits

Many employees rely on unemployment benefits to fill the gaps when they are between jobs at no fault of their own. The current system is a combination of federal and state laws. If an employee quits or is fired for some type of misconduct, that employee is usually ineligible for benefits. To be eligible, an unemployed individual must be available for placement in a similar job and willing to accept a job at a comparable rate of pay. Unemployment is funded through a complex system that employers pay into based on the employee's work rating.

Family and Medical Leave Act

Congress passed the Family and Medical Leave Act (FMLA) in 1993. This law is designed to give employees up to 12 weeks of unpaid leave during any 12-month time period:

♦ In the event of the birth or adoption of the employee's son or daughter

♦ To care for the employee's spouse, son, daughter, or parent in the event of a serious illness or health condition

♦ Because of the employee's serious health condition that affects the employee's ability to do their job

The employer must have 50 employees within a 75-mile area for employees to have access to FMLA's benefits. Employees must have worked for the employer for at least 12 months and worked at least 1,250 hours during that 12-month period to qualify.

The employer must notify the employee that the leave will be FMLA leave, and the employer can require an employee to use vacation and personal time first. Once an employee returns from FMLA leave, the employee is entitled to be restored to the same or equivalent position at the same rate of pay he or she had before.

For example, Donald and his wife are adopting a child from Korea. Donald has worked for his employer for more than a year and accrued sufficient hours to qualify for FLMA leave. As a result, Donald takes FMLA leave for the time he and his wife will be in Korea to receive their daughter and for three weeks after the family returns home. When he returns to work, he should step back into his position, or if his employer had to find someone to do his job, into a similar position.

Social Security

The Social Security system was created by President Franklin Roosevelt and Congress in 1935 as a reaction to the Great Depression and the deep needs it imposed on the elderly. In addition to providing a pension to the elderly, social security provides disability benefits, life insurance benefits, and health insurance. The program is funded by the payment of social security taxes by employees and employers.

Citations
After the 1929 stock market crash, unemployment soared to more than 25 percent and wages paid to workers declined from $50 billion in 1929 to only $30 billion in 1932.

Employees' Health and Safety

The primary federal vehicle that provides for employees' safety on the job is the Occupational Health and Safety Act (OSHA). OSHA provides guidelines for safe work environments and penalties for failing to follow the guidelines. The goal of OSHA and its accompanying regulations is to provide an incentive for employers to provide a safe work environment for their employees and to provide incentives through penalties for failure to do so.

Employee Privacy

Employee privacy is an emerging area of employment law. What rights, if any, do employees have to expect privacy in the workplace? Privacy rights for federal employees grow out of the Fourth Amendment's prohibition against unreasonable search and seizure. When government employees are involved, the government must have a reasonable and genuine reason for conducting the search.

Not all states recognize a common law right to privacy for employees. Those that do recognize some combination of four rights. The first is the right to be left alone in the employee's workspace. Second, there may be a right that prohibits disclosure of the employee's private affairs or medical information. Third, some states recognize a prohibition against defaming an employee. And fourth, some states prevent the misappropriation of an employee's name or likeness.

Tension occurs when employees believe they should have a right to privacy, yet the employer believes it has a valid reason for monitoring the employee. These disputes normally arise in areas of telephone or e-mail monitoring, computer use, locker searches, or drug and alcohol testing. A wise employer will carve out the areas it claims to have a right to search or monitor in the employee handbook. Then, an employee is on notice that the search could occur at any time.

Telephone Call Monitoring

While the Federal Wiretapping Act penalizes the intercepting of oral and electronic communications, it contains an exception for employers monitoring the company's telephones in the ordinary course of business. An employee can also consent to the interception. That consent can occur when the employer gives the employee notice that calls may be monitored. Business calls can be monitored. However, once the employer recognizes that the call is personal, it must immediately stop monitoring.

E-Mail Monitoring

Because so much business is conducted by e-mail in today's business environment, employers may want to monitor their employees' e-mail. The Electronic Communications Privacy Act of 1986 was designed to apply in part to e-mail. However the exceptions just discussed (monitoring e-mails in the ordinary course of business and giving prior notice to employees of a company policy) also apply here. With both telephone and e-mail monitoring an employer is wise to publish its policies regarding monitoring in an employee handbook or by giving the policies in writing to employees.

Stay Out of Jail

Employers should adopt an employee handbook that spells out the policies related to employees' privacy rights as well as other policies that govern the employer-employee relationship. However, if an employer adopts a policy, it must follow that policy or the policy can be used against the employer in a lawsuit.

Property Searches

Public employees receive limited protection from unreasonable search and seizure under the Fourth Amendment to the United States Constitution. Even then, if the government has a valid reason for conducting the search, the search may withstand court scrutiny. Private employees have almost no protection from search and seizure. An exception occurs when the employer provides the locker and tells the employee he can lock the locker. However, if the employer provides a locker key, but keeps the master key, there is no expectation of privacy. Similarly, if the employer has a published policy allowing for search and seizure, the employee has no expectation of privacy.

Drug and Alcohol Testing

Public employees may be protected by the Fourth and Fifth Amendments, however, the government can require testing if there is a reasonable suspicion of abuse. In general, random testing is not allowed of government employees unless they are involved in public transportation or other safety-related areas. In the private sector, random testing is allowed for safety reasons if the employees work in a field that is safety-sensitive. Employers may also test if there is a reasonable suspicion of abuse.

The Least You Need to Know

- ◆ Unless there is a written employment contract, the employee is an at-will employee, and either side can walk away from the employment relationship at any time without a reason.

- ◆ The employer controls the actions of an employee, unlike an independent contractor who can do the job as he or she chooses.

- ◆ Both state and federal governments regulate the employment relationship and provide benefits to employees.

- ◆ An employee's right to privacy is limited by the employer's need to monitor business and provide a safe working environment.

Equal Employment Opportunity Law

In This Chapter

- ◆ Comparing state and federal laws
- ◆ Understanding Title VII
- ◆ Sexual harassment
- ◆ Affirmative action and reverse discrimination
- ◆ Disability law
- ◆ Age discrimination

While people have served as employees since the dawn of time, it's only since the 1960s that federal laws have existed to prohibit discrimination in employment. These laws were an outgrowth of the Civil Rights movement and Title VII of the Civil Rights Act of 1964. Since 1964, Congress has passed several additional laws to define discrimination and penalties for that discrimination.

This chapter will examine the role of the state and federal governments in regulating employment discrimination and then examine the key federal laws and their application.

State Versus Federal Antidiscrimination Laws

Since 1964, the federal government has taken the lead in adopting antidiscrimination legislation. This doesn't mean that the states play no role though. Instead, the states often fill the gaps left by federal law. For example, the Americans with Disabilities Act applies to private employers with 15 or more employees. State law might step in to require firms with fewer employees to follow the same guidelines.

State law can usually be more restrictive than the federal law—in a sense applying it to more businesses—but it cannot prohibit the law from applying where the federal law says it does. For example, if the Americans with Disabilities Act applies to private firms of 15 or more employees, a state cannot raise that threshold to firms of only 25 or more employees.

Consultation

Looking for a comparison of state laws? Look no farther than Workplace Fairness, which maintains a page on its website that links to the agencies in each state that oversee anti-discrimination laws. Go to www.workplacefairness.org/stateagencies.

Often the federal government will create legislation in an area the states have ignored or it will standardize varying state laws. For example, California may have taken the lead in antidiscrimination laws, while New York's law applies different standards or rules. As a result, Congress may pass a law that applies the same baseline rules to each state. If a state has stricter laws, those will still apply. But if a different state has more lenient laws, the federal law will not supersede.

Title VII

Title VII of the Civil Rights Act of 1964 is the granddaddy of federal antidiscrimination laws. It is also the broadest. Its goal is to end discrimination on the basis of race, color, religion, sex, or national origin in the employment setting. It applies from the hiring process through termination.

Disparate Impact and Disparate Treatment

To apply its antidiscrimination principles, two theories have developed:

- *Disparate impact* exists when an employer has a facially neutral policy, but the application of that policy results in discrimination against an employee or a class of employees. (A "facially neutral" policy appears neutral by its terms [on its face] but in application the policy discriminates.) To succeed, the discriminated person has to show there is no job related or valid business reason for the requirement or restriction.

◆ *Disparate treatment* arises when an employer treats a class of people differently because of their race, color, religion, sex, or national origin. All the discriminated person has to prove is intent to discriminate.

Okay. Those sound great in theory, but how do these principles apply?

If a company has a policy that states only people five-feet seven-inches or shorter can apply for a position, someone who is denied a position because he is taller could sue under the disparate impact theory. The employer could argue that the policy is required because the assembly line is tight at that point and only small people can fit safely into the space. However, the potential employee could counter that the policy has a disparate impact because it restricts most men from the position for no other reason than that they're men—even if the policy doesn't state no men need apply.

In contrast, if a supervisor in a company says, "this is man's work," and does not hire or consider women, that is disparate treatment. Only men are hired for no other reason than they are men. It has a direct and negative impact on women. The same could be said if an employer requires employees to work on Saturdays or Sundays, and that interferes with employees' religious practices. The employer would not hire a class of potential employees for no other reason than their religion. Both examples result in disparate treatment.

Role of the Equal Employment Opportunity Commission

Because the Equal Employment Opportunity Commission (EEOC) oversees many of the federal laws related to discrimination, an employee or other person who believes he or she was discriminated against must follow the proper procedures in front of that agency. If the state has an agency that oversees antidiscrimination laws, a claim may need to be filed there first. That will depend on the state the alleged action occurred in and its laws. If the claimant must file in front of the state agency first, she must either wait 60 days to file with the EEOC or wait until the termination of the state proceedings to file, whichever occurs first.

Consultation _____

The Equal Employment Opportunity Commission exists to enforce many of the federal equal employment opportunity laws including Title VII, the Americans with Disabilities Act, the Equal Pay Act, and the Age Discrimination in Employment Act. Its website (www.eeoc.gov) is filled with useful information on these laws and their enforcement.

If there is no state agency overseeing the law, a claim must be filed with the EEOC within 180 days of the discriminatory act. At that point, the EEOC will launch an investigation. At the end of its investigation, the EEOC will do one of three things:

♦ Take the case itself and litigate it on behalf of the employee or class affected by the employer's actions or policy.

♦ Issue a right to sue letter, which gives the individual or class the right to proceed on their own if they file in federal district court within 90 days of the date of that letter.

♦ Tell the person or class that there is no violation, and at that point the claim dies.

Protected Classes Under Title VII

Title VII protects several specific classes of individuals from employment discrimination. Those classes are race, color, religion, sex, and national origin. The reason is that an individual cannot control these elements—even religion, because if it is truly a strongly held belief, it has become part of that person's fabric. If the alleged discriminatory practice does not affect one of these classes, then there is no discrimination under Title VII.

Here are the specifics:

♦ **Race and color.** In Title VII the word "race" applies to four groups: white, black, Native American, and Asian Pacific. An employer also may not discriminate against an employee on the basis of their skin color. Race, color, and national origin often overlap in application.

♦ **Religion.** The EEOC has broadly defined religion "to include moral or ethical beliefs as to what is right and wrong which are sincerely held with the strength of traditional religious views." In application, an employer merely has to offer a reasonable accommodation. Most disputes arise regarding whether a reasonable accommodation has been offered. If the employee refuses to accept it, there is no discrimination. For example, if an employee cannot work on Saturday because of religious beliefs, the employer can ask for volunteers to work that shift. That satisfies its obligation to offer a reasonable accommodation.

♦ **Sex.** As used in Title VII, sex relates only to a person's gender. Problems usually arise with employer's policies that place height, weight, and physical ability requirements on a position. If such a restriction is in place, a valid business reason must exist for that policy. A candidate for those positions must be given the opportunity to demonstrate he or she can satisfy that requirement.

Title VII has also been amended by the Pregnancy Discrimination Act to prohibit employers from treating pregnant employees differently because of their medical condition as opposed to other employees with different medical conditions. An employer is not required to provide additional benefits to a pregnant employee, but the same benefits available to other employees.

Sexual harassment is an extension of Title VII, and will be addressed in the next section.

◆ **National origin.** This provision protects people regardless of their nationality from discrimination. Thus, someone cannot refuse to hire people or take other adverse employment actions against them, solely because of their country of origin.

Sexual Harassment Under Title VII

When sexual harassment is alleged, the EEOC and courts look at two categories: tangible employment action and hostile work environment. If the alleged discrimination does not fall into one of these categories, then no matter how uncomfortable, it does not amount to sexual harassment.

Tangible Employment Action

In a tangible employment action, a supervisor must seek a *quid pro quo* from an employee. Essentially, the supervisor tells the employee, "You can keep your job if you agree to an affair with me. If you don't, you will be demoted/reassigned/etc. in a way that is negative to you." The employer is always vicariously liable for the acts of the supervisor—even if it knew nothing about them. The fact an employer has an antiharassment policy does not end the employer's liability. Instead, it will be liable because the supervisor only has the power to threaten because of the position the employer gave the supervisor.

def•i•ni•tion

Quid pro quo is a Latin term meaning something for something. It's usually used to refer to the fact that one party gives something to the other party, expecting something in return.

Hostile Work Environment

In a hostile work environment a supervisor does not threaten direct employment action against the employee. Instead, the supervisor's action (or lack of action) poisons the work environment and allows it to become hostile to an employee. This could include allowing pornography to be in employee lounges, making lewd jokes, and anything else that could create a sexually charged environment that is uncomfortable for an employee. Because the actions are not as direct, this is more difficult to prove because it is so fact-specific. The employee must prove the supervisor acted with severe and pervasive conduct. The employer can defend itself if it has a strong anti-harassment policy in place that the employee failed to utilize, and if the employer acted in a reasonable manner and promptly to remedy the situation.

Employers are only responsible for the sexual harassment caused by employees rather than supervisors if it knew or should have known about the action and failed to remedy the situation. This lines up with Title VII's purpose of preventing harm. If an employer has put in place a mechanism to prevent harm and quickly remedy that harm if it occurs, the employer has done what Title VII requires.

Retaliation

Under Title VII employees are protected from retaliation for raising a Title VII claim. An employee should be able to challenge the potentially discriminatory acts of the employer without fear of additional repercussions. The EEOC has extended the same theory to the other laws it enforces.

Exceptions to Title VII

Employers can raise defenses to Title VII claims. The three key defenses are the bona fide occupational qualification exception, testing and educational requirement exception, and the seniority system exception.

For an employer to satisfy the bona fide occupational qualification (BFOQ) exception it must show that the alleged discrimination is actually the result of a BFOQ necessary for its business to operate. A BFOQ is never a valid reason to discriminate on the basis of race or color. An example of a BFOQ is when an employer requires that resident assistants in an all-male dorm be men. However, the Supreme Court found that it was not a BFOQ for an employer to restrict a woman from a job that was hazardous to her baby if she was pregnant. Because the policy could only apply to women, the court said that women should be given the right to choose whether to take the position.

The testing and educational requirement exception can apply when the alleged discriminatory policy is actually the result of a job requirement. For example, a county can require its firefighters to pass tests that are tied to valid educational requirements. These tests should be backed by valid studies.

Finally, an employer may use a bona fide seniority system that contains no intention to discriminate. A seniority system is generally a set of rules that gives preference to employees who have served longer in the company. These systems are often parts of collective bargaining agreements since those agreements provide enhanced job security to employees with long periods of service.

Affirmative Action Policies and Reverse Discrimination

An employer might institute an affirmative action plan to ensure it has a diverse workforce. These plans traditionally lead to targeted efforts to attract employees from underrepresented minorities. When Congress passed the Civil Rights Act of 1964, one of its main purposes was to eliminate discrimination in the workplace. Many employers implemented affirmative action plans, either voluntarily or under court order, as a way to remedy the racial discrimination of the past.

The Supreme Court has defined racial discrimination as preferring members of a group for no other reason than race or ethnic origin. While recent landmark cases have dealt with university admission policies, similar principles apply to employment. As the Supreme Court has examined affirmative action plans at universities, it has emphasized that valid affirmative action plans must have an end point as well as consider more than race in giving a preference to individuals. An employer can't fix past discrimination by now discriminating against another racial group.

Without that fixed end point, the affirmative action policy risks instituting reverse discrimination in which someone is discriminated against because she is not a minority.

> ## Citations
>
> The United States Supreme Court determined that universities could not set aside a specific number of admissions slots for individuals of certain ethnic backgrounds in its landmark case of *Regents of the University of California v. Bakke*. Instead, the court suggested that achieving diversity should encompass "a far broader array of qualifications and characteristics."

Permissible affirmative action plans must meet five criteria:

- The plan must be part of an overall employment plan.

- The plan must be justified as a remedial measure.

- The plan must be voluntary.

- The plan must not trample the interests of whites (or other majority, like men).

- The plan must be temporary.

If the plan meets those criteria, a court will likely uphold it. When a nonminority group is unnecessarily trammeled, then the plan has instituted reverse discrimination.

Americans with Disabilities Act

In 1990 President George Bush signed the Americans with Disabilities Act (ADA). Many hoped it would be groundbreaking legislation that continued the civil rights work of Title VII and the Rehabilitation Act by extending protections to the disabled. Almost 20 years later, the application of the law has not lived up to expectations.

While the Americans with Disabilities Act applies to state and local governments, public accommodations, telecommunications, and transportation, I'll focus on employment law here. Unlike the earlier Rehabilitation Act that only applied to the federal government, the ADA applies to all private employers with more than 15 employees. It also applies to all state and local governments regardless of the number of employees.

The ADA provides protections to qualified disabled individuals as they apply for, work in, and are terminated from positions. To have a disability under the ADA, the person must have a physical or mental impairment, which significantly impacts or limits a major life activity, have a record of that impairment, or be regarded as having that impairment. Major life activities include walking, seeing, hearing, thinking, concentrating, and even breathing.

Consultation

In the employment context, the key to applying the ADA is whether the disabled person is unable to perform the job's function with or without reasonable accommodation.

For the disability to substantially limit a major life activity, it must, when compared to others, significantly restrict or prohibit a major life activity. Courts and the EEOC will look at each case on an individual basis. Thus, the law provides guidance, but whether a person has a disability will depend on the facts of their case.

Employers who are covered by the ADA must make reasonable accommodations for qualified individuals unless those accommodations would create a hardship for the employer. Whether an accommodation is used, the disabled employee must be able to perform the essential functions of the job. If they can't, the ADA does not apply. As with so many aspects of law, the application is very case specific. The result of years of court decisions is a law with narrowly defined application.

The regulations limit the questions an employer can ask a potential employee about any disabilities that person has. An employer may not ask if the individual is disabled in any way. However, the employer may ask whether the potential employee has the ability to complete required tasks of the job, such as lifting 50 pounds. The employer may also make a job offer contingent on the potential employee passing a medical exam, but that position must pose a direct threat to the worker's health or safety.

Employers have a duty to provide reasonable accommodations to the disabled unless it creates an undue hardship. An undue hardship is defined under the ADA as significant difficulty or expense and looks at the circumstances and resources of the employer in relation to the cost or difficulty of the proposed accommodation. As with defining a disability, what constitutes a reasonable accommodation is determined on a case-by-case basis. A reasonable accommodation can include making existing locations accessible to and usable by the disabled, restructuring jobs, providing modified work schedules, and modifying equipment or devices. In this context, reasonable means the accommodation is plausible or feasible.

The employee generally must request the accommodation. Then, the employer has a duty to provide it if the requested accommodation is reasonable. For example, if an employee with lupus requests a stool at her cash register station so that she can endure through her entire shift, that is a reasonable accommodation. In contrast, an employer is not required to eliminate an essential job function or lower production goals if that standard is applied equally to all employees. If either is needed, the disabled person is not qualified. There is a recognition in the ADA that what is reasonable for a large Fortune 500 company is not reasonable for a small company.

> **Stay Out of Jail**
>
> Impairments caused by current illegal drug use are not covered by the ADA. However, if the drug use was in the past, even if the impairment was caused by that use, the disability may be covered.

Age Discrimination in Employment Act

The Age Discrimination in Employment Act (ADEA) applies to private employers with 20 or more employees and federal, state, and local governments. The ADEA protects most workers between the ages of 40 and 70 from discrimination in the employment process. Specifically, it prohibits employers from discriminating against people who fall within that age parameter during employment. This covers hiring, firing, pay, promotions, fringe benefits, and other aspects of employment.

For example, if an employer fires an employee who is 55, that employee may sue for age discrimination if his position is filled by someone who is 35. The employee will still have to prove that age is the motivation—the employer fired him because it was cheaper to replace him with someone younger. The employer can raise many defenses like the employee violating employer policies, but an ADEA claim can be raised.

The Least You Need to Know

♦ Title VII provides employment protection against discrimination for five classes: race, color, religion, sex, and national origin.

♦ Title VII prevents employment policies that result in disparate treatment and disparate impacts against a protected class of individuals.

♦ Sexual harassment can occur through tangible employment action or the creation of a hostile work environment.

♦ The Americans with Disabilities Act prohibits discrimination against people with qualified disabilities when a reasonable accommodation can be made by the employer without inflicting an undue hardship on it.

♦ The Age Discrimination in Employment Act provides protection to individuals between the ages of 40 and 70 against discrimination in employment.

Part 6

Property Law Basics

Own a house? Rent an apartment? Then you own or lease real property. Own a car? Lease a truck? Bought a high-definition television this week? Then you've bought or leased personal property.

This part will examine the law as it applies to real and personal property. It may be near the end of this book, but the concepts are foundational to the law.

Chapter 19

Understanding Real Property Law Basics

In This Chapter

- ◆ What is real property?
- ◆ Real property ownership
- ◆ Liability to third parties
- ◆ Transferring real property by deed
- ◆ Understanding landlord-tenant law

Real property consists of the land and structures on that land. Then there are the integrated equipment and anything grown on the land. Oh, and don't forget the mineral rights and possibly air rights. That about covers it. Real property is a complex system of law that controls the ownership and transfer of ownership of land, structures, etc. This layered complexity has caused some to call property rights a bundle of rights.

This chapter will explore those complexities and break them down into understandable chunks.

Types of Real Property

Real property is literally a multilayered concept. It would be easy to think of it as simply the land itself. Soil and rock. However, it's much more complicated. So let's dive in.

Land

When I say *land*, you probably think the soil. That's merely the surface layer. There's much more to land in a legal sense. It includes the mineral rights that theoretically extend to the center of the earth as well as to limitless heights in the sky. The term also includes any bodies of water on that parcel. Finally, it includes those things that are embedded in the ground: grass, plants, trees, and other growing things.

def•i•ni•tion

Real property refers to land and all rights to that land and in the land. **Land** is the earth, including air, mineral rights, and anything that grows on that earth.

Easements

An *easement* is the right to use somebody else's real property for a specific purpose. The title to the property remains with the original owner, but the easement holder has dominant rights. This area has its own vocabulary, which I'll discuss in more detail in the next section.

The easiest way to picture an easement is to consider two parcels of land. Let's say Charlie owns both parcels, but decides to sell one. He keeps the front piece that borders the road, and sells the back portion. When Janice buys the back property, an easement can arise in one of two ways. First, the easement can be surveyed and entered into the legal description of the property, often as a second document. Or her property can have an easement by way of necessity—for example, if the easement is the only way to get off her property and onto a road. If the only way to reach her property is with an easement, then she has one regardless of whether it is carved out in legal documents.

> **Stay Out of Jail**
>
> Because an easement involves an interest in land, the grant must be in writing or the grant is invalidated by the Statute of Frauds (SOF). For more on the Statute of Frauds, see Chapter 12. If an oral grant is made, it's not an easement but a license.

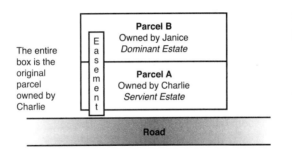

Example of an easement by way of necessity.

Types of Easements

Easements by implication are created when the owner of a parcel divides it in a way that an already existing and obvious use of one parcel is necessary for the reasonable use and enjoyment of the other. For example, if the septic tank is on the second piece of land, then the first can access it when it is clear that is what was intended.

Other times easements by implication are called *way of necessity*. This type arises when the grantor gives the grantee the right to cross his land in order for the grantee to go to and from his or her parcel. If a farmer subdivides a section of his land and sells those parcels to others but there is no access to the road, then a way of necessity is created for the parcel owners to cross the farmer's land to reach the road.

An *easement by prescription* arises when one party uses the property in a way that is obvious and hostile to the other party's rights for a long period of years, usually 20. Let's say Janice from the earlier example has a home office that people need to find. She puts a sign off the driveway that remains there for 20 years. It's not on her property. Both parties know of it, but Charlie never does anything to stop her. When he dies, his kids sell to a man who wants the sign removed. It can't be removed as long as Janice continuously uses the land, because she has gained a prescriptive easement.

An *easement in gross* is an easement that does not require the holder to own the dominant estate. An example of this is utility companies' easements for pipes and wires. They don't own the ground the easement is on. Instead, they own one of the bundle of property rights: the right to dig underground and bury a cable or conduit.

Terminating an Easement

A grantor or *servient tenement* can't terminate an easement on his or her own. Instead, the termination can only happen if the grantee or *dominant tenement* agrees. An easement can also be terminated if the grantee ceases to use the easement and the circumstances indicate the grantee intended to abandon the easement.

def•i•ni•tion

A **dominant tenement** is the property right of the easement holder. The easement holder's land is benefited by the easement on the **servient tenement**.

Licenses and Profits

Licenses and profits are temporary rights that are given to others by the property owner. A profit is the right to take part of the soil or produce of another's land. This could be taking a mineral from under the surface or taking a crop. Licenses are a personal and revocable privilege to perform an act on the land of another. A movie ticket is a license for the holder to be in the movie theater for the purpose of viewing that particular movie.

Liens

Liens are a claim or right against real property that arise in many situations. One example of a lien is a mortgage. That type of lien is one that the owner of the real property enters voluntarily. Other liens arise involuntarily. A tax lien is created when property taxes are unpaid. A mechanics' lien arises when a contractor or subcontractor's labor or materials for improvements to the real estate is unpaid. A judgment lien arises when a creditor wins a verdict against the owner in court.

Fixtures

Fixtures are personal property that become so attached to the real property that they cannot be separated from the real property without causing harm to the building or land. It becomes part of that real property. The challenge with fixtures is determining when an item crosses from personal property to an extension of the real property, whether that's land or a building.

The question of whether something is a fixture can arise in many situations. What if the real estate tax assessor values property more highly because of an addition of personal property? Or if a buyer purchases a piece of property believing the personal property stays with the real estate but the seller takes it with him or her? What if a tenant adds the personal property and tries to take it with her when she leaves but the landlord says it should stay?

When evaluating these types of questions, there are three general tests that should be applied:

- ◆ **Annexation.** Has the piece of personal property become so attached to the real property that if the personal property was removed it would damage the real property? If removing the personal property results in material damage, it has been annexed. A chandelier that cannot be removed without severe damage to a ceiling has been annexed. Bricks that have been adhered to a wall are a fixture.

- ◆ **Adaptation.** If the personal property was created or adapted for that particular piece of real property, it is a fixture. Custom cabinets are created for that home and real property and can't be removed from the home when it's sold.

- ◆ **Intent.** If the intent when the personal property was added was that it become a fixture, then it is. The courts will consider the intent at the time the fixture was affixed and will resort to secondary evidence if direct evidence doesn't exist.

Trade fixtures are those that a tenant attaches to a rented building and uses in their trade or business. Unlike other fixtures, trade fixtures can usually be removed by the tenant when they vacate the premises.

Forms of Real Property Ownership

Real property ownership can take several different forms. The varied strands contained in the ownership have caused many to call it a bundle of property rights. An owner can give up one or more of those rights without losing all ownership interest in the property.

Fee Simple Estate

A fee simple estate means that the owner takes the title to the land clear and free of any other ownership claims. The person owning land this way can sell or pass it on to another by will or inheritance. A fee simple ownership is transferable during life, transferable by will, transferable to heirs if there is no will, subject to the surviving spouse's rights, and can be used to satisfy the owner's debts.

A fee simple defeasible estate is an interest that the grantee has as long as he or she complies with conditions. For example, Dad could grant Junior a fee simple defeasible estate in the family farm so long as Junior continues to farm the land. If Junior stops farming, the property reverts to Dad.

Life Estate

A life estate gives the holder the right to use or occupy the land for the holder's life. With a life estate, the original owner stipulates that one person has a life estate, usually followed by a future interest in a second person or the property reverting to the original holder. Junior is a successful businessman who wants to provide a home for his mother for the rest of her life. He can purchase a condo and give her a life estate in it. When she dies, the home will either revert to him or be given to someone he chooses to hold the future interest.

Future Interest

A future interest in real property is the right to receive that property at some point in the future. This right will be triggered either by a date or an event. For example, the trust document could state that when he reaches the age of 25 or graduates from college with a bachelor's degree, whichever occurs first, Junior will inherit Grandpa's cabin. If Junior is 15 at the time Grandpa dies, this interest in Grandpa's cabin is a future interest.

Real Property Liability to Third Parties

Owners of property bear a responsibility to those who are injured on their property. The common law set the liability according to the status of the injured party. The duty owed depended on whether the third party was a trespasser, a licensee, or invitee.

Trespassers

A trespasser is one who enters property without authorization. Under the common law, a property owner only owed a trespasser a duty not to cause intentional harm. For the most part, landowners were required to post notices about known *traps*, such as a boarded-up mine or an abandoned well, but that was about it.

The key exception to this broad rule involves children. If there exists on the property a condition or something that reasonable people know would attract children, the landowner must take steps to protect children from the attraction. This is known as the *attractive nuisance doctrine*. Let's say Paula has a swimming pool on her property and refuses to put a fence around it. If a child comes onto her property, falls in the pool, and is injured or killed, she is responsible even though she didn't know the child or invite him or her over. Reasonable people know that children are attracted to swimming pools.

def•i•ni•tion

A **trap** is a hazard that is known to the landowner but not obvious to others. The **attractive nuisance doctrine** imposes liability on landowners for injuries sustained by small children playing on the land when the landowner permitted the condition that reasonable people would know attracts children.

Some states have incorporated the five requirements for an attractive nuisance contained in the Restatement of Torts:

- The landowner must know or have reason to know that children are likely to trespass.

- The condition should be one that the owner knows or should know or realize that could involve an unreasonable risk of death or serious bodily harm to children.

- The child because of his or her youth doesn't discover the condition or realize the risk involved.

- The burden of eliminating the risk is slight compared to the risk to children.

- The owner fails to use reasonable care to eliminate the danger or protect children.

As the common law has evolved, a new category has developed regarding frequent or known trespassers. Under this theory, if the landowner is aware of frequent trespassers crossing his or her land, he or she must warn them of nonevident, manmade conditions that could lead to serious bodily harm or death. Let's say Shelton has purchased a piece of land that borders the Appalachian Trail. Because he's camped on it, he's aware that people frequently stray from the trail to his land. Construction has started on his cabin, but right now, all that exists is a hole where the basement will go, but trees partially hide the hole. He should post a sign to warn the trespassers about the change in his land.

Licensees

Licensees are invited on to property for a specific use with the permission of the owner. For example, moviegoers purchase a ticket to see the latest movie. Once they have the ticket, the movie theater has given them permission to be in the theater for that showing only. To see another movie, they need to buy a second ticket.

Licensees also includes social guests. When that's the case, the owner has a duty to the licensee to warn them of dangers that are not obvious. The landowner must know of the danger. Then he or she must make the condition safe or warn the licensee of the risk. If the licensee didn't know of the danger and wouldn't be expected to discover the condition and the landowner has failed to act, the landowner is liable if he or she failed to use reasonable care. However, the landowner does not have to go on a hunt to discover all potential dangers.

Invitees

Invitees enter the landowner's property at the landowner's invitation. For example, McDonald's invites the public into its restaurants when it's open. Those who accept that invitation and enter the building are invitees. Therefore, the landowner owes the highest duty to them. Business invitees are on the property to conduct business, and public invitees are those who cannot reasonably be expected to make an inspection before using the land and property. In those instances, the owner has a duty to take reasonable steps to discover any danger and a duty to warn invitees of that danger. For example, if you go to the Grand Canyon you will see fences to keep people away from the rim and signs warning of the dangers of going beyond the fences. A mail carrier is also an invitee for the purposes of delivering letters and parcels.

Citations

Some courts are doing away with the common law distinctions between trespassers, licensees, and invitees. In those jurisdictions a landowner is liable under normal negligence standards. Should the landowner as a reasonable person have foreseen the possibility for harm and taken steps to prevent that harm from occurring? Other courts have only abolished the distinction between licensees and invitees.

Transfer of Real Property by Deed

The statute of frauds requires a written document for the transfer of property. A *deed* is the document by which the grantor transfers an interest in land to the grantee. While the document is the same from state to state, the way it is publicly recorded varies. Recording the deed is important when there is a dispute about who actually owns the property. In general, though, the deed must identify the grantor and grantee, contain words of conveyance, and describe the land. If there is a problem interpreting the deed, the court will try to determine the intent of the grantor and grantees. If that can't be done, then the court will consider extrinsic evidence.

Executing Deeds

For a deed to be official, the grantor must sign the deed. Most statutes also require that two witnesses sign the deed. Statutes often require the grantor to acknowledge the deed in front of a notary public as well. If a step is missed, as long as it is signed by the grantor it will bind the grantor and grantee. It just may not have any effect against others.

Delivering and Accepting Deeds

Even if the deed is perfectly executed by the grantor, it will not be considered conveyed unless it is *delivered* by the grantor to the grantee and the grantee *accepts* the deed.

The grantor can ask someone to act on his or her behalf to deliver the deed to the grantor upon the completion of an event or requirement—this is *delivering in escrow*. However, the deed must actually be received to be delivered. Entrusting it to a trusted advisor is not sufficient. In addition, the deed must be handed over with the intent that it be conveyed. The deed should also be delivered prior to the death of the grantor or the property will be divided according to the will or intestate statute. The reason the law hesitates to recognize a deed that is not delivered is that until delivery has occurred it is impossible to know whether the grantor has changed his or her mind and the intent element has changed.

Finally, the grantee must *accept* the deed. If the grantee does not, then the delivery is ineffective.

def•i•ni•tion

Delivery is the actual handing of an object to another with intent to convey the deed to that person or entity. **Delivery in escrow** means that the deed is delivered to a third party to be held in trust until the grantor and grantee have complied with the terms of the contract. **Acceptance** is unqualified assent by the grantee to accept the delivery of the deed, receiving something from another with intent to keep it.

Recording Deeds

To protect the conveyance against the rest of the world, the deed must be recorded. If it is not, the deed can be enforced between the parties, but there recourse is limited if a problem arises. The default position is that deeds are recorded. When this fails to happen, problems arise.

The states take four different approaches to who wins if there is a problem with a deed. Let's say that Jason owns a piece of property and sells it to Anna, who receives the deed but fails to file it. He then sells it to Samantha, who knows about the sale to Anna, but agrees to purchase the property anyway since it has not been recorded yet. The question is, who owns the property?

If the state has a *race statute*, whoever reaches the courthouse and records the deed first is the rightful owner of the property. In race statute states, it doesn't matter if Samantha files first and knowingly bought land that Jason didn't own. If a *notice statute* is in place, the last good-faith or bona-fide purchaser holds title. The fact that Samantha files first doesn't matter because she didn't purchase the land in good faith. Some states combine the two types of statutes. If the state were a *notice-race* or *race-notice* state, Anna would be the owner, because she was the last grantee who did not know of any problems with the property and she recorded the deed.

Remember, a deed holder does not need to record the deed. If it's a race statute state, Anna can still sue Jason for breaking their contract. However, she will not be able to reclaim the property. So the prudent grantee will file the deed as promptly as possible.

Grantor's Warranties and Grantee's Covenants

When the grantor transfers title to property, he or she makes the following warranties about the property:

- ◆ **Covenant of seisin.** Guarantee that the grantor owns the property.

- ◆ **Covenant of right to convey.** The grantor has the right or authority to make the conveyance (this comes into play when a third party is the owner).

- ◆ **Covenant against encumbrances.** Guarantee the land is not subject to the rights or interests of third parties: liens, easements, etc.

- ◆ **Covenant of quiet enjoyment.** The grantee's passion of the land will not be disturbed by the grantor or anybody else claiming title to the property.

- ◆ **Covenant of further assurances.** The grantor will execute any additional documents that are needed to complete the conveyance.

These five covenants are routine, and many statutes assume these covenants are part of the deed unless explicitly excluded by the language of the deed.

There is also an implied warranty when a new home is sold or built that the home is fit for use as a home. This warranty will flow beyond the first buyer to the second, but the first buyer will not be accountable under the statute. Instead, the responsibility remains with the builder and contractor.

The grantee can make any covenant that he or she agrees to in the deed.

Additional Ways to Convey Property

There are two primary additional vehicles for conveying property. The government can take property through *eminent domain* if it can show that the private property will be used for a public purpose, such as a public highway. The Fifth Amendment to the U.S. Constitution governs eminent domain. *Adverse possession* occurs when someone who is not the title holder uses property; for example, to place a sign on another's property. For adverse possession to be obtained, the possession must be actual, visible and notorious, exclusive, hostile, and continuous for a period of time (usually 20 years). The idea is that the owner knew or could have known of the use, but failed to do anything about it.

Landlord-Tenant Law

Leases are an option when someone is unable to purchase property. A lease is an agreement between the owner of property and someone who wants to use that property that sets the terms for the use of the property. When the lease involves real estate, the owner is called the *landlord* or *lessor* and the person seeking the temporary use of the property is the *tenant* or *lessee*.

Creating a Lease

A *lease* is the contract between the landlord and tenant regarding the use of real property. As a contract, leases and landlord-tenant law are governed by common law as well as adjusted by statute and court opinions.

To create the contract, the parties can either enter a written or oral contract, though some statutes require leases to be in writing to be valid. The threshold for requiring a written lease varies by state but is usually between one to three years.

The federal Fair Housing Act and other state and federal laws prohibit discrimination on the basis of race, color, religion, or national origin. And the Uniform Commercial Code prohibits terms that are unconscionable. Beyond these areas, landlords and tenants have great freedom in setting the terms of the lease.

Types of Tenancies

A *tenancy for years* is one where the lease establishes a definite duration. *Periodic tenancy* exists when a lease has an indefinite duration, but rent is paid annually, monthly, or weekly. To terminate a periodic tenancy, a party must give notice at least one period prior to ending the lease. A tenancy for years can transfer to a periodic tenancy if a tenant stays beyond the length of the original lease.

> **Stay Out of Jail**
>
> Don't misunderstand the term "tenancy for years." Years does not mean that the length of the lease is actually one for years. Instead, it is simply for a fixed duration.

A *tenancy at will* exists when the lease has an indefinite period and may be terminated at any time by either party. Finally, a *tenancy at sufferance* exists when a tenant stays after termination of the original lease and does not have the permission of the landlord to remain on the property. The landlord can evict the tenant or transform the tenancy into a different form.

Terminating a Lease

There are several ways that a lease can be terminated. Either party can provide *notice* of intent to terminate the lease under the terms of the lease. If the lease is a tenancy for years, the lease is terminated when the term expires. If the lease is a periodic tenancy, the lease terminates under the terms of the lease or according to statute. Usually at least 30 to 60 days notice is required. If the tenant breaches or engages in misconduct, the landlord may terminate the lease. Also if the property is destroyed, the tenant is usually released from the lease either by statute or the terms of the lease. Think of property destroyed by fire. Once it's destroyed, there is nothing for the tenant to lease. A lease may also be terminated if it was obtained by fraud on the part of either party.

A lease may have terms that allow the lease term to renew automatically unless notice is given of intent to terminate the lease. Otherwise, a new lease will be entered into by the parties.

Rights and Duties of Landlord and Tenant

Rights and duties flow between the parties to a lease. Because leases are being treated more like other commercial contracts, general contract principles are being increasingly used:

- **Possession.** A tenant has the right to possess the property and remain there through the term of the lease, and if the landlord interferes, then remedies are available to the tenant. The tenant also has the right to quiet enjoyment of the property, which means the landlord will not interfere with the tenant's possession of the land but does not extend to other's interference with that enjoyment. And a tenant is entitled to use the property without *constructive eviction*, a condition of the property is such that it is impossible for the tenant to continue to possess the property.

> **def•i•ni•tion**
>
> **Constructive eviction** is when by an act or omission, the landlord substantially deprives the tenant of the use and enjoyment of the premises.

- **Use of premises.** The tenant is also entitled to full, lawful use of the premises during the term of the lease. This is a general right, unless the terms of the lease limit the uses of the property. If the use is changed, the landlord can terminate the lease.

- **Rent.** The tenant is under a duty to pay the landlord rent in exchange for the use of the property. Payment must be made according to the terms of the lease. If the lease is assigned, the assignee is responsible to pay the rent to the landlord. If the property is subleased, the original tenant is still responsible to the landlord for rent.

- **Repairs and condition of premises.** Unless the lease requires, the tenant has no duty to make repairs. If the landlord makes repairs, he or she must take reasonable care to make sure the repairs are properly done. Because a landlord makes a warranty of habitability when leasing the premises, the building must have running water, heat in winter, and free from structural defects. In contrast, neither party has a duty to make improvements to the property.

- **Taxes.** If there is no agreement, the landlord is required to pay all taxes and other assessments.

- **Landlord's remedies.** If the lease or statute allows, the landlord may be able to acquire a lien on the property of the tenant for unpaid rent and other damages. The landlord can also sue for unpaid rent. Another remedy available to the landlord is to regain possession of the premises through eviction or other legal means. In any of these situations, the landlord has a duty to mitigate its damages. Generally, that mitigation occurs by re-renting the premises and applying any rent to the amount owed by the tenant.

Liability for Injury on Premises

So, who is liable if someone is injured on rented premises? It depends on the facts. The common law did not impose a duty on the landlord to repair damage, so if a tenant was injured there was no liability. The current trend is to impose a duty on the landlord to keep the premises repaired.

If a third party commits a crime that harms the tenant, the landlord is generally not liable. Think about a parking garage attached to an apartment building. Generally, if there is no notice to the landlord that crime is a problem in that vicinity, there is no liability to the tenant if he or she is injured by the criminal attack of another. However, if the landlord has security systems in place that it does not maintain, or the landlord should have otherwise been aware of a rise in crime, then the landlord would be liable to the tenant.

The lease can limit the liability of the landlord to the tenant. Leases frequently contain a term that requires the tenant to indemnify the landlord for harm to third parties from the tenant's use of the premises.

The landlord may be liable to third parties for the condition of the rented portions of the building and premises. However, the landlord may be liable for harm to third parties that occurs in common areas under the landlord's control.

The tenant is liable to third parties who are licensees and invitees if the harm occurs in property that is under the control of the tenants or the tenant failed to use due care. Even if the landlord promised to fix the problem and failed to do so, the tenant is liable if the injury occurred in an area he or she controls.

Transfer of Rights

The tenant's rights under the lease may be transferred in certain situations, usually an assignment or lease. An assignment occurs when the tenant transfers its entire interest in the property to a third party. Most leases will only allow this with written permission of the landlord. With a sublease, less than the tenant's entire interest is transferred to a third party and the original tenant is still liable to the landlord under the terms of the lease. He has simply found a party to assume part of his responsibilities under the lease.

The landlord may transfer its interest by selling the property. It may also be transferred by judicial order or sale. If either occurs, the tenant simply becomes the tenant of the new owner, but under the original lease.

The Least You Need to Know

- ◆ Real property is the bundle of rights that are attached to the land, extending to the center of the earth up to the heights of space.

- ◆ Easements are a right of way or right to use a portion of land given to a non-owner of a parcel of land.

- ◆ The owner of real property is responsible to third parties who are injured on the property according to the status of the third party.

- ◆ Deeds are the legal document used to transfer title to the property and must be properly filed and recorded to protect the interests of the owner.

- ◆ Leases govern the relationship between the owners of real property and tenants given the right to temporarily use the property.

20

Personal Property Law Basics

In This Chapter

- ◆ What is personal property?
- ◆ Determining ownership of personal property
- ◆ When the property has more than one owner
- ◆ Understanding bailments

Personal property is often defined by what it isn't: real property. Personal property includes things like cars, clothing, and appliances. With that in mind, let's examine the principals that govern this area.

Types of Personal Property

Personal property consists of everything that is not real property. It can be movable. It can be intangible. It can also be the right to do something with that property. Tangible personal property consists of items like furniture, textbooks, computers, and clothes. It's something you can touch and feel. Intangible personal property includes items like negotiable instruments and intellectual property, which I'll discuss in Chapter 21. A trademark is something that can't really be held or moved around. Instead, it is basically protection of an idea or advertising mark about a good. A negotiable instrument represents the intangible concept, for example, that there is a lien on property. You can't see a lien, but it exists in a legal sense and provides a right to the creditor.

def•i•ni•tion

Personal property is property that is movable or intangible, in contrast to land and buildings attached to the land. Examples of personal property include cars, patents, insurance policies, and furniture.

Title

We don't often think of personal property having title unless it's a big-ticket item like a car, boat, or airplane. But you have title to the clothing filling your closet. It's yours until you choose to sell, discard, or gift it.

The Uniform Commercial Code Article 2 provides the general framework for how title passes when personal property is sold. For a look at sales, turn to Chapter 14. Here we'll examine a few other situations.

Gifts

If someone gifts personal property, all that is required is a voluntary act on the part of the owner. At the time of the gift, the owner expects nothing in return from the recipient. There are several types of gifts.

Stay Out of Jail

If a gift is made, the donor may have to pay a federal gift tax. Currently, a donor can give up to $12,000 per person a year under an annual exclusion. Anything beyond that is subject to taxation.

An inter-vivos gift is one that is made during the life of the donor. To make such a gift, the donor must express intent to make the gift and actually deliver control of the item that is gifted. The recipient must accept the gift.

To have intent, the donor cannot be forced to make the gift. That ceases to make a gift a true gift. The intent to do something in the future does not give the recipient a right to the gift if it's personal property. Instead, the intent must exist at the time the gift is made and be immediately effective.

Delivery can be symbolic or constructive. A symbolic gift occurs when, for example, the donor gives the recipient keys to a safety deposit box that contains stock and bonds. The recipient now controls the box and its contents, so the delivery is effective. If the donor handed over an envelope containing the bonds, then the gift is constructive.

All three elements—the donor expressing intent to make the gift, the donor delivering the gift, and the recipient accepting the gift—must be present to have an inter-vivos gift be successfully completed. If any is missing, the recipient has not received the gift, and the donor retains it. And if the donor dies prior to exercising intent and delivery, there is no completed gift.

Gifts causa mortis are made in contemplation of death. For example, your grandmother has a heart attack and fears she will die during surgery. The children come to her hospital room, and she asks what they would like to have. They identify items of furniture and jewelry with minimal fighting, and she tells them it's theirs. These would be gifts causa mortis. However, if the surgery is successful and she recovers, she can revoke the gifts because the peril of death induced her to make the gift. Specifically, the donor can get the gift back if 1) he or she does not die, 2) the donor revokes the gift before dying, or 3) the recipient dies first.

There are laws that provide for gifts to minors for the support, maintenance, education, and benefit of the minor. A custodian will be appointed over the property and will manage it for the benefit of the minor.

Citations

The Uniform Gifts to Minors Act allows transfers of cash and securities to be made to a minor without setting up an elaborate trust. Instead, a custodian is appointed over the assets and distributed them to the minor. The Uniform Transfers to Minors Act is essentially an extension of UGMA and allows additional items like real estate, paintings, royalties, and patents to be transferred to minors.

Conditional gifts are made upon the happening or avoiding of something. For example, if Grandpa tells you he'll give you a brand new car if you graduate from college with honors, that is a conditional gift. The condition must be satisfied before the gift will be given. Grandpa might also tell his grandson he'll give him a sum of money if he avoids drinking until he's 25. In that case, the grandson has to avoid doing something the law allows as a condition of the gift.

Anatomical gifts include those made during life such as donating a kidney or post-death gifts. The Uniform Anatomical Gift Act covers these gifts and provides guidelines.

Potential Problems Regarding Who Owns Personal Property

Several situations can arise that make it difficult to determine who owns particular personal property. The common law and courts have established general principles that apply. The key is the intent of the owner of that property.

Finding Lost Personal Property

Now that you understand what personal property is and the basics of how personal property is titled, let's turn our attention to some of the problems that arise with personal property. One is what happens when you find someone else's personal property.

Something like this probably happened when you were a kid. You rode your bike to the park, and when you arrived it was empty. As you skidded to a stop next to a picnic table, you noticed an electronic game resting on it. You glanced around, unsure what to do. Nobody was around, so you couldn't identify an owner. You picked it up, and noticed it wasn't marked in any way but it worked. It's found personal property without a clear owner. Someone has to own it, but who is a mystery. I don't know what you did, but there are clear rules for the lost property.

First, lost property is only lost when the owner intends to keep the title to the item. She may not know where it is, but she wants to find it because it's still hers. Let's look at that game. The kid who left it did not intentionally abandon it or throw it in the trash. Instead, it is misplaced. He's probably tearing his room apart hunting for it. If that's the case, the general rule is that the property must be surrendered to the original owner if he can show he was the rightful owner.

If you took the game to him, as the finder you aren't entitled to a reward or other compensation for finding the property unless the owner offered the reward ahead of time.

But what about if the item is left in a hotel? Recently, I was in Ohio on business, and left my favorite necklace in a hotel when I checked out. I didn't intend to, but I forgot to put it on. In that kind of instance, it's clear that the owner (me) did not intend to dispose of the property. The maid should turn it over to the proprietor of the hotel, who could then identify that the hotel had it if I called to locate it. Now because I placed it in a cup, it might not be clear to the hotel that I intentionally left it there. The staff doesn't know the cup held my rings and watch, too. If it's not clear the owner intentionally left an item there planning to reclaim it, this exception requiring the item to be turned over does not apply.

Stay Out of Jail

These rules, as with any other area of the law, are subject to change by state stat- ute. Some states no longer require the finder to retain the found personal property indefinitely. Instead, after the close of a stated period of time, the property can be sold or claimed as its own, if notice is attempted to be given to the owner. Notice can be made through newspaper publication.

The finder of lost property is entitled to possess it against everyone but the true owner. If someone finds the lost goods on property that belongs to someone else, the finder can possess them until the true owner is found unless he trespassed.

Mislaid property differs from lost property. If property is mislaid, the owner places it somewhere fully intending to come back and reclaim the property. However, the owner forgets where he placed that property. With lost property, the owner involun- tarily loses it.

Abandoned Property

With abandoned property the owner intentionally relinquishes rights to it. Think about the old couch in your apartment. When you move, are you going to take it with you? Or would you rather leave it in the apartment for someone else or put it at the street to be collected as trash? If you put it at the street and someone carts it away, you can't reclaim it. By disposing of it with the trash, you relinquished your owner- ship. The person who finds and claims the abandoned property becomes the new owner of that property.

If lost, misplaced, or abandoned property is found by an employee while the employee is on the clock and doing his or her job, the employer holds the item until the true owner is found.

Consultation _____

Treasure trove, otherwise known simply as treasure, is the stuff of pirate tales. Often its bounty of gold and silver remains hidden until discovered by a treasure hunter. If the person who buried it can't be determined, the person who has found it becomes its owner. As with other lost property, title rests with the finder unless the true owner can be determined.

Accession

Personal property can lose its nature if it is accessed into other property. This happens when the personal property is blended with, altered by, improved by, or commingled with other property that belongs to other owners. Essentially, the property is so blended with another that it loses its separate identity. A fixture is an example of this. When the chandelier is drilled into the ceiling, the chandelier, which was personal property, has now blended with the home and lost its unique identity.

Conversion

When personal property is converted, someone steals the property of another and puts it to the stealer's use. This can happen when someone who finds lost property refuses to return it to the true owner. The convertor may also give the impression that the property actually belongs to him or her. In each instance, that person has taken property that does not belong to him or her, and the true owner can sue for the return of that property and any damages that result from the conversion.

Escheated Property

Personal property is escheated when the owner fails to claim the property and it reverts to the state. Escheated property is unclaimed. The Uniform Unclaimed Property Act provides a mechanism for states to resolve issues with unclaimed property. The most common types are bank accounts, insurance proceeds, traveler's checks, stock holdings, and other funds that the owner fails to claim. Under this and similar laws, organizations hold the unclaimed funds for a period of years before releasing them plus interest to the state. The state then holds the funds in a central location until the rightful owner or his or her heirs claim the property.

Wild Animals

Most of us don't spend a lot of time worried about who owns wild animals. That's because in the true wild, those animals aren't owned by anyone. Sometimes statutes will control how ownership of a wild animal is obtained. Without that, the animal is owned when it is dominated by someone. This domination could come if it is killed, subdued, gentled, or caged. In those cases the person has exercised dominion and control over the animal.

In addition, if you're the landowner, you own the animals on your land. So any time Mr. Bunny hops across your backyard, you own him. At least as much as a person can own a wild rabbit.

If you have posted no-trespassing signs on your field, yet a hunter enters the land and kills a deer, the deer is yours even though you weren't the one who shot it. But once the hunter has taken the animal off your land, he owns it.

Consultation

If you've caged and tamed a wild animal, it is owned by you to the extent that it exhibits signs it plans to return to your land any time it is released. However, if the animal would return to the wild, any title of ownership you had disappears. The animal has reverted to its truly wild state.

Issues of Multiple Ownership

As with real property, personal property can be owned individually or by multiple people or entities. When the property is owned by more than one person, it is called co-tenancy. There are several types of co-tenancy that mirror those with real property:

◆ *Tenancy in common* is the relationship between owners when they each own an undivided interest in the property. In this form, each tenant has an equal right to possess the whole property, but none has a right to survivorship, meaning the individual owners can will his or her share to his or her children.

Let's say several friends go together to purchase a small place. If they own it as tenants in common, each of the four friends has an equal right to the property. But if one dies, his interest can be gifted to someone else in his will.

◆ *Joint tenancy* is the joint ownership of property by two or more people when they share interest, possession, time, and title to the property. When a joint tenant dies there is a right to survivorship, meaning the remaining owners receive that owner's share in the property. The last surviving joint tenant owns the property individually. Also unique to this form of ownership, if one owner sells his or her share to someone outside the tenancy, the joint tenancy dissolves, replaced by a tenancy in common.

With joint tenancy, those four friends still own the place. But when one of them dies, the other three share his portion of the place.

◆ *Tenancy by entirety* applies only to husbands and wives in limited common-law states. It allows spouses to hold property together and prohibits a creditor of one from taking property both own. An alternative in many states is the concept of *community property*. In those states any property acquired during the marriage is considered community property regardless of who paid for the property.

Bailments

As I mentioned in Chapter 15, a bailment is a special relationship between the owner of property (bailor) and someone (bailee) that the owner entrusts the property to. Under a bailment, the bailee accepts a duty to hold the property, deliver it, or dispose of it as agreed between the parties. A dry cleaner can be a bailee because it holds the clothes, which are personal property, for the bailor until the bailor returns to claim the cleaned clothes. At no time does the bailor relinquish his or her ownership of the clothing. For a bailment to be created the bailor and bailee must reach an agreement regarding the property and details of the bailment. Then the bailor must deliver the goods, and the bailee must accept the goods.

While the bailor is usually the owner, that is not always the case. Sometimes he or she will merely control the property for the owner. The bailee only obtains possession of the property. The title never changes hands. The bailee might be paid to hold the property, but not always. A constructive bailment may also arise. This occurs when someone obtains possession of someone else's property, and must hold it until the owner may claim it. Consider the dry cleaning example. Let's say Joan sends her assistant Rose to pick up her dry cleaning. Rose is Joan's bailee until Rose delivers the clothing to Joan. Rose is also the bailor as far as the dry cleaner is concerned.

While the bailee has the property, the bailee has a duty to care for the property in its possession. This duty will fluctuate depending on whether the bailee holds the property for a fee or for free. If the bailment is for the benefit of the bailee, the bailee owes a higher standard of care than if the bailment is for the bailor's or both parties' benefit.

If the bailor fails to pay the bailee for holding the property after the parties agreed to a fee, the bailee has a lien on the property. This is why storage places often have auctions. They plan to be compensated for the lease of the premises.

The Least You Need to Know

- Personal property encompasses everything but real property.

- Personal property can be gifted by its owner.

- If personal property is lost or mislaid, the true owner retains title to the goods though they can be held by the finder until the owner returns. The true owner relinquishes title to abandoned goods.

- Personal property can be owned by more than one person in ways that mirror real property: tenants in common, joint tenancy with right of survivorship, and tenancy by the entirety.

- When the owner turns property over to a third party to hold it for the owner, the property is held in a bailment.

Chapter 21

Intellectual Property

In This Chapter

♦ Protecting marks that identify goods

♦ Protecting artistic works

♦ Protecting scientific advances

♦ Protecting business secrets

Intellectual property refers to creations of the mind. It covers areas like music, the arts, inventions, and designs. It also falls into basically two areas. We'll call the first industrial property, which includes inventions, patents, and trademarks. The second category contains the more artistic areas and is covered by copyrights. This chapter will address both.

Trademarks

A trademark (™) is a word, phrase, symbol, or design, or a combination of words, phrases, symbols, or designs, that identifies and distinguishes the source of the good of one party from those of others. These signs are commonly used in combination with marketing, though it's certainly not the only use. Think of the Nike Swoosh. Just seeing the Swoosh telegraphs the shoe is a Nike product. An individual or company can also trademark phrases. For example, the New England Patriots filed an application to trademark the phrases "19-0" and "19-0 Perfect Season." Author Brandilyn Collins has trademarked the phrase "Seatbelt Suspense."

A service mark is identical to a trademark, except it identifies and distinguishes the source of a service. Where a trademark identifies Nike, a service mark identifies a service like a dry cleaners.

Citations

A company or individual can use the trademark (™) designation at any time to alert the public to the fact that they claim special use of that phrase or mark. However, they can only use the registered mark (®) if the trademark is registered with the Patent and Trade Office (PTO) and receive all the protections from that extra designation.

Why get a mark? Because registering it with the U.S. Patent and Trademark Office (USPTO) provides the owner with extra protections—once registered, the owner is the only entity that can use the mark. Others can challenge the exclusivity of the mark during the first five years of registration. After that, the right of the registrant is incontestable. An entity can also register a mark in advance, but no earlier than three years before actually using the mark.

What Can Be Registered?

Descriptive terms, surnames, and geographic terms may not usually be registered. Descriptive terms are a characteristic or quality of the article or service, such as color, odor, size, or use. This general rule changes if the descriptive terms, surnames, or geographic terms have acquired a secondary meaning. An example of this secondary meaning is Philadelphia when used with cream cheese. Philadelphia is the name of a city, but if you say Philadelphia Cream Cheese, most people automatically think of the little silver bricks available at grocery stores. It has acquired value independent of the city. However, the Supreme Court decided that "Shredded Wheat" had not acquired a secondary use and denied trademark protection to that term.

Registration Not Required

Simple use of the mark will provide some protection to the user. However, by registering the mark with the USPTO the owner receives several benefits. The public is given constructive notice that the registrant claims ownership of the mark. The registrant is presumed to own the mark and receives the exclusive right to use the mark in connection with the listed goods or services. The registrant can bring an action in federal court and file with the U.S. Customs Service to prevent infringing products from coming into the United States.

A mark is infringed when another uses a mark in a way that causes confusion about the origination of the goods or services. A mark can be used by different parties only if the goods are not so similar that consumers will be confused. If a trademark is not registered with the USPTO, but protected by common law, the same mark can be used by multiple parties as long as the geographic regions do not overlap. If a product has a brand name, common-law trademark protections exist. In contrast, those marks registered with the USPTO receive nationwide protection.

One challenge for those seeking trademark protection is identifying whether a mark has been used in a geographic region. Thus, detailed searches must be made in conjunction with the application to register a mark with the USPTO.

Benefits of Federal Registration

In addition to having nationwide protection of a mark, a registered mark (®) obtains several substantive benefits. First, the mark holder can recover profits, damages, costs of infringement, and attorneys' fees for infringement actions. As mentioned, after five years a registered mark becomes incontestable, eliminating many arguments that registrants don't have the right to exclusive use of the mark. Registrants can use the registered mark. It is also easier for others to find the mark in use through trademark searches. Finally, the holder of the registered mark can sue infringers in federal district court and have the Customs service block imported goods that bear the mark.

Not every mark can be registered. The USPTO will block confusingly similar marks. It's possible that a common law trademark could prevent the registration of a similar mark even though the geographic areas don't overlap.

Merely descriptive marks may not be protected. These include marks that describe goods or the quality or a feature of the goods, describe the geography, or use an individual's surname. There are also prohibitions against immoral and deception marks; marks that disparage a person or falsely suggest a relationship with that person; marks that include a living person without his or her consent; marks that are a government's flag or coat of arms; and marks that use the name, likeness, or signature of a U.S. President during the life of his widow.

Trademark Infringement

To prove trademark infringement the plaintiff must prove the defendant's use of the mark has created a likelihood of confusion about the origin of the defendant's goods. The court will look at several factors including the similarity of the marks and the goods or services involved. If the court finds there is an infringement, the court can issue an injunction against further infringement. The plaintiff may also get attorneys' fees and in the rare case monetary damages.

> ### Citations
> The Internet has made it simpler for companies to monitor trademark infringement by making it easier to monitor the use of its mark. Something as simple as a programmed Google search can run each day to search for uses. But this ease of searching also makes it easier for a registrant to enforce infringement or risk dilution of its mark.

Registrants should rigorously protect its marks against infringement or risk abandoning the mark. Nonuse for three consecutive years is prima facie, on its face, evidence of abandonment.

Trademark Dilution

The Federal Trademark Dilution Act of 1995 (FTDA) provided a cause of action for the use of a trademark where there is no competition between the two users, but there is the likelihood of confusion for the consumer. After a Supreme Court case that changed the standard, Congress updated the law by passing the Trademark Dilution Revision Act in 2006.

The new law addresses many of the problems with defining terms such as "acquired distinctiveness" and "famous." When a registrant proves that dilution occurred, the court can issue injunctive relief against the diluting use. In this context, dilution refers to the lessening of the capacity of a famous mark to identify and distinguish goods or services, regardless of the presence or absence of 1) competition between the owner of the famous mark and other parties, or 2) likelihood of confusion, mistake, or deception.

Copyrights

A copyright (©) is the exclusive right under federal statute to the creator of a literary or artistic work to use, reproduce, or display the work. Under the 1976 Copyright Act, original works of authorship include literary, dramatic, musical, and artistic intellectual works, whether published or unpublished. The copyright protects the "form of expression" rather than the "subject matter." The copyright protection lasts for 70 years from the creation of the work.

The owner of a copyright receives several exclusive rights to the product:

  ◆ The right to reproduce the work

  ◆ The right to prepare derivative products, such as turning a novel into a screenplay

  ◆ The right to distribute copies of a recording of the work

  ◆ If it's a play or movie, the right to publicly perform the work

  ◆ If it's a painting, sculpture, or photograph, the right to publicly display the work

Consultation _____

Copyrights are freely exchangeable. A copyright can be sold, licensed, donated to charity, or bequeathed.

Registration

Nothing needs to be filed with the U.S. Copyright Office to obtain a copyright. Instead, a copyright is automatic when the work is created. However, registration provides many protections for the author or creator of the piece. The copyright holder registers the copyright with the Register of Copyrights in Washington, D.C. That registration creates a public record of the copyright claim. Registration is necessary before an infringement suit can be filed in court. If the registration is within five years of the publication of the work, it creates prima facie evidence of the validity of the copyright and the facts on the certificate. If the registration is within three months of publication, the owner can obtain statutory damages and attorneys' fees. Registration also allows the owner to record the registration with U.S. Customs Service to prevent the importing of infringing copies.

Infringement

Copyright infringement occurs when, without the author's permission, a protected work is copied or reproduced, a new work is created that is derived from the original work, the work is sold or given away, or the work is performed or displayed in public. If a copyright is infringed, the remedies available to the copyright holder include preliminary and permanent injunctions, impounding and destroying the infringing articles, and payment of any profits and legal fees to the copyright holder. There are defenses to copyright infringement, the most common being the fair use doctrine.

> **Stay Out of Jail** _____
>
> Copying and disseminating documents and music on the Internet is a copyright infringement. Individuals cannot share files across the Internet or peer-to-peer computer systems without permission or a license from the copyright holder. Any use without that permission or license is copyright infringement.

Fair Use Doctrine

The Fair Use Doctrine, found in section 107 of the Copyright Act, provides a vehicle for certain infringing uses. For example, an excerpt of a copyrighted book can be used for the purpose of critiquing that work. Other allowed limited uses include commenting, news reporting, teaching, and research. Unfortunately, the law does not provide a clear guideline for how much of a work can be reproduced before it violates fair use. Instead, a court will look at the purpose and character of the use, the nature of the copyrighted work, the amount of the portion used in relation to the whole, and the effect of the use upon the potential market for or value of the copyrighted work. For example, a professor may be able to use a chapter from a book in his classroom, but could only reproduce a couple paragraphs of an article.

To determine whether the use falls under the fair use doctrine, the courts will consider four factors:

- What is the nature and character of the use? If the use is educational in nature rather than commercial, it's more likely to fall under the fair use.

- What is the nature of the copyrighted works?

- How much of the work is being used? If it's a substantial portion of the work, it will violate the fair use doctrine.

- How will the use affect the value of the copyrighted work?

Patents

Patents secure to inventors the exclusive right to use their creation for a limited period of time. The Founding Fathers created patent rights to encourage scientific development.

Types of Patents

Patents are available in three types. *Utility patents* may be granted to anyone who invents or discovers a new and useful process, machine, manufactured item, composition of matter, or an improvement to any of those. Utility patents are granted for a period of 20 years from the date of filing. *Design patents* are granted when a new, original, and ornamental design for a manufactured item is developed. Design patents have a duration of 14 years. *Plant patents* are granted when a distinct and new variety of plant is invented or discovered and asexually reproduced and lasts for 20 years from date of filing. Regardless of the type of patent, a patent can only be granted to an actual invention. Ideas and scientific principles cannot be patented.

Consultation

Patent duration in the United States was extended to 20 years from the date of filing to mirror that of the patent law contained in the General Agreement on Tariffs and Trade (GATT).

Requirements to Obtain a Patent

Having an idea or a suggestion is not sufficient to obtain a patent. Instead, the law requires the invention be new. In patent law that means the invention was not known or used by others in this country or patented or described in a publication in another country. It also could not be patented or described in a printed publication or in public use more than one year prior to the application in the United States for the patent. So once an invention is created and in use or described in a publication, the inventor has one year to apply for a patent or forever loses the opportunity to do so for that invention. Finally, the invention needs to be unique enough that it is nonobvious to a person having ordinary skill in the area of technology related to the invention.

Infringement

Once a patent is approved by the United States Patent and Trademark Office (USPTO), it is presumed valid. Once the patent is obtained, the patent-holder's attention shifts to protecting that patent from infringement. The patent holder alone has the right to make, use, sell, or import the patented product or process. The patent holder can license others to make the product, otherwise, the patent is infringed if someone else makes, uses, sells, or imports it during the period of patent protection without the authority to do so.

Making minor changes to the design will not be enough to remove an infringing product from trouble. When determining whether infringement has occurred, the foundational question the court will ask is does the alleged infringing product contain elements identical or equivalent to each element of the patented product?

This doesn't mean that a party sued for infringement can't assert the underlying patent was invalid, usually because it was obvious. However, once the patent is issued, this argument becomes harder. The alleged infringer can also argue that its product does not fall within the claims of the patent. (As applied to patents, *claims* establish the technical boundaries of the patent by describing the patent in technical terms.)

If infringement is proven, the patent holder can seek an injunction against the infringing party and monetary damages.

Business methods may also be patented in limited circumstances. While this area is not as well defined as other areas of patent law, the basic business method patent usually consists of a series of steps related to performing a business process. Courts will examine the scope of prior methods, identify the differences between the prior method and proposed patent, determine the level of ordinary skill in the pertinent art, and evaluate objective evidence of nonobviousness.

Secret Business Information

A business often develops products or information it wants to keep secret but are not protectable by patent, copyright, or trademark. In such cases, state statutes and common law may step in to fill the gap for *trade secrets*. Forty-six states and the District of Columbia have adopted the Uniform Trade Secret Act. That Act protects businesses from having their trade secrets misappropriated, i.e. wrongly used, disclosed, or acquired.

For an employer to protect trade secrets, the employer should have a policy in place alerting employees to the fact it considers the information secret. This can be done through a policy in the employee handbook and a covenant contained in the employment contract. The employer should also treat the information as secret in the way it is handled. For example, employees should have limited access to the written plans for a product. If access to engineering plans is limited to supervisors and those with the right key or password, the employer has treated the plans as secret. The employer should also instruct departing employees during their exit interview what it considers to be a trade secret. Finally, if the trade secret is misappropriated, the employer/company should actively protect those items through litigation.

def•i•ni•tion

A **trade secret** is information (including a formula, pattern, compilation, program device, method, technique, or process) that derives economic value from being secret or not readily ascertainable. It is also subject to efforts that are reasonable under the circumstances to maintain its secrecy.

To avoid future problems with protecting trade secrets, a company should take active steps to protect those secrets as soon as it knows of a potential misappropriation. Failure to do that could waive the protection in future cases.

The Least You Need to Know

◆ Trademarks and service marks provide indefinite protection for registered words, names, symbols, or devices used to identify a product or service.

◆ Copyrights protect original creative works such as writings, movies, recordings, and computer software for a period of 70 years after the death of the creator.

◆ Patents protect registered inventions that are new and nonobvious for a period of up to 20 years from filing.

◆ Trade secrets are protected formulas, devices, or information that have value to the company and its competitors as long as the company takes steps to protect those secrets.

Part

Financial Law

By the time you reach this part of the book, you know a lot. We've covered the background, regulation, types of entities, agency, and employment relationships. We've even talked about property.

Last but not least, this part examines several aspects of business law such as securities law and negotiable instruments. We'll follow those topics with white-collar crime and torts. Let's get on with the learning.

Securities

In This Chapter

◆ Six key securities laws

◆ Federal regulation

◆ State regulation

◆ Rights and liabilities of shareholders

The official definition of securities contained in the Securities Exchange Act of 1934 begins with "any note, stock, treasury stock, bond ..." and continues on for a long list of options. The easier definition is that securities are an investment instrument, other than an insurance policy or fixed annuity, issued by a corporation, government, or other organization, which offers evidence of debt or equity. Stock in a Fortune 500 Company is an example of an equity security. A mortgage would be an example of a security that evidences debt. This chapter will review the major laws that apply to this area of law.

Federal Securities Regulation

Securities laws were passed in the aftermath of the stock market crash of 1929. The sustained losses that created the Great Depression prompted

Congress to enter the securities area in an attempt to provide some protection to citizens who purchased securities in the securities markets.

def•i•ni•tion

Securities are shares of stock, bonds, and debentures issued by corporations and governments as evidence of ownership and terms of payment of dividends or final pay-off. They are called securities because the assets and/or the profits of the corporation or the creditor of the government stand as security for payment.

Major Federal Laws

There are six securities laws you need to be aware of. The Securities Act of 1933 deals with the distribution of securities when they are first offered to the public. The Securities Act of 1934 addresses the secondary market, or resale, for these securities. The other four include the Securities Enforcement Remedies and Penny Stock Reform Act of 1990, Market Reform Act of 1990, Securities Acts Amendments of 1990, and Private Securities Litigation Reform Act of 1995, plus the Sarbanes-Oxley Act, which was discussed in Chapter 3.

The Securities and Exchange Commission (SEC) implements the laws and rules that govern the securities industry in the United States. It sees its goal as enforcing the laws so that all investors, regardless of their size, have access to certain facts about an investment prior to buying it and for the period of time they own the security.

1990 was an active year for Congress to pass laws and amendments that address securities regulation. The Securities Enforcement Remedies and Penny Stock Reform Act of 1990 gives the SEC broader authority to reduce fraudulent financial reporting and financial fraud. For example, the SEC can disgorge a company of ill-gotten profits and gains through tiered civil money penalties. It can also ask a court to prevent people from serving as directors or officers of companies who have engaged in fraudulent activities. The SEC also issues cease and desist orders, temporary restraining orders, and orders for accounting and disgorgement.

The Securities Acts Amendments of 1990 were designed to increase cooperation between the United States and other countries regarding securities law enforcements. As part of that law, sanctions are allowed against companies that violate federal laws. It also allows the SEC to restrict the activities of brokers, dealers, and investment advisers who have violated foreign securities laws.

The Market Reform Act of 1990 gave the SEC power to deal with the volatility of the markets after the October 1987 market decline. For example, the SEC may suspend trading if the markets become volatile and may require large traders to reveal themselves. In emergency situations, the SEC may use these powers for only ten days at a time.

The Private Securities Litigation Reform Act of 1995 applies to private litigation in an attempt to limit abuses and the number of lawsuits. The Act provides procedures that plaintiffs must take when filing to represent a class. It also set new rules for settlements in securities cases.

The Sarbanes-Oxley Act of 2002, discussed in Chapter 3, also contained numerous securities reforms. It was authored to improve the accuracy and reliability of corporate disclosures under the securities laws. To that end, it enhanced disclosure requirements, auditor and accounting provisions, and enforcement and liability sections.

Securities Act of 1933

The Securities Act of 1933 has two objectives. The first requires that investors receive financial and other significant information concerning securities being offered to the public. The second is to prohibit deceit, misrepresentations, and other fraud in the sale of securities. To do this, the law requires the registration of securities. The registration requires the company to provide essential facts, including …

- ◆ A description of the company's properties and business.
- ◆ A description of the security to be offered for sale.
- ◆ Information about the management of the company.
- ◆ Financial statements certified by independent accountants.

These registration statements must be filed with the SEC and become available to the public shortly after filing.

In addition to the registration, the company must provide a prospectus to each potential purchaser. The prospectus contains the key information from the registration, but removes the burden from the investor of seeking the registration from the SEC.

Citations
The registration statements of United States domestic companies are available on the EDGAR database accessible through the SEC's website: www.sec.gov.

There are exceptions to the registration requirement. Private offerings to a limited number of persons or institutions do not require a filing. Nor do offerings of limited size, intrastate offerings, and securities of municipal, state, and federal governments. These are exempt to lower the costs of entry for small firms.

While small companies are technically exempt from the registration requirements, a Regulation A offering involves what can be thought of as a mini-registration. A fill in the box form can register offerings of securities of up to $5 million per 12-month period.

Small businesses may make broad inquiries regarding interest in the offering from proposed investors. The solicitation documents must be factual, but provide a beginning step before the company is forced to incur the expense of complying with Regulation A reporting.

If the requirements of the 1933 Act are not followed, there may be civil or criminal liability. The issuer faces civil liability for providing materially false or misleading statements. The sellers of securities may also face civil liability for employing any device or scheme to defraud or obtain money by making untrue statements of material facts. And criminal liability can be imposed on those who willfully make untrue statements of material fact or fail to omit required facts. There can also be criminal liability for employing any device or scheme to defraud through the offer or sale of securities.

Securities Act of 1934

The SEC was created by the Securities Act of 1934, but the act did much more. Remember that while the 1933 Act deals with the creation of securities, the 1934 Act deals with the secondary market in securities.

Citations

The 1934 Act gave the SEC authority over the securities industry. That authority includes the power to register, regulate, and oversee brokerage firms, transfer agents, and clearing agencies as well as the securities self-regulatory organizations like the New York Stock Exchange. The SEC also oversees periodic reporting of information for companies with publicly traded securities.

Under the 1934 Act, companies with more than $10 million in assets that are held by more than 500 owners must file annual and other periodic reports. It also creates requirements for disclosure which must be made by the company or shareholders groups when they seek a proxy vote on issues. There are also disclosure requirements when someone seeks to purchase more than 5 percent of a company's securities by direct purchase. Because these offers are often made to obtain control of a company, the disclosure allows shareholders to make informed decisions.

The 1934 Act requires the registering of exchanges, brokers, and dealers with the SEC when those entities deal in securities traded in interstate commerce.

Insider Trading and the 1934 Act

The 1934 Act also addresses insider trading. Insider trading occurs when a person trades a security while in possession of material nonpublic information in violation of a duty to withhold the information or refrain from trading. While insider trading can involve corporate officers, directors, and employees who trade the company's securities after learning significant corporate developments, the rules also apply to friends, business associates, family members, and others who hear the tips. It can also extend to employees of law, banking, brokerage, and printing firms who are given the insider information to provide services to the firm. And the same principle applies to government employees who learn the information in the course of regulating the business.

Stay Out of Jail

In 2003 the SEC brought insider trading charges against Martha Stewart, not because her friend Sam Waksal, the founder of ImClone, told her about a problem with his company's cancer drug. The charges were brought because she then ordered her broker to sell her shares in ImClone before the release of that information. That act on the insider information is insider trading. She went to jail for lying about a stock sale, conspiracy, and obstruction of justice.

Sarbanes-Oxley and the 1934 Act

Sarbanes-Oxley amended the 1934 Act to include a requirement that each company's CEO and CFO sign a written certification when filing 10-K and 10-Q reports. The signature certifies that the officer has reviewed the report, based on the officer's knowledge, the report does not contain untrue statement of a material fact or omit a material fact, the financial statements fairly present in all material respects the financial condition of the company, and the signing officers are responsible for internal controls. Information is material if there is a substantial likelihood that reasonable investors would view it as significantly altering the mix of information and considers the fact important when making investment decisions.

If an officer knowingly misrepresents in the certification process, stiff penalties can be assessed. That officer can be fined up to $1 million and imprisoned for up to ten years.

Sarbanes-Oxley also required a change in the way companies present pro forma financial results. In the past, the press release was released in advance of the financials, often with spin because different accounting standards were used. Now, the pro formas cannot contain material misstatements of the financial picture. If the pro forma numbers differ from the official earnings, the company will have to explain why.

State Securities Regulation

Each state has its own blue sky laws designed to protect consumers from fraudulent transactions when they engage in purchasing securities. The SEC is joined by 50 state regulators in overseeing and regulating the securities' industry. The laws vary from state to state, but have similar threads. Often they require registration of security offerings and registration of brokers and brokerage firms. State law may also provide the state regulators with the authority to pursue securities violators. The state law will regulate the offer and sale of securities as well as the registration and reporting requirements for brokers and dealers.

Citations
The National Securities Markets Improvement Act of 1996 strives to bring some uniformity to the states' regulation of securities by creating classes of securities that are not subject to state securities registration requirements at offer and sale.

Shareholder Rights and Liabilities

Shareholders are those who own stock in corporations. By owning that stock, shareholders obtain rights and liabilities in the company. Those rights stem from the shareholder's status as an owner of the company.

Rights

As a result of the stock, shareholders obtain several rights. Those include …

◆ **Ownership right.** As owners, shareholders have indirect control over the company. Accordingly, shareholders have the right to properly executed certificates that document their ownership interest. They also have the ability to transfer their shares unless limited by a valid restriction. Often the restriction will be something like a buy-sell agreement that requires the shares to be offered to the company or other shareholders first.

◆ **Right to vote.** Shareholders also have the right to vote according to their percentage of ownership at the shareholder's meeting. This allows shareholders to participate in the election of directors or other special business. State law will govern how many votes each share receives. Shareholders have the right to give their proxy to another for voting purposes. They also may enter agreements regarding how they will vote. To accomplish block voting, shareholders can establish a voting trust.

◆ **Preemptive offer of shares.** If the capital stock is increased, shareholders often have the preemptive right to subscribe to the same percentage of the new shares that their old shares represented. This allows the shareholders to prevent the dilution of their interest in the corporation.

◆ **Inspect the books.** Shareholders have the right to inspect the books of the corporation. Some, but not all states, require that the inspection be made in good faith, for proper motives, at a reasonable time and place. This right to inspect can be used to gain information for a lawsuit, but not for merely idle curiosity.

◆ **Dividends.** Shareholders have a right to dividends, a portion of the declared profits that mirror the shareholder's interest in the stock of the corporation. To issue dividends the corporation should have earned surplus or retained earnings. The flip side is that the company can't issue dividends if it is insolvent or doing so would make it insolvent.

 Consultation

The exception to the general dividends rule comes from wasting assets corporations. These corporations are designed to exhaust or use up the assets of the corporation—these corporations do things like extract coal, oil, and iron from the earth.

If the money exists, the distribution of dividends is at the discretion of the directors. The directors may choose to accumulate earnings rather than distribute them, especially if the directors know there is a capital project in the future. It is also important for the corporation to maintain an adequate cash reserve and working capital. Directors have broad discretion to choose when to make dividend payments. Those dividends often take the form of cash. The dividend will often be made on a certain date for ease of determining who the shareholders are at that time.

- **Capital distribution.** If a corporation is dissolved, the shareholders are entitled to capital distributions if any capital remains after the winding up of the corporation in proportion to their ownership interest in the company.

- **Shareholder actions.** Shareholders also have the right to bring derivative actions. This means the shareholders can sue the directors, officers, or third parties on behalf of the corporation when the corporation refuses to do so. By doing so, the shareholder is enforcing the rights of the corporation and any proceeds or recovery go into the corporation, not to the shareholders.

Before bringing such an action, the shareholder must show that he or she has exhausted their remedies with the corporation first. They must show the directors refused to enforce the right or that the board is so unable to make an impartial decision that the need to go to the board first is excused. Shareholders can also intervene or join in actions brought against the corporation if the corporation does not defend itself or act in good faith. Finally, minority shareholders can bring suit against majority shareholders if the majority acts in an oppressive way against the minority.

Liabilities

A shareholder will usually have limited liability in a corporation. That liability is limited to the extent of his or her capital contribution to the corporation. However, there are exceptions:

- **Piercing the corporate veil.** A corporation is treated as a separate legal entity—providing that limited liability—only as long as the shareholders and officers treat it as a separate entity. Two corporations can have identical shareholders without being treated as one company. But in certain cases, the court can ignore the general rule and pierce the corporate veil. To do so, the court can consider the following factors: 1) adequate corporate records have not been maintained and the corporate assets have been commingled with other funds; 2) grossly inadequate capitalization; 3) diversion by shareholders of corporate funds or assets; 4) formation of the corporation to evade an exiting obligation; 5) formation of the corporation to perpetrate a fraud or conceal illegality; 6) determination that injustice and inequitable consequences would result.

- ◆ **Alter ego.** Courts will also evaluate whether the corporation is merely the alter ego for the wrongdoer. If that is the case, the court may ignore the corporate form. When the separate personalities of the shareholders, officers, or directors cease from the corporation, then the corporation is merely the alter ego.

There are additional circumstances that will force the liability from the corporation to the individual. Some states' wage claim statutes provide that shareholders have unlimited liability with employee's wage claims, the reason being that its an important public policy to make sure that employees are properly paid. In rare instances, if a subscription of stock has been offered but not fully paid for, anyone who did not pay full value is liable for the unpaid balance if the corporation is insolvent and the money is needed to pay creditors. Unauthorized dividends can also be claimed by creditors if the dividends came out of capital.

The Least You Need to Know

- ◆ Securities are an investment instrument, other than an insurance policy or fixed annuity, issued by a corporation, government, or other organization, which offers evidence of debt or equity.

- ◆ The Securities Act of 1933 deals with the distribution of securities when they are first offered to the public. The Securities Act of 1934 addresses the secondary market for these securities.

- ◆ Insider trading occurs when a person trades a security while in possession of material nonpublic information in violation of a duty to withhold the information or refrain from trading.

- ◆ Each state has its own blue sky laws designed to protect consumers from fraudulent transactions when they engage in purchasing securities.

Chapter 23

Negotiable Instruments

In This Chapter

- ◆ Defining negotiable instruments
- ◆ The requirements that make an instrument negotiable
- ◆ How to negotiate bearer and order instruments
- ◆ Negotiation problems
- ◆ Negotiation warranties
- ◆ What is a holder in due course?

The rules governing negotiable instruments streamline the flow of monetary obligations between entities and individuals. This chapter will define negotiable instruments and then provide an overview of how those instruments are transferred and the common problems that arise.

Negotiable Instruments Defined

The Uniform Commercial Code (UCC) defines a negotiable instrument as an unconditional promise or order to pay a fixed amount of money if …

◆ It is payable to bearer or order.

◆ It is payable on demand or at a definite time.

◆ The instructions are only about the payment of money.

Article 3 of the UCC contains the detailed and often complex rules that govern negotiable instruments. This area of law is filled with definitions. Stick with this section and you'll see how the definitions tie together.

Types of Instruments

There are several types of instruments that qualify as negotiable instruments. Each fills a specific role and can be issued by certain types of institutions or individuals.

Promissory notes are written promises to pay a sum certain to the holder. The holder is the person with possession of an instrument that is 1) payable to that person, 2) indorsed to that person, or 3) bearer paper.

Certificates of Deposit are a bank's promise to pay a set sum of deposited money back to the customer with interest when the customer surrenders the document.

Drafts are an order by one party to another to pay a sum of money to a third party. In general, if you issue a draft, you instruct somebody to make a payment to a third party on your behalf. You are the drawer, the person making the payment is the drawee, and the person receiving the money is the payee. The drawee only needs to pay when he or she accepts the draft from the payee.

> **Citations**
>
> The UCC breaks it down simply: a note is a promise to pay while a draft is an order to pay.

Still confused? Think of a check—you know, the ones you get from your bank. When you fill it out, you essentially order your bank to pay a specific amount to the identified party. A check is a specific subset of drafts.

Then there are teller checks (a draft drawn by one bank on another bank), cashier's checks (a draft drawn by a bank on itself), traveler's checks (drafts that are payable to the bearer if countersigned by the person who originally signed the check), and money orders (draft issued by a bank or nonbank).

Parties to the Instrument

Each instrument has at least two parties to it. However, those parties change based on the type of instrument. Here's the summary of the vocabulary you need to know.

If a note is involved there are two parties: the *maker* signs the note and is responsible for payment while the *payee* is the named person on the note who receives payment. If it's a draft, the *drawer* is the party who writes or creates the draft or check, the *drawee* is the party who is to pay on the draft or note, and the *payee* is the one named on a check to receive payment.

Note	Draft
Maker: obligated under the note	Drawer: writes the draft
	Drawee: ordered to pay on behalf of drawer
Payee: receives the money	Payee: receives the money

There are two additional terms that could come up in this context. The drawee becomes an *acceptor* when the drawee indicates a willingness to pay the draft. And an *accommodation party* is someone who has no original duty under the note but signs to guarantee payment. The addition of the accommodation party strengthens the collectability of the note.

What Makes an Instrument Negotiable?

Just because a document has been drafted that says someone should be paid does not make the paper a negotiable instrument. For that to occur, the note must meet several requirements. If an instrument is negotiable, the rules in Article 3 of the Uniform Commercial Code govern and provide stronger protection than contract law. To achieve those extra protections, the note must be 1) evidenced by a record, 2) signed 3) by the maker or drawer, 4) pay a sum certain, 5) payable in money, 6) payable on demand or at a specific time, and 7) payable to order or bearer.

To receive the protections of Article 3 of the UCC, all seven requirements must be met in the instrument from the time it is written. If it fails to meet all seven requirements, then the note or draft can be enforced under contract law.

A Record

A record essentially means the instrument needs to be in writing. There has to be a physical piece of paper or electronic record that can be taken to court if a dispute arises. Under Article 3 the record can be handwritten, typed, printed, or electronic. The UCC does not dictate that specific forms be used, merely that a record exists and that it contain the other six elements.

Consultation

Why does the law want the instrument in writing? So that if there is a dispute the court doesn't have to rely on personal interpretations of what was supposed to happen—sometimes years after the negotiations and agreement. Courts always prefer written documents to relying on faulty memories that can also be tainted by bias.

Signed or Authenticated

The record must be signed by the person making the promise or order to pay. In this increasingly electronic world, the UCC now requires that the document be signed or authenticated. This can occur by old-fashioned signature, a seal, symbol, electronic mark, or any other device allowed by law. A company or individual may authorize an agent to sign on its behalf, and the agent can use language in their signature that clarifies the relationship. An agent should sign in a way that avoids personal liability. This can be achieved by signing the company name, then "by Don Marks, Director." Without making it clear that the person signing is doing so as a representative or agent, that person becomes personally liable on the instrument.

Promise or Order to Pay

On the face of the document, the promissory note must contain a promise to pay. A draft or check must have an order to pay. For it to qualify the promise or order to pay must not have any conditions. Instead, it must be payable when presented. For example, the payment can come from a specific fund, but the fund must exist at the time the note is written. Otherwise, the payment is conditional on the fund's creation.

Payment in Money

Money includes any currency used by a government or intergovernmental agency. While the parties can agree to use foreign currency, they cannot agree to a non-monetary source like stocks or bonds. If they do, the UCC no longer applies.

Sum Certain

The requirement for a sum certain means that the amount owed must be specific. It must be an exact amount of money that leaves no doubt about what is owed. The note or draft can have a floating or variable interest rate without violating this requirement.

Time of Payment

The due date must be specific to a definite time or the paper must be payable on demand. An instrument is payable on demand if it states that it is payable on demand or at sight, or indicates it is payable at the will of the holder. A definite time is either spelled out on the document or is readily ascertainable from the document. If there is no date, it is taken to be dated when it is issued to the payee. A paper is not due before the date on its face.

Words of Negotiability

The words of negotiability are "payable to order" or "payable to bearer." Usually, you will see phrases like "Pay to the order of Andrew Smith," "pay to Andrew Smith or order," "pay to bearer," or "Pay to Andrew Smith or bearer." Pay to order language indicates that there is no restriction that the payment be made to Andrew Smith alone. He can sign it over to somebody else. Bearer language indicates that anyone holding the paper can be paid if he or she presents it for payment.

Stay Out of Jail

The statute of limitations for most Article 3 UCC issues is three years. So if a problem arises with a negotiable instrument, it must be taken to court within three years. The statute of limitations for certificates of deposit and accepted drafts is six years.

The following table shows whether the language used makes the note order or bearer paper.

Pay to the order of …	Order
Pay to the order of bearer	Bearer
Pay to the order of X or bearer	Bearer
Pay to the order of X, bearer	Order
Pay to the order of X (on a check)	Order
Pay to cash	Bearer

Transfer of Negotiable Instruments

Negotiation is the transfer of possession of paper. The holder of the paper is different from the possessor of the paper. To be a holder, the person must not only have possession of the paper, but it must also be payable to her, indorsed to her, or bearer paper.

Bearer Paper

Bearer paper (remember the magic words: pay to bearer?) is negotiated by delivery. Possession of the instrument is all it takes to acquire the money promised.

Courts have held that even when the note or instrument is transferred by mistake or inadvertently, if the paper is bearer paper, then the holder gets to keep it. Even fraud and embezzlement don't change this general rule as long as the bearer took the paper in good faith without knowledge of the fraud.

Order Paper

If the paper is order paper (contains the magic words "pay to order"), then the paper can be negotiated only by indorsement and transfer of possession of the paper. Possession alone is insufficient.

Indorsements

If order paper is transferred to another with an indorsement alone, that is called a *blank indorsement*. In that case, the order paper is transferred to bearer paper. Think of a check. When you sign the back of the check, it is a blank indorsement. You are not transferring it to the order of another person. If you lose the check, whoever finds it can take it to a bank and cash it. It has become bearer paper.

Special indorsements are those that contain language detailing who the indorser is making the instrument payable to. Take a check. If instead of merely signing your name you wrote "Pay to John Smith" over your signature, the check now has a special indorsement and continues to be order paper. You have left specific instructions about who the money should be paid to. Then if John Smith signs only his name on the back, he has now transferred the order paper to bearer paper.

A *qualified indorsement* places some limit or disclaimer on the liability of the indorser to the maker or drawee. The usual language you will see in this situation is "without recourse." By adding those two words to the signature, the indorser has now told the drawee and maker that he is not accepting responsibility for all of the secondary liabilities for payment of the instrument. Qualified indorsements are used to show an intent to limit liability.

Restrictive indorsements are used to limit or restrict the way the instrument is transferred. This can be used to indicate the funds are in trust or that the funds are "for deposit only." To ensure that the check can only be deposited in your account, you must add your account number to the signature block. Otherwise, the paper is turned into bearer paper and can be deposited into anybody's account. These restrictive indorsements are designed to reduce the risk of theft.

> **Citations**
>
> If an instrument is made out to someone, but misspells the name due to clerical error, the UCC allows the person to sign the name as it should be, to sign the incorrect name, or ask for a new check with the correct spelling.

Banks also endorse notes, but may use any agreed method including listing its Federal Reserve System number. A bank may also indorse for a customer who forgot to indorse the instrument. A customer may stamp the instrument rather than sign it— think of the stacks of checks restaurants take to the bank that are stamped with the relevant information rather than signed by the restaurant's agent.

An instrument can be made out to more than one person or entity. If it is made out to "Adam Smith and Tom Banks," then both parties must indorse the check. If it is made out to "Adam Smith or Tom Banks," then either can indorse it. If there is any doubt, the court will default to the preference that the instrument is made out to *alternate payees.*

---

def•i•ni•tion ──────────────────────────

Alternate payees are multiple individuals or entities that are listed on an instrument as payees; the instrument can be paid to any one of them. Usually signaled by the use of "or": "Adam Smith or Tom Banks."

Instruments That Are Improperly Negotiated

The terminology of indorsements is complicated. So what happens when someone forges a signature on a check? Or embezzles funds? Or other misconduct occurs with negotiated instruments?

Forged Indorsements

A forged indorsement is not authorized or a valid indorsement. If a forged indorsement exists on an instrument, the person with the instrument is not a holder with the added protections. If the payer makes payment on a forged indorsement, the payer is still liable to the original payee, unless that payee's negligence contributed to the forgery.

The imposter rule provides exceptions to the general forgery rule that allow the instrument to continue to be effectively negotiated. This is important because if the rule applies, the signature is treated as a genuine endorsement even though it is not. For the imposter rule to apply, the payee or its agent is impersonated. The imposter rule also applies if a dummy payee is used. A dummy payee may be used to hide why money was taken from a personal account. Or a dummy payee may be used when an agent or employee supplied the name for the payee line intending to take the money for himself. In that situation the employee intends to forge the indorsement of the dummy payee and keep the money. The imposter rule does not apply when there is a valid check but someone forged a signature.

The dummy payee exception as applied to employees is designed to give employers a reason to keep their internal controls in place to prevent employees from committing fraud.

Incapacity and Misconduct

A minor or other incapacitated person can negotiate an instrument unlike contract law. Fraud, mistake, and duress do not make negotiation ineffective. Neither does the fact that the negotiation was illegal or a breach of duty.

Lost Instruments

If a lost instrument is order paper, the finder does not become the holder because the paper is not made to the order of the finder. If a lost instrument is bearer paper, the finder is the holder and entitled to enforce the instrument.

Warranties in Negotiation

The UCC creates a host of warranties that the parties to a negotiated instrument make to each other.

The unqualified indorser makes six warranties. First, he is entitled to enforce the instrument. Second, all signatures are authentic and authorized. Third, the instrument has not been altered. Fourth, the instrument is not subject to a defense or claim that can be asserted against the warrantor. Fifth, in regards to consumer accounts, that if it does not have a handwritten signature, the drawer has authorized the instrument. And sixth, the warrantor does not know the maker is insolvent.

The party submitting the paper for payment makes three warranties. First, the warrantor is entitled to enforce the draft or authorized to obtain payment. Second, the draft has not been altered. And third, the warrantor has no knowledge that the drawer's signature is unauthorized.

What happens if the document becomes forged at some point? The last person who qualified as a holder can go to the transferor she received the paper from to recover under the warranties. It doesn't matter that neither was a party involved with the original instrument.

You may have noticed that the implied warranties do not guarantee payment. Nor is there a guarantee of sufficient funds in an account. The warranties focus on the character of the instrument (that it's not forged, altered, etc.) rather than on payment. All of the warranties pass to the transferee and any subsequent transferees. Warranties may be disclaimed on all instruments *except* checks. The disclaimer may be made with signing by using language like "without warranties." If someone wants to enforce a warranty, notice must be given to the breaching party within 30 days of learning of the breach.

If an instrument is transferred with a qualified indorsement, the indorser does not assume liability for the payment of the instrument as written. All other warranties remain in place. Finally, if the instrument is transferred by delivery rather than indorsement, the warranty liability from the transferor only flows to the immediate transferee.

Holder in Due Course

A holder in due course (HDC) has more protections than a regular holder. These extra protections exist because the HDC takes the instrument and meets additional requirements at the time the note is negotiated to the holder and the holder gives value. The extra requirements to take the note as an HDC fall into three general areas: taking the note for value, in good faith, and without notice.

Value

Value can include performance of consideration, acquisition of the instrument, taking the instrument for payment of a preexisting debt, giving a negotiable instrument for the instrument, or giving the instrument in exchange for an irrevocable obligation. The value does not need to match the face amount of the instrument. The time the value is given determines whether the holder took the instrument in good faith and without notice.

Good Faith

Good faith means that the holder acted honestly in acquiring the instrument. The holder must have also observed standards of fair dealing. Bad faith can come from something as simple as giving too little value for the instrument. The standard for honesty is subjective, while fair dealing is objective—uses the reasonable person standard.

Without Notice

To be an HDC, the holder must obtain the instrument without notice under one of these conditions:

- That the instrument is overdue
- That the instrument has an unauthorized signature or altered signature
- There are claims on the instrument
- There are no defenses or claims in recoupment

The notice must occur in a way that gives the holder a reasonable opportunity to act on that notice. As it often does, the law has decided to balance the scales if there is a problem with who had the best opportunity to prevent the problem from occurring.

If a person is an HDC, then that individual or entity did nothing to perpetuate the problem. He or she cannot have knowledge that anything was wrong. Thus, he or she receives extra protections.

Transferees after the HDC are sheltered by the rights of the HDC. In a sense, the transferee steps into the shoes of the HDC who transferred the instrument to them and acquires all of the rights and protections of the HDC.

Defenses to Payment

An HDC can often obtain payment because of the added protection that status affords despite any underlying problems between the original parties to the instrument. That is why that status is so valuable. The defenses break into two categories: those available against HDCs and those available to everybody else. All of the defenses can be used against a general holder.

One benefit of attaining HDC status is that several defenses cannot be raised against a claim from an HDC. Those include ordinary contract defenses, incapacity of the maker or drawer, and fraud in the inducement. Instead, the defending party has very limited defenses.

However, there are certain defenses that can be used when defending a claim made by an HDC. These defenses are called universal defenses because public policy dictates the defense should apply to everybody. For example, the fact that one party had the inability to contract due to minority or another capacity issue is a universal defense. If the contract was illegal, that is a defense to HDC status, as are forgery, alteration, fraud in the execution or terms of the paper, and duress.

The Least You Need to Know

- ◆ Negotiable instruments fall under two main categories: notes and drafts.

- ◆ A negotiable instrument is transferred differently depending on whether it is bearer or order paper.

- ◆ To be negotiable, an instrument must have a record, be signed or authenticated, with an unconditional promise to pay sum certain of money at a set time with the words of negotiability (pay to bearer or pay to order).

- ◆ A holder in due course has extra protection because that holder takes for value in good faith and without notice that there are certain problems with the instrument.

Chapter 24

Business Crimes

In This Chapter

- ◆ General principles
- ◆ Understanding white-collar crime
- ◆ Types of common law crimes
- ◆ Protection under the Fourth and Fifth Amendments

In this chapter we'll examine what constitutes a crime and the specifics of several white-collar, or business, crimes. Because this book focuses on business law, these crimes aren't the type you'd see as the subject of a TV show. Instead, the crimes are nonviolent crimes that involve some form of cheating or fraud. While they aren't physical crimes like murder or assault, they are equally devastating because they involve people's money.

Background Principles of Business Crimes

In a general sense, a crime is an act that violates a law by harming someone or their property and leads to jail time for the perpetrator. Most crimes require two things: *mens rea* and *actus reus*. *Mens rea* is Latin for "the guilty mind" and reflects the requirement that the lawbreaker knows what he's doing. However, this does not mean that the person is aware of their guilt, but that they understand and voluntarily make the act.

Actus reus is Latin for "guilty act" and involves the physical actions the alleged criminal takes. The statute may define this as an affirmative action on the part of the law-breaker: stealing somebody's car, for example. Or the law may prevent an action: it is a crime to take somebody's life. Either way, if the *actus reus* is combined with *mens rea*, a crime has been committed.

Crimes are classified in two ways. A misdemeanor is one that is punishable by less than one year in jail. Felonies punish the offender with one year or more in jail. It's important to note that the criminal laws are not standardized. What qualifies as a misdemeanor in one state may be a felony in another.

White-Collar Crime

The term *white-collar crime* was coined in 1939 and is synonymous with fraud in all its iterations. Today's scams often use the Internet and other technology to put a new face on old tricks to separate people from their money.

Consultation

The Federal Bureau of Investigation (FBI) investigates white-collar crime at the federal level. Its major programs are focused on corporate fraud, health care fraud, mortgage fraud, securities and commodities fraud, insurance fraud, mass marketing fraud, money laundering, bankruptcy fraud, and hedge fund fraud.

White-collar crime is a costly endeavor. According to the FBI, health care fraud alone has a price tag of $50 billion annually. The fraud can involve anything from a staged car accident to Medicare/Medicaid fraud. Then there's financial institution fraud, including mortgage fraud and identity theft operations.

In the post Enron, WorldCom, and Adelphia world, corporate executives may be held personally liable for the acts of their subordinates—even if they did not know about or knowingly participate in the crime. In the Sarbanes-Oxley world, Congress has decided that the CEO and CFO or the equivalents are the people best situated to stop the fraud. Thus, they have a higher burden.

Also note that in the business setting multiple individuals can be held responsible for committing the same crime. In the "ordinary" criminal context, only those who directly participated in the crime can be held liable. In the business setting the net can go much broader. For example, the manager can be held liable for the acts of his or her subordinates. To be found liable, the manager must have 1) authorized the conduct, 2) known about the conduct and did nothing, or 3) failed to properly supervise the employee to prevent the criminal conduct.

If found guilty of a criminal violation, corporations can pay huge fines. For example, AIG paid a fine of $1.6 billion to settle state and federal charges that it participated in fraud and bid-rigging and failed to pay into workers' compensation funds. If an individual employee or officer is found guilty, that person can spend time in jail and/or pay fines. For example, Bernie Ebbers, former CEO of WorldCom, was sentenced to 25 years in jail in 2005 for accounting fraud at that company.

Penalties

There are several different types of penalties that can be enforced against the defendant. First, the defendant can forfeit any property that was used to commit the crime. Forfeiture is rare in white-collar crimes, but is an option for the court. The more common punishments are fines and jail time. Recently, fines have been adjusted to recognize that what is a significant penalty to an individual may not affect a business. Since the fines are designed to deter criminal behavior this had to be adjusted.

There are also mandatory sentences now for the officers and directors who were in positions of authority at the time of the crime. The U.S. Sentencing Guidelines allow reductions in sentences if the managers were actively engaged in trying to prohibit the crime. Under the November 2003 amendments, the court can take the following factors into consideration when determining sentences:

◆ The seriousness of the offense

◆ The company's history of violations

◆ Its cooperation in the investigation

◆ The effectiveness of its compliance program

◆ The role of its senior management in the wrongdoing

The effect is to encourage companies to take an active role in the investigation to minimize the amount of the penalty for any wrongdoing. Sarbanes-Oxley has increased the criminal penalties. (For more on Sarbanes-Oxley, refer to Chapter 3.)

Stay Out of Jail _____

Not only the corporation and its officers can be found guilty, but so can its agents. During the Enron accounting scandal, Enron's public accountant Arthur Andersen was found guilty of obstruction of justice. Why? Because it shredded documents from the time it was concerned an investigation would start into Enron's accounting until after the investigation opened. Who should have been guilty? The employees who shredded documents? The managers who encouraged it? The company?

Civil Versus Criminal

One misconception is that the victim of the crime can be compensated for any injury in a criminal proceeding. Any penalties are paid to the government, not the victims. On rare occasions the court may order restitution to the victim of the crime. Usually, though, the only way a victim can be compensated is to pursue a civil case.

Conspiracy

A *conspiracy* is an agreement between two or more people to commit an unlawful act or to use unlawful means to achieve an otherwise lawful result. For example, if competing businessmen agree on a price for a product they both sell, they have conspired to violate the antitrust laws by engaging in price-fixing. In most cases, the crime is the actual agreement. Some statutes will require that some act in support of the agreement be taken before the parties commit conspiracy.

Money Laundering

Money laundering occurs when parties knowingly participate in a financial transaction which is designed to hide the origins of those funds. This often occurs with drug money and other profits made from crimes. The Money Laundering and Control Act was amended by the U.S. Patriot Act. The reach of these acts has greatly expanded in many areas. The acts are targeted at controlling bribery, money laundering, and tax evasion.

The acts also cover a broader range of accounts. Those include securities and money market accounts. Banks have additional reporting requirements and must assign one person to follow up on law enforcement information regarding suspicious activity and individuals. It is also clearer that small banks and financial institutions are not exempt from these laws as was thought. To avoid longer sentences if a violation occurs, these institutions should create training programs that teach employees how to identify suspicious customers and transactions.

Citations
The U.S. Patriot Act amends the Money Laundering and Control Act and the Bank Secrecy Act. Passed two months after 9/11, the Patriot Act expands the coverage of the laws to anyone who is involved in a wide array of financial transactions including brokers, travel agents currency exchanges, and car dealers. It also requires the reporting of cash transactions in excess of $10,000.

Bribery

Bribery occurs when an individual or business gives money, property, or any other benefit to a particular person for the purpose of influencing that person's actions and judgment in their favor. Giving a bribe is one crime. Receiving a bribe is also a crime. And if a person tries to coerce a person or entity into giving him or her a bribe, that is also a crime.

Let's say Joe's Bakery needs a building permit to expand. He's got the expansion site and contractor lined up, but City Hall is notoriously slow. Joe takes an official with the permitting office to lunch and offers a bribe in exchange for a permit and the official accepts. They have each committed a crime. However, if the official tells Joe the only way to get the permit is to first pay a bribe, only the official has committed a crime unless Joe follows the advice.

A twist on bribery is commercial bribery. It occurs when one company bribes an official at another company to give the first company business or to let that business do something for the second. Let's say Joe's Bakery is trying to obtain a lucrative contract from a chain of restaurants. If Joe promises a $1,000 gift to the restaurant's COO in exchange for the contract, that is a commercial bribe.

Racketeering

Under the Racketeer Influenced and Corrupt Organizations (RICO) Act, the original intent was to prevent organized crime from investing money obtained through racketeering activity into legitimate businesses.

Racketeering is a broadly defined crime. It consists of kidnapping, gambling, murder, arson, and much more. Because racketeering activity is defined so broadly and *treble damages* are a remedy, the law has been used against legitimate businesses in addition to organized crime. To have RICO apply, the plaintiff or prosecutor must show there is a pattern of racketeering activity. To have a pattern, at least two racketeering activities must be committed within two years.

def•i•ni•tion

Treble damages are actual damages multiplied times three.

Under RICO, a guilty defendant can be fined $25,000 and sentenced to up to 20 years in jail. Any property used in the racketeering can also be forfeited. A civil plaintiff may obtain treble damages and attorneys' fees.

Extortion and Blackmail

Extortion is the illegal demand by a public officer acting with apparent authority. *Blackmail* is a demand made by a private official. In both cases the person demanding the money demands it in exchange to either buy his action or prevent him from acting. Blackmail is usually a threat to make something public if not paid.

Counterfeiting and Forgery

Counterfeiting occurs when a person knowingly makes a document or coin that looks genuine but is not. Traditionally, this crime applies to the creation of what looks like U.S. money, but has expanded to include foreign securities and foreign bank notes.

Forgery is the crime of fraudulently making or altering an instrument that in turn creates or alters the legal liability of another. The easiest way to think of this is forging a check. By forging a check, the forger acts without authority to create a legal obligation on the part of the account holder and bank to pay money to a third party. It can also occur when the forger signs another's name with the intent to defraud a third party. Again think of a check … if the payee's name is forged, the forger obtains funds that are not his or hers while depriving the payee of rightful funds. If a forged check is sent through the stream of commerce with knowledge that it is forged and the intent to defraud, then uttering a forged instrument has occurred.

Perjury

Perjury is the crime of knowingly giving false testimony in judicial proceedings after swearing to tell the truth. This crime occurs if a witness lies on the stand. But to be prosecuted the person must first swear to tell the truth.

Obstruction of Justice and Corporate Fraud Under Sarbanes-Oxley

Under Sarbanes-Oxley, *obstruction of justice* occurs when anyone alters, destroys, conceals, covers up, falsifies, or makes a false entry with intent to impede, obstruct, or influence an investigation of a department or agency of the United States. Sarbanes-Oxley also created a new element of mail and wire fraud, broadening it from the original crime of using the mail or telephone to defraud another. Sarbanes-Oxley requires corporate officers to take extra steps when signing or certifying financial statements. If corporate officers fail to comply with the requirements for financial statement certification or certify financial statements that contain false material information, those officers have committed corporate fraud with stiff penalties and jail time.

Embezzlement

Embezzlement occurs when someone fraudulently coverts another's property or money that has been entrusted to him or her. If an employee takes property or funds for personal use that belong to his or her employer, he or she has embezzled those items. An agent, like a property manager, embezzles when he or she keeps payments from third parties that were intended for the principle.

Other White-Collar Crimes

Here are additional white-collar crimes whose titles explain the crime:

♦ Making false claims to an insurance company, government office, or relief agency

♦ Obtaining goods by false pretenses

♦ Unauthorized use of ATMs

♦ Submitting false information to banks

♦ Writing bad checks

♦ Stealing credit cards and possessing a credit card without the owner's consent

Common Law Crimes

Common law crimes are the more traditional crimes. These crimes involve the use or threat of the use of force. They also cause injuries to people or damage property.

Stay Out of Jail

Classic common law crimes that don't usually involve businesses are murder, rape, and assault. However, if an employer hires someone who they know or should have known had a violent past and that employee commits such a crime, the employer can be civilly liable to the injured parties. There may also be civil liability for violent crimes third parties commit on business premises if the business should have but failed to take security steps.

Common Law Crimes to be Aware Of

Larceny is the wrongful or fraudulent taking of the personal property of another. A common form of this that affects businesses is shoplifting. *Robbery* differs from larceny in that a robber uses force or the threat of force to take personal property from another. *Burglary* occurs when a person breaks and enters the dwelling of another at night with the intent to commit a felony. Though the word *dwelling* is used, this crime has evolved to include many businesses such as banks and warehouses. *Arson* is the willful and malicious burning of another's dwelling.

Crimes Involving Computers

What about computers? Can someone commit a crime against a computer? Using a computer? Through a computer? Yes to all of those. Crimes against the computer include the theft of hardware and software. It can also be violated when someone hacks into a computer to destroy or alter data. Taking information off a computer without authorization is also a crime. It may be stealing a trade secret, computer trespass, or taking information with intent to harm.

Other crimes include violating copyrights with the aid of the computer by circumventing encryption protections on CDs and DVDs. It is also a crime to use the electronic transfer of funds to steal or defraud another. Even spamming, sending unsolicited e-mails, is against the law.

Criminal Procedure Rights Applied to Businesses

The broad constitutional protections apply to businesses and individuals. The Fourth and Fifth Amendments provide key protections.

Fourth Amendment Rights

Under the Fourth Amendment protections, businesses have the right to be secure from unreasonable searches and seizures without a warrant. This protection is enforced by the requirement that the government obtain a search warrant before it can search or seize property if the business has a reasonable expectation of privacy. To obtain a warrant, law enforcement must show a judge that there is probable cause that to believe that evidence of the crime is at the location they want to search. Law enforcement must also list the items they are searching for. If the search is improper, any evidence obtained during the search is inadmissible.

There are several exceptions to the warrant requirement. One is that if the item or evidence is in plain view, law enforcement may seize the item. There are no privacy rights attached to something that a person or business leaves in plain view of the public. Officers may enter a building in order to give aid during an ongoing criminal act like a robbery. They can also enter if the person who lives on the property gives permission.

If law enforcement seeks to obtain business records, law enforcement must obtain a search warrant to seize those records. But what if the records are in the control of an agent such as an accountant or attorney? Attorney-client privilege applies to documents an attorney has and their notes of conversations with a client. Where the privilege exists, then the records cannot be seized—even if law enforcement obtains a warrant.

> **Citations**
>
> Some states recognize privileges in addition to the attorney-client privilege. Those can include an accountant privilege, as well as priest and parishioner or doctor and patient.

Fifth Amendment Protections

The Fifth Amendment provides constitutional protection against self-incrimination and guarantees due process. It's not uncommon to hear people who are called in criminal cases to take the Fifth. That means if forced to testify the individual could incriminate themselves of committing a crime. The Fifth Amendment specifically provides individuals protection against forcing them to testify against themselves. They can choose to take the stand in their defense and may end up testifying against themselves under skillful cross-examination, but the government cannot force someone into that position.

The Fifth Amendment due-process protections require that individuals be given certain warnings when in a custodial interrogation. The Miranda warning informs people in police custody or in an interrogation that they have a right to remain silent, anything they say can and will be used against them in a court of law, they are entitled to counsel, and if they can't afford counsel one will be appointed for them. If law enforcement fails to give this warning, any statements made after the warning should have been given are inadmissible. In addition, any evidence acquired because of the invalid confession or testimony is fruit of the poisonous tree and will not be allowed in at trial either. This is a mechanism designed to deter law enforcement from violating rights with unreasonable searches and seizures.

Finally, the Fifth Amendment due-process rights of an individual must be extended to businesses as well. Those include the rights to be heard, question witnesses, and present evidence. They also include a preliminary hearing or grand jury, arraignment, discovery, and all other steps that lead up to trial as well as full trial rights.

The Least You Need to Know

- All crimes require *mens rea*, the intent to commit the crime, and *actus reus*, the actual physical act of the crime.

- Businesses can participate in and commit crimes just as individuals do.

- Companies that commit crimes are often fined while key officers and employees involved in the crime face penalties and jail time. Sarbanes-Oxley stiffened and enhanced many of the penalties and jail time individuals face.

- Common law crimes have evolved and include crimes like robbery, burglary, and arson.

- The Fourth Amendment's search and seizure requirements and the Fifth Amendment's due process protections extend to businesses and individuals.

Chapter 25

Torts

In This Chapter

- ◆ Understanding the elements of negligence
- ◆ Types of intentional torts
- ◆ Requirements of strict liability
- ◆ Burdens of products liability
- ◆ Defining express warranties
- ◆ Expounding on implied warranties

Torts are a broad and ancient section of the law that allows individuals or entities that are harmed by another to recover damages for that wrong. This harm can occur because of an intentional act or an accident. However, it is not a crime, though sometimes a wrong can be tried as both a crime and a tort. O. J. Simpson is a good example. The state of California failed to prove he murdered his ex-wife and her boyfriend. However, the families prevailed in a civil tort action. You'll see the differences as we dive into this chapter. We'll start with negligence and then turn to intentional torts.

Determining Negligence

At its core, torts are about determining if someone has been *negligent* in their actions, and if that negligence caused harm to someone else. To prove negligence, the plaintiff must show that four conditions existed:

◆ The defendant had to have a *duty*, or legal obligation, to act in a certain way.

◆ The defendant had to *breach* that duty, or fail to fulfill his legal obligation.

◆ That breach had to be the *actual and proximate cause* of the plaintiff's injury—the immediate reason damage was caused, can be acting or failing to act.

◆ The plaintiff must have incurred *damage*, or harm, to his property or person.

def•i•ni•tion

Negligence is the failure to exercise the care a reasonable or prudent person would toward another.

Duty

Duty is the broad concept that someone owes an obligation to another. The duty can be to act or refrain from acting in a certain manner. The standard is that when a person acts they are under a legal duty to act as an ordinary, prudent, reasonable person. This standard presumes that reasonable people act with caution. For example, when you get in your car, the standard is that as a reasonable person, you will follow the rules of the road. Deviating from those rules by running a red light is not reasonable. And if someone is injured because of that deviation, you have broken your duty to them.

However, there is no duty to take precautions against events you can't reasonably foresee and anticipate. So if your car is pushed into the intersection by another car, you probably wouldn't have a duty.

Stay Out of Jail

Most states recognize a duty that extends to unborn children who are viable at the time of injury. That means a duty of care is owed to these children. Some states also allow a wrongful death action.

Duty of care is owed to foreseeable third parties. But what if an unforeseeable person is injured? This situation arises when the duty is breached to someone the defendant could anticipate but also injures another in the process. Let's say Bob drives a car that crashes into Sam's vehicle, injuring Sam. Sam is a foreseeable party. But what if in the collision Sam's car is pushed onto a sidewalk, injuring a pedestrian, Tara? Tara is an unforeseeable party. Under the majority view, Tara would have to show that a reasonable person would have seen the risk of injury to her because she was in the zone of danger.

The reasonable standard of care is an objective standard. Under it the reasonable person is thought to have the same physical characteristics as the defendant, an average mental ability, and the same knowledge as an average member of the community.

Duty in Specialized Settings

If the defendant is a professional, he or she will be required to exercise the knowledge and skill of the reasonable person in the profession or occupation. For example, a doctor is to give enough information to a patient about the risks of a procedure for the patient to make informed consent. Failure to provide that information is a breach of duty. Children are usually held to the standard of care of children of like age, education, intelligence, and experience used in a subjective manner. However, if a child engages in traditionally adult activities, the child will be held to the same standard of care as an adult. Common carriers and innkeepers must exercise a high standard of care toward their guests and are liable for slight negligence.

What about emergency situations? If an emergency arises, the defendant must act as a reasonable person would in the same situation. However, if the emergency is the defendant's creation, the emergency standard will not be used.

There are separate standards for owners and occupiers of land. Generally, a landowner owes no duty to someone who is not on their land for natural or artificial conditions *unless* the condition is unreasonably dangerous or the person is a passerby. For example, if the homeowner allows water to run from his house to the sidewalk, which then freezes into ice, that is an unreasonably dangerous condition. Or if icicles begin to fall from his building onto the sidewalk, he must warn passersby of the hazard, put up a barrier, etc., to alert and protect the passersby.

What about a trespasser? Trespassers are on the property but without permission. If the owner doesn't know about the trespasser, he owed no duty. If he is aware of the trespasser, he has a duty to warn about the danger or correct artificial conditions that could cause serious bodily injury or death.

The owner has a duty to disclose dangerous conditions to a licensee if the owner knew or should have known about the danger. However, this does not translate into a duty to inspect for defects or repair known defects. The duty is merely to warn of the danger.

If an invitee is involved, the owner has a duty to use reasonable and ordinary care to keep the property reasonably safe. This includes the duty owed to licensees *plus* a duty to inspect the premises and repair any dangerous spots found.

See Chapter 19 for more on property law and attractive nuisance.

Affirmative Duty to Act

The general rule is that there is no affirmative duty to act. If someone begins acting, though, they have a duty to continue acting. The reason is that by starting someone else may decide not to act. Claudia is injured when her car hits a tree. Bob races to the car to assist her. Doug and Joan stay behind; since Bob seems to have things under control they see no need to get involved. Then he leaves, and Claudia is further injured by the delay in getting assistance. Bob is liable—not because he originally had a duty to help Claudia, but because by beginning to act, he discouraged others who were willing from helping.

If the danger arises because of the acts of another, that person has a duty to help those that are harmed.

Breach of That Duty

The second element in negligence requires that if a duty exists, the defendant must breach that duty. In its simplest form that means the defendant fails to do something he or she should do. The law says you must stop at red lights, but you fail to do that and cause an accident. You have breached a duty and satisfied the second prong of negligence.

To prove breach, the plaintiff must show what actually happened, and then that the defendant acted unreasonably. The court may consider custom or usage to help determine what is reasonable. It also will consider whether the defendant violated a statute.

Res ipsa loquitur is the Latin phrase for the thing speaks for itself. In practice, it means one is presumed negligent if the injury was caused by something he or she controlled even if there is not specific evidence linking the defendant to the harm other than without that there would be no injury. The plaintiff must show that accident wouldn't normally occur without negligence. An example of *res ipsa loquitur* is if a pane of glass falls from a second story and strikes someone on the sidewalk below. The injury speaks for itself—there would be no injury without someone being negligent in handling the glass.

Even with the *res ipsa loquitur* doctrine, foreseeability of the harm remains a key concept. The classic example here comes from an old case in which a woman was injured at a train depot. Two employees helped a man onto the train. He carried a package of fireworks that got dropped at one end of a train depot causing a scale to drop at the other end, injuring the woman in the process. The person carrying the fireworks knew they were potentially dangerous and did not properly handle them. The woman sued the train company, alleging her injuries were a result of the employees' negligence. The appellate court found the causal link to the harm to be tenuous and unforeseeable.

Causation

In its simplest form, causation means that the harm the plaintiff suffered is a direct result of the defendant's breach of duty. For example, if Tara is injured because Sam runs into her after Bob's vehicle collides with his, Tara has hospital bills. She may also have lost wages. Those damages would not have occurred but for Bob's breach of duty, so his breach is the cause of the damages.

The injury must in fact be caused by the defendant. The courts use a *but for* test, which requires that the injury would not have occurred but for the acts of the defendant. If there are several causes of the injury, the *but for* test applies. The court will ask would the injury have occurred but for the multiple actions. If the *but for* test would lead to no liability, the court may use a substantial factor test. For example, if two fires burn and converge on one home and destroy it, under the *but for* test neither fire caused the fire because the home would have still been destroyed by the other. Thus, no one is liable for the harm. The law doesn't like that, so the substantial factor test comes into play. Now the court will ask if either fire was a substantial factor in the destruction. Since they were, whoever set the fires is liable.

Another form of causation is *proximate cause*. Under proximate cause, also known as legal causation, the injury must actually be caused or tied to the defendant's negligence. Generally, the defendant is liable for all injuries that flow out of his acts as a normal incident or increased risk of that action. Direct cause comes if there is no interruption in the chain from the event to the injury. Think about the speeding car that hits a pedestrian. Nothing occurs in between the negligence and the injury.

Sometimes the defendant's action is interrupted by another action that adds to the injury. These indirect or intervening causes can limit the defendant's liability if the defendant shows that he or she did not actually cause the harm.

Citations

Defendants retain liability if the intervening cause would not happen *but for* the defendant's negligence; for example, medical malpractice that wouldn't have occurred but for the defendant's initial injury to the plaintiff. The negligence of rescuers is also foreseeable. However, the defendant is not liable for independent intervening forces. This includes things like the negligent acts of third parties, the criminal acts and intentional torts of third parties, and acts of God.

Damages

Damages are the final element of negligence and can take several forms. Damages can be monetary damage like Tara's lost wages and hospital bills. They can be loss of property or pain and suffering. They can take the form of punitive damages to punish the defendant for its wrong acts.

Monetary damages for breach fall into several categories. Compensatory damages will compensate the injured party for the injuries from the result of the breach. The goal is to place the injured party in the position they would have been in if the contract had been honored by the breaching party. So the party can seek compensation for past and future pain and suffering, past and future physical impairment, past and future medical care, and past and future loss of earning potential. Punitive damages are used by a court to punish the breaching party for its bad acts that are wanton and willful.

Defendants need to be aware when they are in partnership with others of the type of damages they share with partners. Joint liability arises when two or more people share liability for a debt. The plaintiff can sue both or one, and a defendant can demand that any person who shares joint liability is brought into the lawsuit. Joint and several liability occurs when each debtor or defendant is responsible for the entire debt or amount awarded. The defendant partner can seek contribution when he or she is sued on a debt or judgment that has joint and several liability. The defendant who pays more than his share can demand contribution from the other liable parties. For more on this see Chapter 9.

The plaintiff must take steps to mitigate the damages he or she incurs. Thus, it is in the best interests of the plaintiff to be evaluated by a doctor and start treatment as soon as possible. Failure to do that could make the injury worse than it otherwise would be, and is a failure to mitigate the ongoing damages.

Consultation

In general, plaintiffs are not able to recover for attorneys' fees they incur during the lawsuit. That is why most personal injury cases are taken on a contingent fee basis. The attorney assumes the risk of the plaintiff losing and not being paid or of the plaintiff winning and getting paid a percentage of the awarded amount.

The Defenses

Defendants can raise defenses to their alleged liability. The primary defenses are contributory negligence, comparative negligence, and assumption of risk.

Contributory negligence is a harsh remedy that states if a person was injured in part due to their own negligence, the injured party would not be entitled to collect any damages from the defendant. Under it, if a jury found a plaintiff 10 percent liable and the defendant 90 percent liable, the plaintiff recovers nothing for his or her injuries. It becomes a complete bar to recovery. The defendant must prove the four elements of negligence and that the plaintiff failed to uphold his or her duty to exercise reasonable care.

As a reaction to the harsh results of contributory negligence, many states have adopted *comparative negligence.* Comparative negligence determines the negligence of each party involved in the accident. Let's say a passenger is injured in a car accident. The jury decides that the driver of the other car was 60 percent responsible, but because the plaintiff didn't wear his seatbelt he was 40 percent negligent. Any award has the plaintiff's percentage of fault subtracted from the total award. So if the jury awards $100,000, the plaintiff only receives $60,000.

Assumption of risk can include a written assumption. When you sign up to go bungee jumping you sign a document that says you assume the risk involved in making the jump. By signing that you acknowledge the risk inherent in the activity and release the defendant company from prospective liability for any injuries you sustain as a result of bungee jumping. Implied assumption of risk is more nebulous but occurs if the plaintiff is aware of the risk but accepts the risk prior to the defendant's negligence. However, nothing is in writing.

Citations

Governments are often immune from tort liability. The Federal Tort Claim Act and similar state statutes set the parameters for an individual to sue a government entity for tort. If the statute isn't followed, any right to sue is waived. And if the statute doesn't allow for the suit, the government generally can't be sued for a tort.

Intentional Torts

Intentional torts are civil wrongs that result from the intentional acts of the defendant. The following are intentional torts:

- **Assault.** Intentional conduct that threatens a person creating a well-founded fear of imminent harm coupled with the ability to carry out that threat of harm.

- **Battery.** Intentional, wrongful touching of another without their consent.

- **False imprisonment.** Intentional detention of another without their consent. There is no period of time that is required for false imprisonment. This often arises when shopkeeper's unreasonably detain someone while trying to prove shoplifting.

- **Intentional infliction of emotional distress.** Involves conduct that goes beyond the bounds of decency and causes mental anguish. For example, outrageous collection practices can lead to the intentional infliction of emotional distress if the collection agency continued to call after knowing the plaintiff was recovering from serious surgery.

- **Invasion of privacy.** Consists of three separate torts: 1) intrusion into the plaintiff's private affairs, 2) public disclosure of private facts, and 3) misappropriation of another's name or likeness for commercial gain. The right of publicity is designed to protect celebrities and allow them to profit from their name, image, and likeness.

- **Defamation.** The untrue statements one makes about the plaintiff to a third party. Slander occurs when the defamation is spoken. Libel occurs when the defamation is in writing. In either case, defamation requires a statement about a person's reputation, honesty, or integrity that is untrue; publication of that statement (can be hearing); a statement that is directed at a particular person; and damages from that statement. A defense to defamation is the truth.

- **Product disparagement.** Also called trade libel, product disparagement occurs when someone makes false statements about another business, its products, or its abilities. The first element is the same as defamation with communication of that false statement to a third party and damages.

- **Wrongful interference with a contract.** An intentional tort that arises when parties are not allowed to freely contract by the interference of a third party.

◆ **Trespass.** The unauthorized action with regard to land or property. If land is involved, it's the unauthorized entry on, below, across, or above someone else's land. If property is involved, it is the invasion of the personal property without the owner's permission.

Strict Liability

Strict liability creates an absolute standard of liability that is imposed by statute or courts. If strict liability exists, the defendant will be liable because few if any defenses are available to the defendant. Usually strict liability is enforced when the activity is ultra-hazardous, such as using dynamite to demolish a building. Strict liability is created by statute or product liability. If a product is defective in its design, instructions, or manufacture, the manufacturer is strictly liable to the plaintiff for the injury.

Products Liability

Products liability encompasses the liability of suppliers for the injuries sustained by others because of its products. Another way to look at it is that manufacturers, distributors, and sellers of products have a responsibility to deliver those products free of defects which harm others. Product recalls occur because of this responsibility to provide products that are free from harmful defects.

In this area, a plaintiff has five basic theories he or she can use to recover damages. The first is negligence. This contains the same elements I discussed earlier in the chapter. The plaintiff must show a duty existed, that duty was breached, and the breach caused the damages. Then there's fraud, which requires intent on the part of the manufacturer to make statements they know are false or make them with reckless disregard for whether the statements are true. The plaintiff may also be able to rely on strict liability. We'll spend the rest of this chapter examining the last two options: implied warranties of merchantability and fitness for a particular purpose and express warranties.

Before we get to warranties, though, let's look at defects. A prerequisite to proving product liability is that there is a defect. Manufacturing defects are created when through the manufacturing process a product is made that is more dangerous than it should otherwise be. The question will be whether the product was dangerous beyond the expectation of the ordinary consumer. Design defects arise when a product from its design is dangerous because of mechanical features or packaging. With design defects the question is whether the plaintiff can show a less dangerous modification or alternative was economically feasible.

The problem with defects arises when the plaintiff misused the product. There can also be scientifically unknowable risks that the manufacturer doesn't know about ahead of time. This often happens with new drugs where side effects are unknown ahead of time. Allergies can also be unknown risks to plaintiffs but if the manufacturer can anticipate the allergic reaction, it should post a warning.

Express Warranties

An express warranty is usually a written statement about the quality of the merchandise, but it can include oral communication. The key is that the statement must also be a basis of the bargain. These statements must address the quality, capacity, or other characteristics of the good. An express warranty can be made without using the words "warrant" or "guarantee." Because express warranties grow out of communication, the seller can warrant anything.

Seller's Opinion or Statement of Value

An important exception to express warranties is that a seller can give his opinion or make a statement of the value of the product. This sales talk is part of the process and a buyer is on notice that these statements are merely an opinion. The exception arises if a reasonable person would rely on the sales statements.

Warranty of Conformity to Description, Sample, or Model

The Uniform Commercial Code (UCC) creates express warranties in certain circumstances. Express warranties arises when the seller tells the buyer that the goods conform to any affirmation or promise of fact the seller made to the buyer about the goods. The seller also warrants that the factual description of the goods conform to the actual goods shown. The goods must also conform to any models or samples shown to the buyer before making the purchase.

Implied Warranties

Implied warranties are those that arise when the seller warrants the product will work the way it is supposed to work. Implied warranties exist unless they are expressly excluded. In contrast to negligence, if an implied warranty is involved, the plaintiff does not need to show fault, just that the implied warranty was violated.

Implied Warranty of Merchantability

This warranty applies to merchants and implies that the goods sold are of the same quality generally acceptable among those who sell like goods. It also warrants that the goods are generally fit for the ordinary purposes for which such goods are used.

Implied Warranties in Particular Sales

There is also an implied warranty that goods are fit for a particular purpose that applies to merchants. This warranty is created when the seller tells the buyer the product will fill the buyer's particular need. To exist, the seller must or should know the specific purpose for which the goods are required and that the buyer is relying on the seller's skill or judgment to select or furnish suitable goods.

Additional Implied Warranties

A couple more implied warranties you should be aware of are the warranty of title and the warranty against encumbrances. With the warranty of title, the seller warrants that the title to the goods is good and the seller has the right to transfer the title. The warranty against encumbrances requires the seller to warrant that it can transfer title free of mortgages, security interests, and any other lien or encumbrance.

The Least You Need to Know

- Negligence occurs when a duty exists that is breached by a person if the breach causes the damages suffered by the plaintiff.

- Intentional torts occur when someone chooses to infringe on another's person or property. Intentional torts include assault, battery, and infliction of emotional distress.

- Strict liability arises if the defendant's action is one that is ultra-hazardous.

- Products liability is a type of tort that encompasses the liability of suppliers for the injuries sustained by others because of its products.

- Express and implied warranties protect consumers from defects in products.

Appendix A

Glossary

acceptance   Unqualified assent by the grantee to accept the delivery of the deed; receiving something from another with intent to keep it.

acceptor   With negotiable instruments, drawee becomes this when he or she indicates a willingness to pay the draft.

accommodation party   Party who has no original duty under the note but signs to guarantee payment.

acquisition   A larger company taking over a smaller one.

agency   Relationship between a principal (the person or firm that utilizes an agent) and an agent (the person or firm authorized to act on behalf of the principal with third parties).

agency by appointment   Principal expressly authorizes the agent to act in a specific manner for the principal.

agency by conduct   Develops when a third party is led to believe the agent has authority to act based on the actions of the principal.

agency by ratification   Principal can ratify the unauthorized actions of its agent and honor or deny the contract.

agent   Person or firm authorized by a principal or by law to make contracts with third parties on behalf of the principal.

alternate payee   Multiple individuals or entities that are listed on an instrument as payees; the instrument can be paid to any one of them; usually signaled by the use of "or."

apparent authority   The authority an agent has when the principal's act or words lead a third party to believe that the authority exists.

appeal   Review of a specific case to determine whether it was correctly decided by a lower court.

appellate jurisdiction   The power select courts have to hear appeals from other courts or administrative agencies.

arson   The willful and malicious burning of another's dwelling, which includes homes and business locations.

attractive nuisance doctrine   Imposes liability on the landowner for injuries sustained by small children playing on the land when the landowner permitted the condition that reasonable people would know attracts children.

authority   The permission to act on behalf of a partnership or employer.

bailee   The one who accepts possession of personal property without becoming the owner of the property.

bailment   Relationship that exists between owner of personal property who delivers possession of those goods to another without transferring ownership.

bailor   The owner who delivers personal property to another for purposes of a bailment.

blackmail   An illegal demand made by a private official.

Blanchard and Peale Three Part Test   Test that allows companies and individuals to gauge the most ethical decision: Is the proposed action legal? Is the action balanced? How does the action make me feel?

blank indorsement   Order paper transferred to another with an indorsement alone.

breach   Failure to perform or act as called for by the terms of the contract.

bribery   Individual or business gives money, property, or any other benefit to a particular person for the purpose of influencing that person's actions and judgment in their favor.

burglary   Breaking and entering the dwelling of another at night with the intent to commit a felony.

business ethics Subset of ethics that focuses on the goal of balancing profits with the values of society and individuals.

business stakeholder theory of ethics Examines situations from the viewpoint of a company's constituencies.

case law Law expressed in the published opinions of courts.

causation The third element of negligence that requires the breach of duty to actually cause harm to the injured party.

certificates of deposit Bank's promises to pay a set sum of deposited money back to the customer with interest when the customer surrenders the document.

choice-of-law provision Contract clause that sets which law will apply should a dispute develop.

claim As applied to patents, claims establish the technical boundaries of the patent by describing the patent in technical terms.

close corporation Held by a single or small group of shareholders; shares not traded on a public exchange.

commercial impracticability Under this theory a contract may be discharged because fulfilling the contract is unreasonable and carries an excessive cost.

common carrier Individual or organization that transports goods and is available to the general public for the purpose of shipping at a cost.

common law The body of unwritten principles that were recognized and enforced by the courts.

compensatory damages Damages designed to compensate the injured party for the injuries from the result of the breach.

concurrent condition Conditions to a contract that each party must perform simultaneously.

condition A stipulation or prerequisite in a contract, will, or other legal document.

condition precedent A condition that must occur before something else can occur.

condition subsequent A condition that, if it occurs, will terminate a contract.

conglomerate Subsidiary companies that are not engaged in the core business of the parent.

consequential damages Those not necessarily anticipated before the breach but flow from special circumstances of the injured party.

consolidation Two companies come together and a third company is born; the original companies cease to exist and a new company is created with the assets and property of the original companies.

conspiracy An agreement between two or more people to commit an unlawful act or to use unlawful means to achieve an otherwise lawful result.

construction eviction By an act or omission, the landlord substantially deprives the tenant of the use and enjoyment of the premises.

contract An agreement 1) between two or more parties 2) an offer to perform with 3) an acceptance of that offer. There must also be 4) a set time period, 5) terms for performance, and 6) valuable consideration exchanged for that performance.

contract carrier Individual or organization that transports goods and is available to those that contract with it.

contribution Requires that when one person is sued on a debt or judgment that has joint and several liability, the individual who pays more than his share can demand the other liable parties to pay him their portion of the judgment.

cooperatives Two or more people or entities come together to act through one agent for a specific purpose.

copyright The exclusive right under federal statute to the creator of a literary or artistic work to use, reproduce, or display the work.

corporation An artificial person created by the government to carry on business or other activities; it is its own legal entity separate and distinct from the people who created and invest in the company.

corporation by estoppel Arises if third parties thought the business was a corporation that would profit if the third party was allowed to deny the existence of a corporation.

corporation de jure Incorporation steps are properly followed, and corporation created by operation of law.

counterfeiting Knowingly making a document or coin that looks genuine but is not.

courts Government tribunals or bodies that hear and decide disputes and other matters brought before them.

covenant against encumbrances   Guarantee the land is not subject to the rights or interests of third parties—liens, easements, etc.

covenant of further assurances   The grantor will execute any additional documents that are needed to complete the conveyance.

covenant of quiet enjoyment   The grantee's possession of the land will not be disturbed by the grantor or anybody else claiming title to the property.

covenant of right to convey   The grantor has the right or authority to make the conveyance (this comes into play when a third party is the owner).

covenant of seisin   Guarantee that the grantor owns the property he or she conveys.

customary authority   The authority to do anything that is customary in the community to complete the authorized act.

damages   The fourth element of negligence, which requires the breach of duty to cause actual monetary or other harm.

de facto corporation   A defect in the incorporation is so substantial it cannot be ignored, but the actions of the company or board of directors are such that the corporation will be treated as if it did in fact exist.

deed   The instrument or writing by which the owner transfers an interest in land to a new owner.

deliver   Actual handing of an object to another with intent to convey the deed to that person or entity.

delivery in escrow   Deed is delivered to a third party to be held in trust until the grantor and grantee have complied with the terms of the contract.

design patent   Granted when a new, original, and ornamental design for a manufactured item is developed; good for 14 years.

detrimental reliance   A substitute for consideration that arises when one party relies on the acts or representations of another party to the first party's detriment.

dilution   The lessening of the capacity of a famous mark to identify and distinguish goods or services, regardless of the presence or absence of 1) competition between the owner of the famous mark and other parties, or 2) likelihood of confusion, mistake, or deception.

disparate impact   An employer has a facially neutral policy, but the application of that policy results in discrimination against an employee or a class of employees.

disparate treatment   An employer treats a class of people differently because of their race, color, religion, sex, or national origin.

dissolution   Partnership ceases to exist as a going concern, either by agreement of the partners that they no longer wish to conduct business together or by operation of law.

distribution franchise   Allows the franchisor to sell its products through the franchisees.

dominant tenement   The property right of the easement holder, benefited by the easement; dominant over the right of the property holder.

dormant partners   Partners who have no active role in the partnership and are unknown to the public as partners.

draft   One party's order to another to pay a sum of money to a third party.

drawee   Party who is to pay on the draft or note.

drawer   Party who writes or creates the draft or check.

due process   Principle of fairness under the law; legal procedures must be applied equally to avoid prejudicial or unequal treatment under the law.

duty   The second element of damages, which requires the person who allegedly caused the harm to have an actual responsibility to the injured person.

easement   The right to use somebody else's real property for a specific purpose.

easement by implication   An easement not specifically created by deed, but from the circumstances of the parties and land access and location.

easement in gross   Personal right to use another's land and is not dependent on owning the dominant tenement.

embezzlement   One fraudulently coverts another's property or money that has been entrusted to him or her.

en banc   Full panel of the judges from the Court of Appeals hears the case.

ethics   A system of moral principles that govern individual's actions; the search for right and wrong; provides a framework for making decisions in all contexts.

ethics from the law   Ethical framework that draws moral standards from codified law; the test of whether an action is justified is whether it is legal.

express authority   The authority to take an action because the partnership agreement gives the authority to a partner or because the partners have voted to delegate that authority.

extortion   The illegal demand by a public officer acting with apparent authority.

fee simple estate   The owner takes the title to the real property clear and free of any other ownership claims.

fixture   Personal property that becomes so attached to the real property that it cannot be separated from the real property without causing harm to the building or land.

forbearance   One party to a contract gives up the right to do something they have a legal right to do.

foreign corporation   Incorporated in one state but also operate inside a different state.

forgery   Fraudulently making or altering an instrument that in turn creates or alters the legal liability of another.

franchise   An arrangement in which the owner of a trademark, trade name, or copyright licenses others, under specified conditions or limitations, to use the trademark, trade name, or copyright in purveying goods or services.

franchisee   Purchases the right to use the franchised product, idea, etc.; party receiving the franchise.

franchiser   Owner of the franchised product, idea, etc.; party granting the franchise.

free enterprise   A system where business is regulated by supply and demand rather than government interference through regulations and subsidies.

Freedom of Information Act   Ensures the public access to public records. If a citizen requests records in writing, the federal agency must provide those records unless the request falls within one of nine exemptions.

front-page-of-the-newspaper test   An ethical test which asks the following question when someone is trying to reach an ethical decision: is the result of this decision something I want to read about on the front page of *The New York Times*, *The Wall Street Journal*, or *USA Today?*

future interest   A right in real property to receive that property at some point in the future.

general agent   Given authority to transact any kind of business that can be lawfully delegated.

general jurisdiction   The court can hear most disputes brought before it.

general partner   Visible to the public and active in management of the partnership; must always be at least one in a general partnership or limited partnership.

goodwill   The value of a business beyond the tangible assets; can include items like reputation, strong customer base, desirable location, and name.

holder   Person possessing an instrument that is 1) payable to that person, 2) indorsed to that person, or 3) is bearer paper.

holder in due course   Holder who takes the note for value, in good faith, and without notice and receives additional warranty protection as a result.

incidental authority   Authority to perform any reasonable act necessary to execute the agent's express authority.

incidental damages   Extra expenses the injured party paid as a consequence of the breach or to mitigate damages.

indemnification   The act of making someone "whole" or protected from losses.

independent contractor   A person or business who works for another according to the terms of a contract; not given specific instructions and guidelines on how to complete that job.

integrated industry   Subsidiary companies that are related to the parent company's business; for example, a newspaper company may own subsidiaries that deal in paper and ink.

intellectual property   Creations of the mind that include music, the arts, inventions, and designs.

intentional torts   Civil wrongs that result from the intentional acts of a party.

joint and several liability   Each debtor or defendant is responsible for the entire debt or amount awarded.

joint liability   Two or more people are liable for a debt; the plaintiff can sue both and a defendant can demand that any person who shares joint liability is brought into the lawsuit.

joint venture   Exists when two or more persons or entities combine their labor or property for the purpose of a single business undertaking.

jurisdiction   The power, right, or authority of the court to hear and determine or apply the law.

landlord   Owner of real property who leases it to another.

larceny   The wrongful or fraudulent taking of the personal property of another.

lease   An agreement between the landlord and tenant that sets the terms for the use of the property.

legislative power   As to agencies, the power to make laws by promulgating regulations with public input.

license   A personal and revocable privilege to perform an act on the land of another.

liens   A claim or right against real property that arise in many situations.

life estate   Gives the holder the right to use or occupy the land for the holder's life.

limited liability   Liability limited to the investment in the firm or partnership of the member or innocent partner.

limited liability company (LLC)   Business form that combines the pass-through taxation with the limited liability protection of a corporation.

limited liability partnership (LLP)   Partnership that maintains the pass-through taxation of partnerships, but provides limited liability to innocent partners; developed as a response to the success of limited liability companies.

limited partners   Partners who do not participate in the management of the partnership and do not appear to the public as general partners, and because of that, do not have personal liability for the acts of the partnership or other partners beyond their investment in the partnership.

limited partnership   Partnership that shields some partners from liability. To accomplish this, those partners desiring limited liability contribute capital to the endeavor but do not participate in the management of the firm.

liquidated damages   Contracted for damages that take effect if the contract is breached; usually related to delays in performance or if damages are too difficult to determine without an agreement.

mailbox rule   Acceptance of a contract is effective when put in the mailbox unless the offer states acceptance is only effective when received or an options contract is involved.

maker   Signs the note and is responsible for payment.

manufacturing or processing franchise   Grants the franchisee the right to make and sell the products of the franchisor under its trademark.

meeting of the minds   Key contract term that exists when two parties to a contract have the same understanding of the terms of the contract.

members   Owners of LLC who have an ownership interest in proportion to their capital contribution and the operating agreement or articles of organization.

merger   Two companies combine when one offers its stock or cash to the shareholders of the other company.

money laundering   Parties knowingly participate in a financial transaction which is designed to hide the origins of those funds.

most-favored-nation clause   Any privilege granted to a third country after two parties have contracted on the same subject matter is extended to the other party to the treaty.

mutual mistake   Each party to a contract misunderstands the other party's intent about a material term.

natural law   Standards of conduct derived from traditional moral principles and/or God's law and will.

negligence   The failure to exercise the care a reasonable or prudent person would toward another.

negotiable   Note or other paper becomes negotiable when it is 1) evidenced by a record, 2) signed 3) by the maker or drawer, 4) pay a sum certain, 5) payable in money, 6) payable on demand or at a specific time, and 7) payable to order or bearer.

nominal damages   Token damages awarded for breach that results in no actual loss.

nominal partners   Represented to the public as partners because of something they add to the partnership, usually status or goodwill.

nonprofit corporation   Formed for purpose other than making a profit.

obligee   The recipient of the obligor's promise to perform.

obligor   The promisor is called this when the promise is binding with an obligation to perform.

obstruction of justice   Occurs when anyone alters, destroys, conceals, covers up, falsifies, or makes a false entry with intent to impede, obstruct, or influence an investigation.

operating agreement   LLC's equivalent to a corporation's bylaws.

original jurisdiction   Authority to hear a case when it is brought before the court.

parol evidence rule   Principal of contract law that evidence cannot be admitted in court if it would add to, vary, or contradict a written contract.

partially disclosed principal   The agent tells the third party there is a principal, but does not reveal the principal's identity.

partnership   Two or more persons or entities that pool resources and talent with the purpose of making a profit; exists without approval of the state.

patent   Provide inventors the exclusive right to use their creation for a limited period of time.

payee   Named person on the note or check to receive payment.

periodic tenancy   Exists when a lease has an indefinite duration, but rent is paid annually, monthly, or weekly.

perjury   Knowingly giving false testimony in judicial proceedings after swearing to tell the truth.

personal jurisdiction   Gives the court authority to bring the parties into court and hear the complaint against them.

personal property   Includes things other than real property such as cars, clothing, and appliances; also includes intangibles such as negotiable instruments, patents, and trademarks.

plant patent   Granted when a distinct and new variety of plant is invented or discovered and asexually reproduced; lasts 20 years from date of filing.

precedent   A court decision that becomes the law for a particular problem in the future.

prescriptive easement   Easement upon another's real property acquired by open, notorious, continuous, and hostile and adverse use without the owner's permission, for a period of 20 years or that mandated by statute.

price-fixing   Any agreement to charge an agreed upon price or set maximum or minimum prices.

principal   Person or firm who employs an agent.

private carrier   Individual or organization that transports goods for its owner.

private corporation   Corporation organized for charitable purposes or for business purposes.

private law   The rules and regulations parties agree to in their contracts.

privity of contract   Requirement that there be a connection between parties to a contract in order to enforce the terms of the contract.

procedural due process   Applies to the criminal setting and limits the exercise of power by state and federal governments; has an individual been deprived of life, liberty, or property and what process should be given to that individual.

procedural law   Sets the rules that must be followed to enforce rights and liabilities; deals with the procedure of the legal environment.

professional corporation   Organized so members can practice a profession like law and medicine.

profit   The right to take part of the soil or produce of another's land.

promisee   The person who benefits from the promisor's promise.

promisor   The person who makes the promise in the contract context.

promissory notes   Written promises to pay a sum certain to the holder.

promoter   Person who creates a corporation including the financing; usually the principal shareholder or member of the management team.

public authorities   Companies owned by the government to provide services.

public corporation   Government entities like cities and counties that are created to perform a governmental function.

puffing   A nonspecific, unmeasurable statement about a product; cannot be reasonably interpreted as providing a benchmark by which the veracity of the statement can be ascertained.

punitive damages   Used by a court to punish or make an example of the breaching party for its bad acts.

qualified indorsement   Places a limit or disclaimer on the liability of the indorser to the maker or drawee.

quasi-public corporation   Carries out a government mandate, but may have private investors; regardless of who owns stock, the corporation must carry out its government-directed duties.

quid pro quo   Latin term meaning something for something. Usually used to refer to the fact that one party gives something to the other party, expecting something in return.

racketeering activity   A broad crime that includes kidnapping, gambling, murder, arson, and much more.

real property   Land, the air above it, and the minerals below it extending to the core of the earth.

repudiation   A party to a contract indicates by words or deeds that it has no intention of performing the contract. Anticipatory repudiation means that a party who has an obligation to perform under a contract repudiates before the time of performance, giving the injured party the right to damages for total breach as well as discharging any remaining duty to perform that injured party has.

res ipsa loquitur   Latin phrase for the thing speaks for itself; one is presumed negligent if injury is caused by something he or she controlled even if there is no specific evidence linking the defendant to the harm.

reservation of rights   The assertion by a party that it is not waiving its right to damages for potential nonconformity even though it accepted performance that does not comply with the terms of the contract.

respondeat superior   Principal or employer is vicariously liable for the unauthorized tort of an agent or employee while acting within the scope of the agency or employment.

restrictive indorsement   Used to limit or restrict the way the instrument is transferred; "for deposit only."

reversible error   An error or defect made by a court of original jurisdiction that is so serious it will be set aside.

risk of loss   Determines when the buyer or seller become responsible for goods that are damaged or destroyed en route between the two.

robbery   Using force or the threat of force to take personal property from another.

sale of goods   The sale of personal property as defined in the Uniform Commercial Code Article 2.

secret partners   Partners who may be active in the partnership, but hidden to the public as partners.

securities   Shares of stock, bonds, and debentures issued by corporations and governments as evidence of ownership and terms of payment of dividends or final pay-off.

service franchise   Allows the franchisee to provide a service under the terms of a franchise agreement.

service mark   Identifies and distinguishes the source of a service; similar to a trademark.

silent partners   Not active participants in the partnership on a day-to-day basis; usually add something like money to the partnership and may be known to or hidden from the public.

situational business ethics   Individuals examine the underlying situation and make decisions based on those facts; also known as moral relativism.

sole proprietorship   An individual provides goods or services to others without taking steps to form a corporate entity or partnership.

special agent   Authorized to handle a specific project or transaction only.

special indorsement   Indorsement that contains language detailing who the indorser made the instrument payable to.

special jurisdiction   Reflects the limited nature of some courts like juvenile courts and small claims courts.

special service corporation   Governed by special laws because of specialized area; can include insurance, banking, and savings and loans; heavily regulated by federal and state governments and agencies.

specific performance   Party who has breached a contract is required by the court to perform the actual terms of the contract because merely suing for damages is not adequate to compensate the aggrieved party.

stakeholder   Those who have an interest in the activities of a corporation; may include shareholders, employees, vendors, customers, and governments.

stare decisis   Latin for let the decision stand; the principle that prior case law should serve as a precedent and control future decisions of courts.

statute of frauds   Requirement that certain classes of contracts be in writing to be valid and enforceable.

strict liability   An absolute standard of liability imposed by statute or courts.

subchapter S-corporations   The corporation will be treated as a partnership for tax purposes if it is a domestic corporation with 100 or fewer shareholders, the shareholders are individuals, estates, or exempt organizations, and it has one class of stock; must check a box on IRS Form 2553.

subject matter jurisdiction   Court's ability to hear a case based on the material covered.

substantive due process   Constitutional limits placed on the content or subject matter of state and federal laws.

substantive law   Establishes principles and creates, defines, and regulates rights and liabilities.

surety   A person who accepts primary liablity for the debt or obligation of another, who is the principal debtor; the surety accepts an obligation that is not his or hers.

tariff   Domestically a tariff is a government-approved schedule of charges that can be made by a regulated business like a carrier; internationally a tax imposed by a country on goods crossing its borders.

tenancy at sufferance   Exists when a tenant stays after termination of the original lease and does not have the permission of the landlord to remain on the property.

tenancy at will   Exists when the lease has an indefinite period and may be terminated at any time by either party.

tenancy for years   One where the lease establishes a definite duration for weeks, months, years, or another time period.

tenant   One who holds property by paying rent and the terms of a lease.

tender   To present payment to another or delivery under terms of contract; tender ends a party's obligations under the contract.

third party   Anyone involved in an agency relationship who is not the agent or principal.

tort   A civil wrong or wrongful act which injures another, includes negligence.

trade fixture   Fixture that a tenant attaches to a rented building and uses in their trade or business; can be removed by the tenant.

trade secret   Information (including a formula, pattern, compilation, program device, method, technique, or process) that derives economic value from being secret or not readily ascertainable; subject to efforts reasonable under the circumstances to maintain its secrecy.

trademark   Word, phrase, symbol, or design, or a combination of words, phrases, symbols, or designs, that identifies and distinguishes the source of the good of one party from those of others.

trap   A hazard that is known to the landowner but concealed to others.

treble damages   When imposed, results in the party paying three times the actual amount of damages incurred.

trust   Customers and other businesses can rely on the character, strength, and integrity of a company.

tying   The seller forces the buyer to purchase an item it doesn't want in order to purchase the one it does.

ultra vires   Beyond powers; the corporation or officers have exceeded the powers granted by law.

undisclosed principal   Principal remains hidden from the third party.

unilateral mistake   Mistake about a contract made by one party; will not effect the contract when the nonmistaken party is unaware of the mistake.

unincorporated associations   Two or more people come together for a specific nonprofit purpose.

universal agent   Principal has delegated to the agent everything that can be lawfully delegated most often through a power of attorney.

universal standards for ethics   Holds that ethics are set and cannot be changed by the shifting winds of the law; natural law sets the standards individuals should live by.

unjust enrichment   A benefit is incurred to one person either by mistake, chance, or someone's misfortune, and the person who benefits fails to pay for the benefit.

utility patent   Granted to anyone who invents or discovers a new and useful process, machine, manufactured item, composition of matter, or an improvement to any of those; good for 20 years.

vicarious liability   Imposing liability on one for the fault of another.

way of necessity   The right to access land retained by the grantor to gain access and leave property.

white-collar crime   Nonviolent crimes that involve some form of cheating or fraud.

winding up   Period after termination or dissolution of partnership in which the remaining partners only have authority to finish work in progress and cannot accept new work.

Appendix B

Resources

Books

If you're interested in learning more about the topics discussed in these chapters, the following books are a great place to start.

Goldstein, Paul. *Intellectual Property*. Portfolio, 2007.

Harper, Tim. *The Complete Idiot's Guide to the U.S. Constitution*. Indianapolis: Alpha Books, 2007.

Paulson, Edward. *The Complete Idiot's Guide to Starting Your Own Business, 5th Edition*. Indianapolis: Alpha Books, 2007.

Websites

The following websites are excellent resources.

Antitrust

Department of Justice Antitrust Division: www.usdoj.gov/atr

Federal Trade Commission (FTC): www.ftc.gov

Corporate Formation

The secretary of state for each state oversees the formation and continuation of businesses. Be sure to check each state's website for the needed statutes, rules, and forms.

Employment

Equal Employment Opportunity Commission: www.eeoc.gov

U.S. Department of Labor: www.dol.gov

Federal Agencies

Consumer Litigation branch of the Civil Division of the Department of Justice: www.usdoj.gov/civil/ocl/index.htm

Department of Justice: www.usdoj.gov

Department of Labor: www.labor.gov

Environmental Protection Agency: www.epa.gov

Equal Employment Opportunity Commission: www.eeoc.gov

Federal Communications Commission: www.fcc.gov

Federal Trade Commission: www.ftc.gov

Fish and Wildlife Service: www.fws.gov

Food and Drug Administration (FDA): www.fda.gov

National Labor Relations Board: www.nlrb.gov

Occupational Safety & Health Administration: www.osha.gov

Portal for consumers: www.consumer.gov

Portal to all federal agencies: www.usa.gov

Securities and Exchange Commission: www.sec.gov

U.S. Patent and Trademark Office: www.uspto.gov

Secretary of States

This site serves as a portal to each state's secretary of state: www.coordinatedlegal.com/SecretaryOfState.html

Index

contribution and indemnity, partners and, 97
contributory negligence, 291
conversion, 236
cooperatives, 74-75
copyrights, 245
Fair Use Doctrine, 246
infringement, 246
Internet downloads, 246
registration, 245
corporate fraud, 281
corporation by estoppel, 85
corporation de jure, 85
corporations, 73, 80
acquisitions, 87
application for incorporation, 84-85
bond issue, 82
borrowing money, 82
close, 81
conglomerates, 88
consolidation, 87
contracts, 82
corporation by estoppel, 85
creating, 83-85
creation, 81
de facto corporation, 85
domestic, 80
dissolving, 85-86
foreign, 80
liabilities
shareholders, 89-90
successor, 88
mergers, 86-87
name, 82
negotiable instruments, 82
nonprofit, 81
perpetual life, 82
private, 80
professional, 81
promoters, 83
public, 80
public-authorities, 80
quasi-public, 80
Revised Model Business Corporation Act, 81
special service, 81

stock issue, 80, 82
subchapter S-corporations, 81
ultra vires act, 83
counterclaims, 19
counterfeiting, 280
counteroffers, contracts, 124
court
counterclaims, 19
defendant, 19
discovery, 20
federal
district courts, 16
jurisdiction, 16
U.S. Courts of Appeals, 16
United States Supreme Court, 17
federal compared to state, 18
lawsuit, steps in, 19-20
parties, 19
plaintiff, 19
state court
appellate courts, 18
jurisdiction, 17-18
small claims courts, 18
specialty courts, 17
supreme courts, 18
trial courts, 17
court reformation, breach of contract, 151
courts, 14
small claims, 14
covenant against encumbrance, 225
covenant of further assurances, 225
covenant of quiet enjoyment, 225
covenant of right to convey, 225
covenant of seisin, 225
covenants not to compete, state employment law, 195
creditors claim to goods, 172

crimes, 275
actus reus, 276
agents, principals liability, 188-189
blackmail, 280
bribery, 279
computers and, 282
conspiracy, 278
corporate fraud, 281
counterfeiting, 280
embezzlement, 281
extortion, 280
felonies, 276
Fifth Amendment protections, 283
fines, 277
forgery, 280
Fourth Amendment protections, 283
fraud, corporate, 281
larceny, 282
mandatory sentencing, 277
mens rea, 275
misdemeanors, 276
money laundering, 278
multiple persons for one crime, 276
obstruction of justice, 281
penalties, 277
perjury, 280
racketeering, 279-280
white-collar, 276, 281
criminal cases versus civil cases, 278
Criminal Division (DOJ), 61
criminal procedure, 20
currency, 9

D

damaged goods, 172
damages, negligence, 290
de facto corporation, 85
debts, contracts, 130
Declaration of Independence, 4
declaring war, 9